BUILDING PARTNERSHIPS

India and International Cooperation for Maritime Security

BUILDING PARTNERSHIPS

India and International Cooperation for Maritime Security

Captain Himadri Das

First published in 2024 by
PENTAGON PRESS LLP
206, Peacock Lane, Shahpur Jat
New Delhi-110049, India
Contact: 011-26491568 • 011-26490600

Typeset in Adobe Garamond, 11.5 Point
Printed by Aegean Offset Printers, Greater Noida, U.P.

ISBN 978-93-90095-94-0 (HB)

Disclaimer: The publication has been developed with the support of the Indian Naval Despatch Foundation (INDEF) and the Naval War College (NWC), Goa. The opinions expressed and inferences drawn in this book are the personal views of the author and do not represent the official policy of any of the organisations, or the Government of India.

www.pentagonpress.in

To Rajkumari

CONTENTS

Foreword

That the seas unite what land borders divide is an assertion that is widely accepted by all those who have been maritime analysts and especially those fortunate enough to have been seagoing practitioners within the maritime domain. The author of this book, Captain Himadri Das, Indian Navy, has been and remains a highly competent practitioner and a deeply respected former Research Fellow of the National Maritime Foundation, as also a member of the faculty of the Naval War College. As such, he fits into both categories and his authorship of this book offers unambiguous proof of the opening assertion.

There is an undeniable and unique bond amongst practitioners of maritime security that easily transcends geographies. Its origins and developmental contours are complex sociological phenomena in and of themselves but, as a net result, maritime security forces in general and navies in particular tend to be naturally gifted at military diplomacy through their ability to generate, appreciate, and sustain a variety of international partnerships distributed over both time and space. Military diplomacy itself is the exploitation by a country of military institutions (the primary source of Hard Power) to convince (rather than coerce) a recipient State—especially its government—that what the practitioner wants is also what the recipient actually wants. Consequently, military diplomacy may be described as the exploitation by a nation of its primary instrument of hard power (the military establishment) to exercise soft power (diplomacy) upon the government of another nation so as to shape the latter's thinking and institutions in a manner designed to yield a desired strategic result. Military diplomacy is often simultaneously at play at the strategic level as well as the level of 'operational art'—the latter denotes the deployment of tactical assets in sequences of time and/or space and/or event to achieve a desired strategic result. For instance, driven by the need to pursue, preserve, promote, and protect India's core national interest which, derived from the Constitution, is *"to assure the societal, economic, and material well-being of the People of India"*, India's military diplomacy reflects the desire of the nation to gain and sustain a favourable geopolitical position.

Indeed, 'diplomacy' and the (usually peaceful) deployment of 'military force' are the two principal instruments by which a nation executes its foreign policy, i.e., its political interaction in the international arena. When a variety of geoeconomic goals non-geoeconomic ones (examples of the latter are prestige, cultural- and people-to-people connectivity, etc.) and the strategies that nation-states evolve across multiple policy-fields to attain these goals are factored into this international political interaction, the result, of course, is what is called *geopolitics*. Strategic convergence in these various policy fields leads to partnerships between and amongst nations. The sheer *number* of policy fields involved and the depth to which strategic convergence can be discerned and sustained give rise to a hierarchy of strategic partnerships that have emerged as alternatives to the military treaty alliances that characterised the Cold War period and which still endure, albeit with considerably less adhesion and cohesion amongst their member States.

Thus, India, like several other geopolitical entities has established "Strategic Partnerships" with several States (Afghanistan, Brazil, Canada, China, EU, France, Germany, Iran, Italy, Kazakhstan, Malaysia, Mongolia, Nigeria, Oman, Russia, Saudi Arabia, Seychelles, Singapore, South Africa, Tajikistan, and Uzbekistan) and "Special Strategic Partnerships" with a couple (South Korea, and Denmark with whom we have a 'Green' strategic partnership). We also have "Comprehensive Strategic Partnerships" with ASEAN, Australia, Indonesia, the UAE, the UK, and Vietnam; a "Strategic and Global Partnership" with Japan; a "Special and Privileged Strategic Partnership" with Russia; and a "Comprehensive Global Strategic Partnership" with the USA.

There are a number of manifestations of military maritime diplomacy within this hierarchy of partnerships. These include, inter alia, bilateral and multilateral officer-exchanges; periodic or regular exposure of personnel to foreign military and defence civilian organisations, structures, platforms, and units; periodic or regular contacts amongst senior officers and civilian officials; the appointment of defence attachés in foreign countries; bilateral defence cooperation agreements; the training of foreign military and civilian defence personnel; sharing of expertise and advice on the control and management of defence assets and organisational structures; warship visits; and 'combined' (as well as 'combined' and 'joint') military exercises. In fact, within the paradigm of maritime activity, exercises with foreign militaries are frequently options of choice to demonstrate the strength, cohesion, and adhesion of partnerships and are designed to yield, particularly over time, desired strategic results.

As Das succinctly explains in this book, *"The 3Cs of 'coordination,' 'cooperation,' and 'collaboration' are often used in the context of partnerships"*. While 'cooperation' (such as through information-sharing, training, capacity-building, and capability-enhancement) is often the first step to develop partnerships, tangible manifestations of such maritime-security partnerships frequently begin with 'coordination' (*"such as in the case of the anti-piracy mission in the Gulf of Aden, which is coordinated amongst all the deploying navies through the Shared Awareness and Deconfliction (SHADE) mechanism"*). Within a strategic partnership (as opposed to a treaty alliance) 'collaboration', typically reflects the higher end of the partnership spectrum. International law provides the legal underpinning for international cooperation in several areas of maritime security. This is quite comprehensively exemplified by regional cooperation to stop illegal, unreported, and unregulated (IUU) fishing.

Maritime manifestations of international partnerships are also important in the broader geopolitical context. As Das points out, the *"need to hedge against an adversary, potential adversary, or a rival; countering growing influence of a competitor, or arresting diminishing influence with some partners; developing dependencies; enhancing defence exports and supporting domestic industries etc are unstated, but clearly discernible associated factors for expanding cooperation."* Obviously, international partnerships are not without their hidden agendas and the trade-offs between perceived gains and costs such as, for instance, the development of dependencies. While adhering strongly to the principle of *Vasudhaiva Kutumbakam* (**वासुधैव कुटुम्बकम्**)—which translates to 'the world is one family'—in its espousal of international partnerships, India's ongoing drive towards *atmanirbharta*, that is, self-reliance, seeks to mitigate precisely these sorts of costs.

Perhaps the clearest manifestation of India's pragmatism while pursuing and strengthening international partnerships is to be found in India's maritime policy itself, which is encapsulated in the acronym SAGAR (Security and Growth for All in the Region) and, like every good policy should, unambiguously articulates India's desired end state. The seven deeply interconnected spokes of the complex cooperative and collaborative web that constitutes the Indo-Pacific Oceans Initiative (IPOI) offer first-order-specificity to the maritime policy of SAGAR. All seven of these spokes or pillars—and therefore the IPOI as a whole—are founded upon the enormous value that India places upon international partnerships, especially those that are relevant to the one domain that will overwhelmingly determine India's socio-economic progress and success over the foreseeable future—the maritime domain.

That India and its government recognises and has internalised the centrality of the maritime domain to the future wellbeing of the people of India is clearly evidenced in the 09 August 2021 address by Prime Minister Modi at the UN Security Council, in which he set forth five principles to develop a global roadmap for partnerships to enhance maritime security cooperation: developing an 'inclusive structure for maritime security' in the IOR based on the vision of SAGAR; the peaceful settlement of disputes; cooperative efforts at fighting natural disasters and non-State actors; the preservation of the environment and resources; and, the promotion of maritime connectivity. Building upon these very principles, the concept of 'collective maritime competence' had been brilliantly articulated by Admiral Karambir Singh, the then Chief of the Naval Staff, who described it as the ability to "*collectively promote maritime interests in the global commons by collaborating with like-minded nations to build capacities and deepen linkages.*" The enduring rationale underpinning the concept of collective maritime competence is that maritime threats are transnational, that no single nation has the resources to harness all the opportunities or to address all the challenges, and that safe and secure seas are in the interest of all nations. The various lines of effort towards achieving this collective maritime competence all coalesce into 'constructive engagement'. This, in turn, involves strengthening partnerships with friendly countries, enhancing maritime situational awareness (MSA), integrating MSA to yield maritime domain awareness (MDA), and enhancing reach and sustenance. These partnerships can be meaningfully progressed through established platforms and frameworks at bilateral, trilateral, minilateral, and multilateral structures. These include the seven trilaterals that India has established (India-Brazil-South Africa; India-US-Japan; India-Japan-Australia; India-Japan-Italy; India-Indonesia-Australia; India-Australia-France; and India-France-UAE), minilaterals such as, *inter alia*, BIMSTEC, IONS, I2U2, the Quad, the Colombo Security Dialogue, etc., and a host of larger, multilateral partnerships such as IORA, EAS, ARF, the DCoC-JA, ReCAAP, the IMO, and so forth.

In this latest book of his, Captain Himadri has competently and compellingly set forth supportive and cautionary arguments relevant to each of these types and classes of partnership. This is the sweep of his magisterial vision, and it finds rich expression in the pages and chapters that follow. I commend this book and the magisterial vision contained within it to all categories of stakeholders in and beyond the maritime domain.

Jai Hind

Vice Admiral Pradeep Chauhan
AVSM & Bar, VSM (Retd)
Director-General
National Maritime Foundation
New Delhi -110010

Preface

In August 2021, the Indian Prime Minister, Shri Narendra Modi, chaired a High-level Open Debate on 'Enhancing Maritime Security – A Case for International Cooperation' during India's rotating presidency of the UN Security Council. This was the first time that maritime security was discussed exclusively as a holistic concept, and this was also the first time that an Indian Prime Minister had presided over a UN Security Council open debate. However, this marked the progressive upscaling of efforts by India to shape the discourse on maritime security.

In the 21st century, the concept of maritime security has evolved, and continues to evolve, encompassing wider dimensions of security. Increasing threats to maritime security, have also underscored the need for enhancing international cooperation to ensure freedom of the sea. Over the years India has taken on a stewardship role in fostering international maritime security cooperation through policy pronouncements, such as Security and Growth for All in the Region (SAGAR) in 2015. It has gone on to provide first-order specificity to this maritime policy through the Indo-Pacific Oceans Initiative (IPOI) of 2018, and is developing second, third, and ever-greater orders of specificity through a series of cooperative, constructive, and where feasible, collaborative practical actions, dispersed over time and space. These incorporate not merely anti-piracy taskings, but also broader ones that seek to generate and maintain stability operations involving, *inter alia,* anti-crime missions in the Gulf of Aden and its environs, information-sharing, Humanitarian Assistance and Disaster Relief (HADR) operations, etc.

Against this backdrop, this effort aims to comprehensively explore the 'nuts and bolts' of multidimensional maritime security cooperation. In doing so, it also endeavours to link India's vision, policy, doctrine, strategy, and action. The focus of the study is particularly on aspects related to governance for cooperation from an Indian perspective, as it is derived from my own effort to understand maritime security governance in India. In short, this book examines the *India Way* for maritime security cooperation.

I am hopeful that this effort will facilitate a better understanding of how India in the 21st century has advanced its efforts at strengthening maritime security cooperation through a holistic approach focused on partnerships, and possibly also ways of furthering cooperative endeavours for public good.

Captain Himadri Das

ACKNOWLEDGEMENTS

The overwhelming majority of this effort was written during my tenure at the National Maritime Foundation (NMF) on study leave from 2020-2022 and was further updated in 2023 while I was at the Naval War College (NWC), Goa. Therefore, I am indebted to the Personnel Branch of the Indian Navy for having spared me on study leave, and to the NMF and NWC for facilitating this study.

In particular I would like to place on record my gratitude to the Director-General of the NMF, Vice Admiral Pradeep Chauhan, AVSM & Bar, VSM; Executive Directors of the NMF, Captain Sarabjit S Parmar and Commodore Debesh Lahiri; Commandant of the NWC, Rear Admiral Rajesh Dhankhar, NM; and Deputy Commandants of the NWC, Commodore Nitin Kapoor and Commodore Prashant Chandrasekharan. My gratitude also extends to a long list of members of both the institutions who in their own ways have contributed to this effort, but in particular the production and administrative teams at the NMF.

I owe a special debt of gratitude to Vice Admiral Pradeep Chauhan for his tireless evangelical efforts in respect of all 'matters maritime' and for readying the next generation(s) to take forward his legacy. I have been enriched through the numerous lectures that I have attended, and interactions that I have had. I also a debt of gratitude to Vice Admiral Sanjay J Singh, AVSM, NM, who has guided me through several academic and doctrinal pursuits over close to two decades. I have also been enriched by my interactions with friends and colleagues who provided their valuable inputs.

Finally, I would like to thank my family, without whose everyday support and sacrifices, I would not have been able to pursue this, and other efforts.

Captain Himadri Das

List of Figures and Tables

Figures

Tables

List of Abbreviations

ABNJ	Areas Beyond National Jurisdiction
ACNS(FCI)	Assistant Chief of the Naval Staff (Foreign Cooperation and Intelligence)
ADMM+	ASEAN Defence Ministers' Meeting Plus
AEW&C	Airborne Early Warning and Control
AI/ML	Artificial Intelligence/ Machine Learning
AIS	Automatic Identification System
ALH	Advanced Light Helicopter
ANDEP	Deployment off Andaman and Nicobar Islands [Indian Navy]
APFIC	Asia-Pacific Fishery Commission
ARF	ASEAN Regional Forum
ASEAN	Association of Southeast Asian Nations
ASEM	Asia-Europe Meeting
AUKUS	Australia-United Kingdom-United States Trilateral Security Partnership
AWACS	Airborne Warning and Control System
BDA	Big Data Analytics
BECA	Basic Exchange and Cooperation Agreement for Geo-spatial Cooperation
BEL	Bharat Electronics Limited
BIMSTEC	Bay of Bengal Initiative for Multi-Sectoral Technical and Economic Cooperation
BMP	Best Management Practices
BOBLME	Bay of Bengal Large Marine Ecosystem
BOBP-IGO	Bay of Bengal Programme Inter-Governmental Organisation

C4ISR	Command, Control, Communications, Computers, Intelligence, Surveillance, and Reconnaissance
CASEVAC	Casualty Evacuation
CBI	Central Bureau of Investigation
CBM	Coordinated Border Management
	Confidence Building Measures
CCSBT	Commission for the Conservation of Southern Bluefin Tuna
CDS	Chief of Defence Staff
CENTDEP	Indian Naval Deployment off Maldives and Sri Lanka
CGPCS	Contact Group on Piracy off the Coast of Somalia
CINCAN	Commander-in-Chief Andaman and Nicobar Command
CISMOA	Communication and Information on Security Memorandum of Agreement
CMF	Combined Maritime Forces
CMM	Conservation of Management Measures
CNO	Chief of Naval Operations
CNS	Chief of Naval Staff
COMCASA	Communications Compatibility and Security Agreement
CORPAT	Coordinated Patrols
CRS	Coastal Radar System
CSC	Colombo Security Conclave
CSG	Carrier Strike Group
CSI	Container Security Initiative
CSN	Coastal Surveillance Network
CUES	Code of Unalerted Encounters at Sea
DA	Defence Attaché/ Advisor
DCG	Defence Consultative Group
DCNS	Deputy Chief of the Naval Staff
DCoC	Djibouti Code of Conduct
DCOC/ JA	Djibouti Code of Conduct/ Jeddah Amendment
DEFEXPO	Defence Exposition
DFC	Directorate of Foreign Cooperation
DGCG	Director General Coast Guard
DIB	Defence Industrial Base
DIC	Directorate of International Customs
DLEA	Drug Law Enforcement Agency
DoD	Department of Defence

DRI	Directorate of Revenue intelligence
DSRV	Deep Sea Rescue Vehicle
E&SA	Eastern and Southern Africa
EAM	External Affairs Minister
EAMF	Expanded ASEAN Maritime Forum
EAS	East Asia Summit
EEZ	Exclusive Economic Zone
ENC	Electronic Nautical Chart
ESG	Executive Steering Group
EU	European Union
EUNAVFOR	EU Naval Force
FAC	Fast Attack Craft
FFC	Friendly Foreign Countries
FFPU	Female Formed Police Unit
FIC	Fast Interceptor Craft
FoGG	G7++ Group of Friends of the Gulf of Guinea
FOIP	Free and Open Indo-Pacific
FPC	Fast Patrol Craft
GISIS	Global Integrated Shipping Information System
GMC	Goa Maritime Conclave
GMCP	Global Maritime Crime Programme
GMS	Goa Maritime Symposium
GoG-MCF	Gulf of Guinea Maritime Collaboration Forum
GoI	Government of India
GSI	Geological Survey of India
GSOMIA	General Security of Military Information Agreement
GULFDEP	Persian Gulf Deployment [Indian Navy]
HACGAM	Heads of Asian Coast Guard Agencies Meeting
HADR	Humanitarian Assistance and Disaster Relief
HALE	High Altitude Long Endurance
HLM	High Level Meeting
HOSTAC	Helicopter Operations from Ships Other Than Aircraft Carriers
HQANC	Headquarters, Andaman and Nicobar Command
HQIDS	Headquarters, Integrated Defence Staff
HRA	High Risk Area
IAF	Indian Air Force
IB	Interceptor Boat

IDY	International Day of Yoga
IFC	Information Fusion Centre
IFC-IOR	Information Fusion Centre – Indian Ocean Region
IFN	Information Network System
IFR	International Fleet Review
IHO	International Hydrographic Organisation
IIHL	International Institute of Humanitarian Law
ILO	International Liaison Officer
IMEX-22	Indian Ocean Naval Symposium (IONS) Maritime Exercise 2022
IMF	Indian Maritime Foundation
IMLI	International Maritime Law Institute
IMMSAREX	IONS Multilateral Maritime SAR Exercise
IMO	International Maritime Organisation
IMSF	Indian Marine Special Force
INDU	Indian National Defence University
INHD	Indian Naval Hydrographic Department
INT	International [Charts]
INTERPOL	International Criminal Police Organisation
IOC	Indian Ocean Commission
IODEP	Indian Naval Deployment Mauritius, Seychelles, and Madagascar
IOFMC	Indian Ocean Forum on Maritime Crime
IOMOU	Indian Ocean Memorandum of Understanding on PSC
IONS	Indian Ocean Naval Symposium
IOR	Indian Ocean Region
IORA	Indian Ocean Rim Association
IORIS	Indian Ocean Regional Information Sharing and Incident Management Network
IOTC	Indian Ocean Tuna Commission
IPKF	Indian Peacekeeping Force
IPOI	Indo-Pacific Open Initiative
IPRD	Indo-Pacific Regional Dialogue
IRIS	IFC Real-time Info-sharing System
IS&IIWG	Information Sharing and Interoperability IONS Working Group
ISC	Information Sharing Centre
ISL	International Shipping Lane
ISPS	International Ship and Port Facility Security

ISR	Intelligence, Surveillance, Reconnaissance
ISRO	Indian Space Research Organisation
ISSR	Indian Search and Rescue Region
ITEC	Indian Technical and Economic Cooperation
ITLOS	International Tribunal for the Law of the Sea
IUU	Illegal, Unreported, Unregulated (fishing)
IWG	IONS Working Group
JWG	Joint Working Group
KLE	Key Leader Engagement
LAC	Line of Actual Control
LEMOA	Logistics Exchange Memorandum of Agreement
LMO	Liquid Medical Oxygen
LRIT	Long-Range Identification and Tracking
LRMP	Long Range Maritime Patrol
MALDEP	Strait of Malacca Deployment [Indian Navy]
MARCOs	Marine Commandos
MARPOL	International Convention for the Prevention of Pollution from Ships
MDA	Maritime domain awareness
MEDEVAC	Medical Evacuation
METOC	Meteorology and Oceanography
MIO	Maritime Interdiction Operation
MIEVOM	Maritime Information Exchange Vessel Operators Meeting
MISTA	Maritime Information Sharing Technical Agreement
MLEA	Maritime Law Enforcement Agencies
MLSA	Mutual Logistics Support Agreement
MNDF	Maldives National Defence Force
MNDF-CG	Maldives National Defence Force Coast Guard
MoD	Ministry of Defence
MoES	Ministry of Earth Sciences
MOU	Memorandum of Understanding
MRC	Maritime Research Centre
MRCC	Maritime Rescue Co-ordination Centre
M-SAR	Maritime Search and Rescue
MSC	Maritime Security Committee
MSC	Maritime Security Council
MSC-HOA	Maritime Security Centre-Horn of Africa

MSG	Military Subgroup
MSIS	Maritime Safety Information Services
MSIS	Merchant Shipping Information System
MSS	Maritime Safety and Security
MSSR	Maritime Security Sector Reform
MTC	Maritime Theatre Command
MTF	Marine Task Force
MV	Motor Vessel
NA	Naval Attaché/ Advisor
NACIN	National Academy of Customs, Indirect Taxes and Narcotics
NATO	North Atlantic Treaty Organisation
NAVAREA	Maritime Geographic Area for Navigation and Weather Warnings
NAVCENT	US Naval Forces Central Command
NC3IN	National Command Control Communication and Intelligence [Network]
NCB	Narcotics Control Bureau
NEO	Non-combatant Evacuation Operation
NGO	Non-Governmental Organisation
NHO	National Hydrographic Office
NIH	National Institute of Hydrography
NIOHC	North Indian Ocean Hydrographic Commission
NIOT	National Institute of Ocean Technology
NMDA	National Maritime Domain Awareness [Project]
NMF	National Maritime Foundation
NMSC	National Maritime Security Coordinator
NORDEP	North Bay of Bengal Deployment [Indian Navy]
NSA	National Security Agency
NWC	Naval War College
OFC	Overall Force Commander
OOAC	Out-of-Area Contingencies
OPV	Offshore Patrol Vessel
ORF	Observer Research Foundation
OSD	Overseas Deployment
OTR	Operational Turn Around
PASSEX	Passage Exercise
PLA(N)	People's Liberation Army (Navy)

PME	Professional Military Exchange
PMI	Permanent Mission of India
PMSA	Pakistan Maritime Security Agency
POC	Point of Contact
POGDEP	[Piracy off] Gulf of Aden Deployment [Indian Navy]
PSC	Port State Control
PSI	Proliferation Security Initiative
PSM	Presence and Surveillance Mission
PSO	Peace Support Operations
QEN	Qatari-Emiri Navy
QUAD	Quadrilateral Security Dialogue
R&D	Research and Development
ReCAAP ISC	ReCAAP Information Sharing Centre
ReCAAP	Regional Cooperation Agreement on Combating Piracy and Armed Robbery Against Ships in Asia
RFB	Regional Fisheries Bodies
RFMO	Regional Fisheries Management Organisations
RMSI	Regional Maritime Security Initiative
RPSS	Reciprocal Provisions for Support and Services [Agreement]
SAARC	South Asia Association for Regional Cooperation
SACEP	South Asia Co-operative Environment Programme
SAGAR	Security and Growth For all in the Region
SAIHC	Southern African and Island Hydrographic Commission
SAR	Search and Rescue
SARCOMEX	SAR Communication Exercise
SAREX-22	National Maritime Search and Rescue Exercise
SASP	South Asian Seas Programme
SHADE	Shared Awareness and Deconfliction
SIMBEX	Singapore-India Maritime Bilateral Exercise
SIOFA	Southern Indian Ocean Fisheries Agreement
SOLAS	International Convention for the Safety of Life at Sea, 1974
SOP	Standard Operating Procedure
SRP	Southern Route Partnership
SSIFS	Shushma Swaraj Institute of Foreign Service
STCW	International Convention on Standards of Training, Certification and Watchkeeping for Seafarers
TFG	Transitional Federal Government

T-RMN	Trans-Regional Maritime Network
TTX	Table-Top Exercises
UAE	United Arab Emirates
UDA	Underwater Domain Awareness
UK	United Kingdom
UN	United Nations
UNCAP	UN C4ISR Academy for Peace Operations
UNCLOS	United Nations Convention on the Law of the Sea
UNIFIL	UN Interim Force in Lebanon
UNODC	United Nations Office on Drugs and Crime
UNREP	Underway Replenishment
UNSC	United Nations Security Council
UNSOM	United Nations Assistance Mission in Somalia
USSR	Union of Soviet Socialist Republics
VBSS	Visit, Board, Search and Seize
WANA	West Asia and North Africa
WCO	World Customs Organisation
WGMSS	Working Group on MSS
WLM	Working Level Meeting
WMD	Weapons of Mass Destruction
WMU	World Maritime University
WoG	Whole-of-Government
WPNS	Western Pacific Naval Symposium
WSIE	White Shipping Information Exchange Agreement
WTO	World Trade Organisation

1

Maritime Security Cooperation

The reality is that in maritime policy too, India could succeed in doing more with less. A lighter footprint, applications of technology, embrace of partnerships and a propensity towards frugality have come together. The net impact of all this has been very much more because working with international partners has provided a multiplier effect.

—S Jaishankar[1]

Background and Context

The concept of 'maritime security' has diverse interpretations, with no universally accepted definition, and its usage is largely contextual.[2] Its evolution, since the late 20th century, has been associated with, but is not limited to, events such as the attack on the USS *Cole* (2000), '9/11' attack (2001), piracy off the Gulf of Aden (2008), and the Mumbai Attack (2008), etc. Conceptually, maritime security is increasingly considered as an inclusive, interconnected, adaptable and diffusive concept, with a web of linkages to other concepts and dimensions of security, such as geopolitics, national security, maritime law enforcement, economy, energy, environment, diplomacy, human security, etc.[3]

A host of malicious actors, such as terrorists, pirates, smugglers, traffickers, etc., threaten maritime security worldwide, including through transnational networks of organised crime.[4] In addition to threats to 'good order at sea,' the established 'rules-based order' is also under threat in some parts of the world, such as in the South and East China Seas, by militarisation of disputed features, dangerous manoeuvres by State vessels inconsistent with international rules, deployment of militia, and efforts to disrupt economic activities.[5] In addition to the loss of human lives, maritime insecurity can adversely impact international trade, energy security, and the global economy.[6] In a globalised world, insecurity in one region can have global effects, as seen in the cases of piracy off the Horn of Africa (2008) and the Ukraine crisis (2022). The emergence of 'hybrid threats' (especially state-supported ones), cyber threats, and climate change, have only complicated the threat and response matrix. It has, therefore, been recognised that countering threats to maritime security necessitates international and regional cooperation, such as through information sharing, capacity building, technical assistance, etc.[7]

While 'maritime security' is a widely used term, it is a contextual concept that means different things to different stakeholders. 'Cooperation' literally means "the fact of doing something together or of working together towards a shared aim."[8] Put together, 'maritime security cooperation' broadly refers to working with foreign partners for ensuring a safe and secure maritime environment. From the early years of the 21st century there has been an increasing international focus on international maritime security cooperation. Some of the main drivers for enhancing maritime security cooperation have been the '9/11' attack, and the increasing risks to the global commons emanating from non-traditional threats, such as piracy in the Gulf of Aden. The rise of China, widely regarded to be a threat to the established international rules-based order and the present global order, particularly in view of its unilateral actions in the South China Sea and its disregard for international dispute resolution mechanisms, has also galvanised cooperative partnerships in the maritime space. The Quadrilateral Security Dialogue (QUAD) and the Australia-United Kingdom-United States Trilateral Security Partnership (AUKUS) are examples of such partnerships. In August 2021, for the first time in history, a case was made out in the UN Security Council for enhancing international cooperation for maritime security.

Over the past five decades a host of 'non-traditional' maritime security threats have threatened maritime security in India, including smuggling, trafficking, terrorism, piracy, and armed robbery.[9] India's maritime security construct has, over the years, evolved to respond to such threats, not just domestically, but also regionally.[10] Since the latter half of the 1980s, the Indian Navy has been engaged in several operations overseas. Some notable ones include that in Seychelles in response to an intelligence input about a possible coup in Seychelles (1986); Indian Peacekeeping Force (IPKF) operations in Sri Lanka (1987-90); the intervention in Maldives in response to an attempted coup (1988); UN peacekeeping operations in Somalia (1993); the intervention in an incident of piracy involving MV *Alondra Rainbow* in the Arabian Sea in coordination with Japan (1999); the escort of US ships in the Malacca Strait (2002); naval patrols off Mozambique (2003); Humanitarian Assistance Disaster Relief (HADR) assistance to maritime neighbours, particularly in the aftermath of the Tsunami (2004), Non-Combatant Evacuation Operation (NEO) from Lebanon (2006), Libya (2011), and Yemen (2015), anti-piracy missions in the Gulf of Aden (2008), and maritime security deployment in the Persian Gulf (2019).[11] The comprehensive, pan-regional HADR assistance rendered by the Indian Navy, in coordination with other navies, across South Asia and South East Asia in response to the *tsunami* of 2004, is considered by many as being an inflexion point in respect of the global recognition of the Indian Navy's cooperative effort.[12] The Indian Coast Guard, in addition to cooperating with maritime security agencies of Asian/neighbouring countries to counter maritime crimes, such as piracy and drug trafficking has, more recently been a first responder to maritime environmental disasters in South Asia, and beyond, and has also been nominated as the nodal Indian agency for Search and Rescue in the Indo-Pacific.[13]

The 3Cs: Coordination, Cooperation, and Collaboration

The 3Cs of 'coordination,' 'cooperation,' and 'collaboration' are often used in the context of partnerships, sometimes even interchangeably. 'Collaboration' literally means, "the act of working with another person or group of people to create or produce something" and the term 'coordination' means "the act of making parts of something, groups of people, etc. work together in an efficient and organized way."[14] The meanings reflect the differences, sometimes nuanced, between the three activities. In developing partnerships for maritime security, especially in an operational context, 'coordination' is often the first step, such as in the case of the anti-piracy mission in the Gulf of Aden, which is coordinated amongst all the deploying navies through the Shared Awareness and Deconfliction (SHADE) mechanism; however, outside of operational contexts, 'cooperation' is often the first step to develop partnerships, such as through information sharing, training, capacity building, etc. Cooperation may be an end by itself, but could also lead to collaborative efforts, such as joint patrols, etc. Outside of an alliance mechanism, hierarchically, collaboration reflects the higher end of the partnership spectrum. In the context of regional cooperation to stop illegal fishing, an indicative matrix of approaches, relative resources required, and success probability, while not being applicable to all situations, is instructive of the advantages of a partnership approach vis-à-vis individual approaches.[15]

Table 1.1: Approaches to Partnerships

Approach	Relative Resources	Success Probability
Independent	High	Low
Coordination	Moderate/High	Moderate
Cooperation	Moderate	Moderate/High
Collaboration	Low	High

Legal Basis

International law provides the basis for international cooperation in maritime security. The Charter of the UN for the maintenance of international peace and security *inter alia* provides for taking *"effective collective measures for the prevention and removal of threats to the peace, and for the suppression of acts of aggression or other breaches of the peace."*[16] It is a fact that in the 21st century there has been an exponential increase in maritime-security-related interventions by the UN Security Council, such as those undertaken to counter piracy in the Gulf of Aden.[17]

From a maritime context, the United Nations Convention on the Law of the Sea (UNCLOS) provides the legal framework for maritime cooperation, including for maritime security.[18] Several provisions in UNCLOS require states to cooperate bilaterally, multilaterally, regionally, or internationally, in several areas. These include, *inter alia*, cooperation in the countering of maritime crimes such as piracy and drug-trafficking (Articles 100 and 108), the conservation and management of living resources (Article 118), cooperation between States bordering enclosed or semi-enclosed seas (Article 123), the protection and preservation of the marine environment (Article 197), marine scientific research (Article 242), and the development and transfer of marine technology (Articles 270 to 274). Accordingly, several regional cooperative mechanisms have been established in different parts of the world, in diverse areas such as anti-piracy, countering maritime crime, marine scientific research, marine environmental protection, fisheries management, conservation of living resources, etc.[19]

Regional approaches to cooperation, often in advance of global responses, potentially involve a variety of approaches, including political ones (through regional institutions), binding legal instruments, as also non-binding (soft law) instruments such as declarations; and, a host of informal processes.[20] Progress notwithstanding, it has been assessed that there is room for furthering cooperative endeavours in a number of areas, including Search and Rescue (SAR), oil pollution preparedness and response, cooperation in Areas Beyond National Jurisdiction (ABNJ), fisheries management, etc.[21] Domestically, principles enshrined in the Indian Constitution also engender the promotion of international peace and security, the fostering of respect for international law and treaty obligations, and the peaceful settlement of international disputes.[22] A non-exhaustive list of international instruments that facilitate maritime security cooperation from an Indian perspective are enumerated at **Annexure A**.

Drivers and Impediments

Overall, the drivers for maritime security cooperation are many. In the 21st century, it is widely acknowledged that no individual nation has the capacity to ensure maritime security, especially in a regional or global context. This necessitates partnerships as even securing one's own maritime zones can be a challenge. Broadly, maritime security cooperative efforts aim to bridge the gap between required and available capacities and capabilities to deal with security threats. Shared concerns in the maritime space such as maritime crime, especially transnational organised crime, proliferation of Weapons of Mass Destruction (WMD), etc. have also led to the rise of issue-based "coalitions of convenience."[23] The counter-piracy efforts off the Gulf of Aden/Horn of Africa is an exemplar of such a 'coalition.'

In response to a call from the United Nations (UN) Security Council urging States to deploy naval assets, in addition to task forces from the European Union (EU), North Atlantic Treaty Organisation (NATO), and Combined Maritime Force (CMF), individual countries, like India, also deployed naval assets, not only to protect national shipping, but also to ensure protection of international trade through global commons. The modest mechanisms for coordination, led by the deployed task forces through the SHADE forum, have remained informal, yet, importantly, effective. The institution of a similar forum in the Gulf of Guinea in 2021, the Gulf of Guinea Maritime Collaboration Forum (GoG-MCF/SHADE), more than a decade after the institution SHADE mechanism in the Horn of Africa only validates the global need for practical cooperation. On the other hand, some other formal cooperative endeavours with relatively grandiose visions, have made little practical progress, beyond pronouncements. It, therefore, appears that states actively come together to respond to real and immediate crises for common good, than for perceived crises that may or may not happen in a distant or not so distant future (or area).

Despite the pragmatism, there is also often an underlying realism in pursuing several cooperative endeavours. The need to hedge against an adversary, potential adversary, or a rival; countering growing influence of a competitor, or arresting diminishing influence with some partners; developing dependencies; enhancing defence exports and supporting domestic industries etc are unstated, but clearly discernible associated factors for expanding cooperation. Therefore, despite the allure of expanding maritime security cooperation, there is also reason for caution. Partners, therefore, need to undertake their own assessments of hidden agendas and the perceived immediate gains against possible hidden long-term costs from cooperative efforts, such as development of dependencies, etc. The *Atmanirbhar* [self-reliant] initiative is a move towards moving away from dependencies, but not an anathema to defence cooperation.

From a governance perspective, the US Maritime Security Sector Reform (MSSR) Guide, lists "diplomatic and foreign affairs support,' as a governance sub-function, and defines it as "the tasks required to coordinate between civil and criminal law enforcement and foreign affairs entities to ensure effective attainment of national maritime goals." The capabilities required for this function include participation in international and multilateral bodies (maritime and non-maritime), negotiation and implementation of treaties, and deployment of knowledgeable diplomatic personnel in pursuance of maritime-related interagency activities. While the articulation in the MSSR is restrictive to law enforcement and foreign affairs entities, and to law enforcement activities, the scope is wider and naval forces *de facto* continue to lead maritime security cooperation efforts, duly supported by other maritime stakeholders. It is also instructive to note that coordination is also needed with agencies that may not have a primary maritime focus ['non-maritime agencies'].

The diplomatic role is one of the roles of navies, including the Indian Navy. 'Naval diplomacy' entails the "use of naval forces in support of foreign policy objectives to build 'bridges of friendship' and strengthen international cooperation on the one hand, and to signal capability and intent to deter potential adversaries on the other."[24] However, in the 21st century, it has been realised that strengthening international cooperation for maritime security needs more than naval diplomacy.

The US, the only 'superpower' at that time, articulated the need for cooperation for maritime security in the mid-2000s. In 2005, the US Chief of Naval Operations (CNO), Admiral Mike Mullen, introduced the concept of '1000-ship navy' as a global partnership for maintaining international order at sea and combating non-military threats.[25] Towards achieving the aims of a '1000-ship navy,' it was envisaged that the US Navy would contribute 300 of the ships, with the balance being contributed by other navies/maritime security forces.[26] According to Gurpreet Khurana, the 'overstretch' of the US to deal with multiple global threats to its mainland led the US to take up a series of cooperative initiatives primarily to secure the US homeland.[27] This included the Proliferation Security Initiative (PSI), the Container Security Initiative (CSI), the Regional Maritime Security Initiative (RMSI), and the '1000-ship navy' concept. Two years later, in 2007, the idea of a '1000-ship navy,' was replaced by 'A Cooperative Strategy for 21st Century Sea Power' that also focused on cooperation in a globalised world, with lesser focus on US leadership.[28] The subsequent 2015 strategy was however different and focused largely on naval cooperation, and lesser on wider maritime security cooperation.[29] By 2022, the US Navy, to meet its own commitments, was looking at a 500-ship US Navy focused on aircraft carriers, large amphibious ships, frigates, destroyers, submarines, support ships, and even unmanned ships.[30] The 2020 maritime tri-service strategy, *Advantage at Sea*, focusing on China and Russia, also highlights the need for collaboration with "allies and partners to build capability, enhance interoperability, and generate unity of effort."[31]

In about twenty years, the US Navy's approach shifted its focus from non-traditional threats to military threats, indicating the changing strategic dynamics. Notwithstanding, military threats too need be dealt with through cooperative endeavours such as alliances and partnerships with like-minded partners. In about the same period, India's naval strategy as a developing regional power, focused significantly on expanding international naval cooperation for maritime security, along with strengthening domestic structures for governance through better interagency coordination, particularly after '26/11.'

Notwithstanding the need for cooperation, there are broad impediments in maritime security cooperation. In 2018, Shishir Upadhyaya in his thesis on "Maritime Security Cooperation in the IOR: Assessment of India's Maritime Strategy to be the Regional 'Net Security Provider,'" identified four broad impediments to maritime security cooperation: first, inter-state relations particularly mistrust and suspicion, as well as domestic issues, such as governance and national approach to international cooperation; second, wide disparities in force levels (capacity) and technological gaps between partners; third, linguistic and cultural barriers, such as between Anglophone and Francophone countries; and, finally, costs associated with furthering maritime cooperation efforts.[32]

In 2020, Ranendra Sawan, a serving officer, while exploring the same theme with a focus on the multilateral IONS construct, added some more challenges, including: the lack of a understanding of maritime security; absence of shared interests; the wide geographical expanse; and, the interplay between resident and extra-regional powers.[33] Pratnashree Basu, in 2021, identified other impediments, such as balance between 'blue-water' and 'brown-water' responsibilities (operational stretch); the China factor and the continuing continental focus of the security establishment; and, budgetary constraints and resultant impact on force levels.[34] In sum, progressing maritime security cooperation comes with a host of challenges which need to be addressed.

Typologies

Based on the nature of engagement, cooperative frameworks for maritime security can be described in different ways, informal, *ad hoc*, and temporary arrangements at one end of the spectrum, such as SHADE, to treaty-based mechanisms at the other end, with formalised and institutionalised mechanisms, such as NATO and the EU Naval Force. Voluntary coalitions, such as the CMF, led by the US Navy, is an example of a contemporary arrangement of working together outside a treaty mechanism.[35] Unlike security alliances in the past, the emerging architecture for security cooperation in the 21st century is relatively diffused, as exemplified by the QUAD. Maritime security cooperation can also be categorised depending on the number of partners (bilateral/multilateral [plurilateral]), level of partnership (strategic or non-strategic), geographical focus (regional/'sub-regional'), etc. Notably, a 'region' while reflecting a geographical space, is essentially an academic construct.

Shishir Upadhyaya, a naval veteran, has classified maritime security cooperation based on three traditional roles of navies viz. diplomatic, constabulary, and military, and under three levels viz. normal cooperation (Level 1), cooperation in crisis (Level 2), and cooperation in war (Level 3).[36] The typology essentially extrapolates the three naval roles with the spectrum of conflict (peace to war). In this context, a few of the more important elements from his exhaustive classification are reproduced in the table below:

Table 1.2: Levels and Types of Maritime Security Cooperation

	Level 1 (Normal)	Level 2 (Crisis)	Level 3 (War)
Diplomatic	• Visits/exchanges/talks • Constructs (IONS) • CBMs/CUES[37]	• OTR agreements • Exercises • Training • Foreign policy support 'gunboat diplomacy' • HADR	• Diplomatic support at international fora • Advanced training • Sanction enforcement

	Level 1 (Normal)	Level 2 (Crisis)	Level 3 (War)
Constabulary	• Coast guard functions and exercises • SAR	• Classified information sharing • Joint/coordinated patrols	• Non-military intelligence sharing, e.g., enemy shipping
Military	• Defence/security agreements • Logistic agreements • Technical support (repairs/refit) • Covert activities e.g., 'listening posts' • Sale of military hardware	• Classified information sharing • Advanced Exercises • Development of doctrines/SOPs • ISR operations • Transfer of military technology/hardware	• Treaty/alliance • Military intelligence sharing • Transfer of critical military technology/['strategic'] platforms • Sharing of crucial intelligence

Source: Shishir Upadhyaya.[38]

While there could be some discussion on the typology, as well as on the additions and omissions of certain activities, this elucidation is an important one in understanding the wide range and spectrum of maritime security cooperative effort, as well as the limitations to which certain partnerships can be taken forward. Considering India's overbearing reluctance to be part of 'alliances' outside the UN framework, some of the higher-level cooperative activities could be undertaken under the framework of 'strategic partnerships.'

Figure 1.1: Three Levels of Cooperations

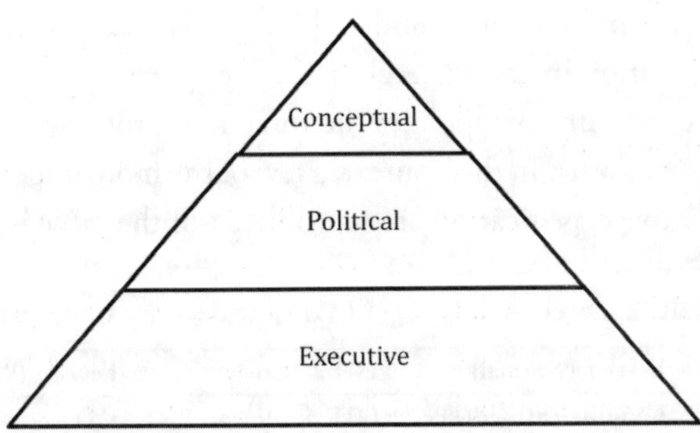

Source: Vice Admiral Pradeep Chauhan (Retd.).

Another typology, as espoused by the National Maritime Foundation (NMF), is to look at it as a pyramid comprising three levels: a conceptual level, a political level, and an executive level.[39] The conceptual level, at the top, includes broad policy articulations, such as Security and Growth for all in the Region (SAGAR) and Free and Open Indo-Pacific (FOIP); the political level, in the middle includes political-led groupings, such as Association of Southeast Asian Nations (ASEAN), Indian Ocean Rim Association (IORA), and QUAD; and, the executive level includes groupings, such as SHADE, and to some extent Indian Ocean Naval Symposium (IONS)/Western Pacific Naval Symposium (WPNS). However, *ex post facto*, harmonising an executive-level which has developed outside a political grouping, with a political group, is a challenging prospect, primarily because the political group, such as IORA, did not choose to have an executive-level grouping, such as IONS at the first place. However, it would be unwise if the executive level was not leveraged to further the interest of a political group.

Overall, there is no standard typology or classification of maritime security cooperation. However, the term 'maritime security cooperation' is an umbrella term to describe the entire spectrum of activities between two or more countries, international organisations, regional bodies for furthering shared maritime security objectives. Practically, it includes cooperative efforts by maritime security agencies, such as the Indian Navy and Coast Guard, as also sectoral initiatives. Increasingly, the inclusive paradigm for maritime security cooperation also includes a host of maritime stakeholders.

Overall, opinions are divided on maritime cooperation in the Indian Ocean, an area of primary interest for India: one view is that of "a strong track record of international cooperation," and the polar opposite is that of "the story of maritime security cooperation in the Indian Ocean Region (IOR) is, ironically, that of its absence."[40]

Having provided an overview of maritime security cooperation including the legal basis, the drivers and impediments, and the typology, subsequent chapters will endeavour to explore and evaluate the mechanisms for maritime security cooperation which have been adopted by India, and investigate possible imperatives for strengthening measures for maritime security cooperation.

NOTES

1 S. Jaishankar. *The India Way: Strategies for An Uncertain World* (Harper Collins, 2020), 95.

2 Christian Bueger, "What is maritime security?," *Marine Policy* 53, (2015): 159-164, https://www.sciencedirect.com/science/article/pii/S0308597X14003327, accessed on 20 August 2022; C. Dedeoglu, "The Ontology of Security and its Implications for Maritime Security,"

Güvenlik Stratejileri Dergisi 15 (2019): 631-654, DOI: 10.17752/guvenlikstrtj.668182, accessed on 20 August 2022,

3 Bueger, "What is maritime security?"

4 United Nations Security Council, "Statement by President of the Security Council," [UN S/PRST/2021/15] 09 August 2021, https://documents-dds-ny.un.org/doc/UNDOC/GEN/N21/220/62/PDF/N2122062.pdf? OpenElement, accessed on 20 August 2023.

5 Ministry of External Affairs, Government of India, "Joint Statement: Quad Foreign Ministers' Meeting," 03 March 2023, https://mea.gov.in/bilateral-documents.htm?dtl/36323/Joint_Statement_Quad, accessed on 20 August 2023.

6 United Nations Security Council, "Statement by President of the Security Council."

7 United Nations Security Council, "Statement by President of the Security Council"; Ministry of External Affairs, Government of India. "Joint Statement"

8 *Oxford Leaner's Dictionaries* (online), s.v. "cooperation," https://www.oxfordlearnersdictionaries.com/definition/english/cooperation?q=Cooperation+

9 Himadri Das, "India @75: Reflections on the Homeland Dimensions of Maritime Security in India," National Maritime Foundation, 08 August 2022, https://maritimeindia.org/15395-2/, accessed on 20 August 2023.

10 Das, "India @75."

11 Collated from multiple sources.

12 Author's interaction with former naval officer.

13 Coast Guard, "Indian Coast Guard Holds 19th National Maritime Search & Rescue Board Meeting," Press release, https://indiancoastguard.gov.in/WriteReadData/Tender/202111250217462790657NMSAR_Press_Brief_2021.pdf, accessed on 20 August 2023.

14 *Oxford Leaner's Dictionaries* (online), s.v. "collaboration," https://www.oxfordlearnersdictionaries.com/definition/english/collaboration?q=collaboration+ ; Oxford Leaner's Dictionaries (online), s.v. "coordination," https://www.oxfordlearnersdictionaries.com/definition/english/coordination?q=coordination.

15 FISH-i Africa and West Africa Task Force, *Stop Illegal Fishing (2021) Regional Cooperation to Stop Illegal Fishing: A Tale of Two Task Forces*, (Gaborone, Botswana: 2021), 14, https://1ae03060-3f06-4a5c-9ac6-b5c1b4a62664.usrfiles.com/ugd/1ae030_adff42091e77403db1f894ff1d17f986.pdf, accessed on 04 January 2022.

16 Charter of the United Nations, Article 1(1), https://legal.un.org/repertory/art1.shtml, accessed on 04 January 2022.

17 Brian Wilson, "The Turtle Bay Pivot: How the United Nations Security Council Is Reshaping Naval Pursuit of Nuclear Proliferators, Rogue States, and Pirates," *Emory Law Scholarly Commons* 33, no. 1 (February 2021), https://scholarlycommons.law.emory.edu/eilr/vol33/iss1/1, accessed on 20 August 2023.

18 James Borton, "UNCLOS Remains the Gold Standard in Maritime Security Cooperation," Geopolitical Monitor, 13 August 2021, https://www.geopoliticalmonitor.com/unclos-remains-the-gold-standard-in-maritime-security-cooperation/, accessed on 21 August 2021.

19 Donald R Rothwell, "Issues in Maritime Cooperation in the Region," Presentation at the 3rd ASEAN Regional Forum Workshop on UNLCOS, 01 June 2021.

20 Rothwell, "Issues in Maritime Cooperation in the Region."

21 Rothwell, "Issues in Maritime Cooperation in the Region."

22 Constitution of India, Section 51, https://www.constitutionofindia.net/

constitution_of_india/directive_principles_of_state_policy/articles/Article%2051, accessed on 14 March 2022.

23 Jaishankar, *The India Way*, 35.

24 Integrated Headquarters of Ministry of Defence (Navy), *Indian Maritime Doctrine* (New Delhi: 2004), 105.

25 Jo Inge Bekkevold and Geoffrey Till, eds., *International Order at Sea: How it is challenged; How it is maintained* (London: Palgrave Macmillan, 2016), 275.

26 Bekkevold and Till, *International Order at Sea*, 275.

27 Gurpreet Khurana, "'Thousand-Ship Navy': A Reincarnation of the Controversial P.S.I.?," Institute of Defence Studies and Analyses, 28 December 2006, https://www.idsa.in/idsastrategiccomments/AReincarnationoftheControversialPSI_GSKhurana_281206, accessed on 10 January 2022.

28 Bekkevold and Till, *International Order at Sea*, 276.

29 Bekkevold and Till, *International Order at Sea*, 276.

30 Sam LaGrone and Mallory Shelbourne, "CNO Gilday: 'We Need a Naval Force of Over 500 Ships," US Naval Institute News, 08 February 2022, https://news.usni.org/2022/02/18/cno-gilday-we-need-a-naval-force-of-over-500-ships, accessed on 09 March 2022.

31 US Navy, "Navy, Marine Corps, Coast Guard Release Maritime Strategy," *America's Navy*, 17 December 2020, https://www.navy.mil/Press-Office/Press-Releases/display-press releases/Article/2449829/navy-marine-corps-coast-guard-release-maritime-strategy/, accessed on 13 March 2022.

32 Shishir Upadhyaya, "Maritime Security Cooperation in the Indian Ocean Region: Assessment of India's Maritime Strategy to be the Regional "Net Security Provider"," Doctor of Philosophy Thesis, Australian National Centre for Ocean Resources and Security (University of Wollongong, Australia, 2018), 118-20, accessed on 20 August 2023, https://ro.uow.edu.au/theses1/297.

33 R.S. Sawan, "Problems and prospects of maritime security cooperation in the Indian Ocean Region: a case study of the Indian Ocean Naval Symposium (IONS)," *Sea Power Soundings,* no. 15 (2020), https://www.navy.gov.au/sites/default/files/documents/Soundings_Number_15.pdf, accessed on 31 December 2021.

34 Pratnashree Basu, "Maritime India: The Quest for a Steadfast Identity," *Observer Research Foundation Occasional Paper,* no. 339, November 2021, https://www.orfonline.org/research/maritime-india-the-quest-for-a-steadfast-identity/, accessed on 31 December 2021.

35 Upadhyaya, "Maritime Security Cooperation in the Indian Ocean Region," 117-20.

36 Upadhyaya, "Maritime Security Cooperation in the Indian Ocean Region," 121-22.

37 CBM: Confidence Building Measures; CUES: Code of Unalerted Encounters at Sea; IONS: Indian Ocean Naval Symposium; ISR: Intelligence, Surveillance, and Reconnaissance; HADR: Humanitarian Assistance and Disaster Relief; OTR: Operational Turn Around; SOP: Standard Operating Procedure.

38 Adapted from Upadhyaya, "Maritime Security Cooperation in the Indian Ocean Region," 121-22.

39 The author was a Researcher at the National Maritime Foundation.

40 Stable Seas, *Challenges and Solutions for Maritime Security in the Indian Ocean*, 6, https://www.stableseas.org/post/challenges-and-solutions-for-maritime-security-in-the-indian-ocean, accessed on 10 January 2022; Sawan, "Problems and Prospects of Maritime Security Cooperation."

2

The Indian Approach

The best ally is one who has the following six qualities: an ally of the family for a long time, constant, amenable to control, powerful in his support, sharing a common interest, able to mobilise [his forces] quickly, and not a man who betrays [his friends].

—Kautilya[1]

Ancient scriptures and wisdom underline the Indian approach to international cooperation. Indian leaders have also repeatedly extolled the importance of the Indian ethos underlying the phrase *Vasudhaiva Kutumbakam* (**वासुधैव कुटुम्बकम्**), which translates to 'the world is one family' in various contexts, but especially in the context of international relations and international cooperation. This approach, described as a "positive normative philosophical approach," is advocated as a way to develop trust and solidarity.[2] The Honourable Raksha Mantri, delivering the keynote address at a seminar focused on building collective maritime competence towards SAGAR during Aero India 2021, also highlighted ancient Indian wisdom encapsulated in the phrase *Aikyambalansamajasya, tadbhaveshdurbalah* (**ऐक्यंबलंसमाजस्य, तद्भावेसःदुर्बलः**), which translates to 'Unity is Strength of any Society, and a Society is weak without it' as the ethos of India's cooperative endeavours.[3]

As one of the oldest civilisations in the world, India has an ancient history of diplomacy, with scriptures and texts providing evidence of ancient Indian diplomacy.[4] The narrative of diplomacy in ancient India is incomplete without reference to *Arthasthatra,* considered as the world's first comprehensive work on diplomatic practice.[5] The treatise provides some basic principles of foreign policy which continue to be relevant today.[6] Allies are considered as an important aspect of foreign policy, and described as 'constituent of a state.'[7] Kautilya goes on to provide a comprehensive analysis of the types of kings with whom alliances are desirable, and the types of alliances based on their character and motivation.[8] Further, in addition to making peace, waging war, staying quiet, preparing for war, and a dual policy of making peace with one king and ware with another, one of the methods of foreign policy is described as seeking protection in the form of alliances [Samasrya].[9]

On becoming a republic, the promotion of international peace and security was enshrined in the Directive Principles of State Policy.[10] The Directives of State Policy although not enforceable by any court, lay down principles that are "fundamental in the governance of the country."[11] Article 51 of the Constitution (Promotion of International Peace and Security) states that India must endeavour to (a) promote international peace and security; (b) maintain just and honourable relations between nations; (c) foster respect for international law and treaty obligations in the dealings of organized peoples with one another; and (d) encourage settlement of international disputes by arbitration. It is no surprise, therefore, that India's approach to security cooperation, including for maritime security, is based on these principles. In the framing of the article, members of the Constituent Assembly felt that India should play a role in effectuating world peace, as Indian history and culture were steeped in peace, non-aggression, and spirituality.[12] The draft article was viewed as expressive of India's intention to pursue an independent foreign policy, and it was envisioned that "India would not be dragged into the quarrels of other countries and would not align with power blocs."[13] While India has maintained an independent foreign policy, and not joined any formal 'power block,' increasingly India is aligning itself with likeminded countries through robust strategic partnerships, such as through the QUAD, which is being perceived by China as an anti-China clique.[14]

Since independence, Indian foreign policy has undergone significant changes driven by the changing world, a changing India, and its own outlook to the world. India's External Affairs Minister (EAM) has divided the seven decades since independence into six phases: first, 1946-62, as a phase of optimistic non-alignment that ended with the China war; second, 1962-71, as a phase of realism and recovery, and a movement beyond non-alignment; third, 1971-91, as a phase of regional assertion with interventions in the neighbourhood; fourth, 1991-99, as a shift to strategic autonomy in a unipolar world; fifth, 2000-13, marked the shift to a balancing power in an increasing multi-polar world, and the sixth phase, commenced in 2014, when India chose to play a wider role in the global order.[15]

Writing on the ninth anniversary of the government in 2023, the EAM highlighted that Indian diplomacy was far more influential, and it is handling of a volatile world much more sophisticated.[16] He went on to highlight that India's growing influence comes from the powers of ideas and initiatives, and cited amongst others, maritime security as an arena where India has shaped discussions and outcomes.[17] The SAGAR initiative, the IPOI, and UN Security Council debate on maritime security are reflective of some of the foreign policy initiatives taken by India. These pronouncements have also been followed by expanding engagement of Indian agencies in strengthening maritime security, beginning from the neighbourhood, and transcending oceans to distant seas. He further underscored that under the leadership of PM Modi, the focus has been on "building greater capabilities, assuming greater responsibilities, and shaping the big issues of our day."[18] Maritime security is one such issue, and India's maritime security cooperation efforts have indeed concentrated on the focus areas.

Notwithstanding India's changing world-view, the key principles of *Panchsheel* (five principles), non-alignment and strategic autonomy continue to influence India's foreign policy.[19] Progressively, India's foreign policy has adopted a multi-aligned approach which permits India to have conversations with diverse players.[20] As India's foreign policy focus evolved and India's maritime capacities and capabilities grew, India has taken on a wider role in regional maritime security. Progressively beginning with the fourth phase, the ways and means to achieve maritime security cooperation have also evolved and expanded. India's approach to maritime security cooperation received a significant fillip commencing the fifth phase, and with it, India's engagement for maritime security and safety with the international community has also expanded exponentially, particularly in the sixth phase.

CONTEMPORARY POLICIES

> *We stand for open, free, rule-based maritime borders in Indo-pacific, in which no nation, how-so-ever big, may be allowed to appropriate the global common or exclude others from its fair use. We are always ready and forthcoming to work with all the like-minded partner countries across various forums towards this endeavour.*
>
> —Shri Rajnath Singh, Raksha Mantri[21]

While the 'Look East Policy' and the need for greater engagement with IOR nations were the primary drivers for India's engagement in a new world order in the 1990s, the decade 2011-2021 has been an especially important one for the development of India's approach to maritime security cooperation. One of the most important facets of this period was the articulation of the vision for maritime security (and cooperation) by the political leadership. These include: 'net security provider' (2011), SAGAR vision in Mauritius (2015), the free open and inclusive Indo-Pacific and the five 'S' principles at the Shangri La Dialogue (2018), the Indo-Pacific Oceans' Initiative (IPOI) at the East Asia Summit (EAS) (2019), and the five principles for maritime security cooperation at the high-level open debate on maritime security at the UN Security Council (2021).

2011: Net Security Provider

In 2011, the then Raksha Mantri, Shri AK Anthony, while addressing the Naval Commanders' Conference, stated that the Indian Navy has been "mandated to be a *net security provider* to island nations in the IOR [emphasis added]." In the same breath, he also highlighted that this must not be to the detriment of the core responsibilities of the Indian Navy.[22] Subsequently, in 2013, at the foundation laying stone of the Indian National Defence University (INDU), Prime Minister Manmohan Singh said:

> Our defence cooperation has grown and today we have unprecedented access to high technology, capital and partnerships. We have also sought to assume our responsibility for stability in the IOR. We are well positioned, therefore, to become a *net provider of security* in our immediate region and beyond [emphasis added].[23]

Over time there have been nuanced differences in the articulation of the concept: while the initial articulation by the Raksha Mantri in 2011 related to India being a "*net security provider* to island nations in the Indian Ocean Region," in 2013 the articulation was modified to "*net provider of security*," and the geographic scope was expanded to the "immediate region and beyond." In 2015, the *Indian Maritime Security Strategy*, gave a much required maritime focus to the articulation, and it was expressed from a naval perspective as "*net maritime security provider*," the geographic extent of the Indian Navy's areas of interest also included regions beyond the IOR.[24] The *Indian Maritime Security Strategy* described 'net security' as the security available upon balancing threats, risks, and challenges in the maritime domain, against the ability to monitor, contain and counter them.[25] In other words, India seeks to address the security deficit in regional security capabilities. The strategy document also highlights that the maritime security objective of "shaping a favourable and positive maritime environment" facilitates "net security in India's areas of maritime interest."[26] Amplifying further, the strategy identified preservation of peace, promotion of stability, and maintenance of security as the three key principles of 'net maritime security.'[27] Further, to actualise the three principles, presence and rapid response, maritime engagements, capacity building and capacity enhancement, developing regional Maritime Domain Awareness (MDA), maritime security operations, and, strategic communication were identified as the key actions.[28] With the reiteration of the concept by the Prime Minister at the UN Security Council in August 2021, wherein he stated that "India's role in the Indian Ocean Region has been as a *Net Security Provider* [emphasis added]," the concept remains at the heart of India's approach to maritime security in the India Ocean, albeit with some variations in the articulation. In 2022, the *Indo-Pacific Strategy of the United States* also endorsed the 2011 pronouncement, by supporting India in "its role as a net security provider."[29] Furthermore, the articulation by successive governments, despite ideological differences, also reflects a continuity in government policy.

2015: SAGAR

In 2015, Prime Minister Modi, during a visit to Mauritius, articulated the SAGAR vision, which is the foundational paradigm for India's Indo-Pacific policy.[30] The EAM has described SAGAR as the "first integrated maritime outlook."[31] While 'net security' focused extensively on security, SAGAR conceptually integrated growth (development) with security. Further, according to the minister, it is India's belief is that "advancing cooperation and using our capabilities for larger good would benefit India," and that it "comes with a willingness to assume responsibilities as a net-security provider."[32] He further established four elements of the outlook:

> First, safeguarding own territory and interests, and ensuring a safe, secure, and stable Indian Ocean;
>
> Second, deepening economic and security cooperation with maritime neighbours aimed at strengthening capacities;
>
> Third, advancing collective action and cooperation to advance peace and security and respond to emergencies;
>
> Fourth, a more integrated future that enhances sustainable development;[33] and
>
> A fifth point relates to partnerships with extra-regional powers with interests in the region.

In a similar vein, in 2021, the Raksha Mantri, Shri Rajnath Singh identified deepening of security and economic cooperation, capacity-building for safeguarding territories, sustainable development, and collective action to deal with non-traditional threats, HADR, and SAR as related elements of the SAGAR vision.[34]

He also emphasised the need for prioritisation, which he described as four 'concentric circles,' including the homeland and immediate neighbours, maritime island neighbours (including Seychelles), the wider IOR, and finally the wider Indo-Pacific.[35] The concept of 'maritime neighbourhood' is a flexible concept, at one end it could include those neighbours with whom India shares maritime borders (immediate neighbourhood) and on the other those countries with which India is a separated by intervening seas, especially those in the IOR (extended neighbourhood).

Five years after the enunciation of the vision, in the words of the EAM, there is indeed a better understanding of maritime geography and the SAGAR doctrine.[36] He also contended that India has responded with new grit to security challenges and is shaping global conversations, including on maritime security.[37] He specifically cited relief operations undertaken in various parts of the IOR and beyond as statements of capability and responsibility.[38] It is therefore no surprise that in 2021 India steered the maiden UN Security Council high-level open debate on maritime security.

2018: The 'Five S' Vision/Free Open and inclusive Indo-Pacific

In 2018, Prime Minister Modi, delivering the keynote address at the annual Shangri-La Dialogue in Singapore articulated India's vision for a free open and inclusive Indo-Pacific. Further, he also highlighted that India's engagement with the world is based on the principles of *Samman* (respect); *Samvad* (dialogue); *Sahayog* (cooperation), *Shanti* (peace), and *Samriddhi* (prosperity).[39] This was later described by the Raksha Mantri, Shri Rajnath Singh, as the 'Five S' vision to tackle global challenges.

On the keynote address, Rahul Roy-Chaudhury, one of India's earliest writers on comprehensive maritime security, highlighted three other major facets of the Prime Minister's speech: one, the articulation of the Indian perspective on the geographic scope of the Indo-Pacific and India's approach to the region; second, the importance of a rule-based order and ASEAN centrality; and, finally, from a maritime security cooperation perspective, the importance of naval diplomacy in the overall Indo-Pacific vision.[40] Rahul Roy-Chaudhury also raised two concerns: first, the challenges in being a 'first responder' and 'net security provider' east of the Straits of Malacca-Singapore where India has little defence/security leverage; and second, the lack of clarity about the how regional cooperation and collective security could be progressed through the framework of IORA and IONS, whose performance for these objective were describe by him as "underwhelming."[41]

2019: IPOI

In November 2019, Prime Minister Modi announced the Indo-Pacific Oceans' Initiative (IPOI) at the East Asia Summit (EAS) held in Bangkok.[42] The IPOI is an open, inclusive, cooperative global initiative focused on finding solutions to global changes and draws on existing regional architecture and mechanisms.[43] Like the QUAD, bereft of a formal structure, the IPOI is a 21st century response to a 21st century challenge. It focuses on seven central pillars conceived around maritime security; maritime ecology; maritime resources; capacity building and resource sharing; disaster risk reduction and management; science, technology, and academic cooperation; trade connectivity, and maritime transport.[44] It has been argued that viewing the focus areas of the framework as 'pillars' may be constrictive silos approach, and therefore the seven dimensions of cooperation need to be viewed as a web of interlinkages between seven webbed 'spokes,' rather than seven 'pillars.'[45] While at the conceptual-level, an interlinked approach is certainly desirable, from an implementation perspective, a pillared approach may in fact be more pragmatic.

The initiative is significant in that while it geographically expands the SAGAR vision of the IOR, beyond the IOR to the Indo-Pacific, it also provides an actionable framework for cooperation. While maritime security is only one of the seven pillars of cooperation; maritime security itself is a facilitator and enabler for the other dimensions of the IPOI which have a predominant maritime focus.

India is the lead partner in two pillars focused on maritime security and disaster risk reduction; consequently, Indian agencies responsible for maritime security and disaster relief reduction would be the lead agencies to support the MEA in its implementation, along with other resources, such as academic institutions, think tanks, etc.[46] Australia, France, and Japan are lead partners for the maritime ecology, maritime resources, and trade connectivity pillars respectively. It still means that two pillars viz. capacity building and academic cooperation are yet to find leaders, and consequently to be taken forward.

2021: Five Principles for Maritime Security Cooperation

In 2021, under Indian presidency of the UN Security Council, a high-level open debate on the topic "Enhancing Maritime Security: A Case for International Cooperation" was held on 09 August 2021. India, during its presidency, had chosen maritime security as one of the areas of focus; the other two areas being peacekeeping and counter-terrorism. This was the first time that maritime security was discussed in a holistic manner at the Security Council and the open debate highlights the importance that the world in general, and India in particular, attaches to maritime security, and specifically maritime security cooperation. In another first, the Indian Prime Minister chaired the meeting and laid out five principles for developing a global roadmap for maritime security cooperation. These included:

(1) Developing an 'inclusive structure for maritime security' in the IOR based on the vision of SAGAR;
(2) Peaceful settlement of disputes;
(3) Cooperative efforts at fighting natural disasters and non-state actors;
(4) Preservation of the environment and resources; and
(5) Promotion of maritime connectivity.[47]

During this speech at the UN Security Council, Prime Minister Modi highlighted some of India's most notable contributions for maritime security: India's peaceful resolution of its maritime boundary dispute with Bangladesh; India's proven capability as a regional first responder to contingencies, such as natural calamities; India's anti-piracy efforts in the Gulf of Aden; India's efforts at developing MDA through white-shipping agreements and through the Information Fusion Centre-Indian Ocean Region (IFC-IOR); and, training support in hydrography and maritime security. He also highlighted that India's efforts are promoting sustainable fisheries and advancing ocean sciences through the 'Deep Ocean Mission'. Finally, he also underscored India's role in the Indian Ocean of a net security provider.

The Presidential Statement adopted by the UN Security Council emphasised the need for international cooperation for maritime security, including on specific facets. In particular, the Council commended the role of regional and sub-regional organisations, and extolled them to continue their endeavours to assist in capacity building and in sharing practices to prevent and combat terrorism at sea.[48] The Council also welcomed the establishment of specific regional cooperative frameworks under the aegis of the UN Office on Drugs and Crime (UNODC) to counter maritime crime, and reiterated the need for information sharing. Recognising the importance of enhancing international and regional cooperation to counter threats to maritime safety and security, the UN Security Council also called upon Member States to participate in regional and global initiatives to counter transnational organised crime and in capacity building.[49] Further, the Council also called upon Member States to foster cooperation in mutual legal assistance and to 'share experiences' on possible gaps and vulnerabilities.

The lead taken by India at the UN Security Council has been lauded by several analysts, and is reflective of the important role that India can play to shape in the discourse on global governance through multilateral institutions.[50]

It is another matter that repeatedly abstaining from voting against the Russian invasion of Ukraine in the Security Council and other UN bodies has led to calls for a more 'forceful' role from India in the UN Security Council.[51] The presence of the Russian President, despite India's own increasing closeness with its arch-rival the US, and India's acknowledgment of the Russian role in maritime security, underscores India's continued advocacy of strategic autonomy in foreign policy; likewise, the decision to procure the S-400 Triumf Air Defence System is another example.[52] The UN debate was unprecedented, and reflected the importance of maritime security to international peace and security, and India's stewardship of maritime security, not just at the regional level, but also at a global level. Overall, the debate is reflective of growing diplomatic heft, and "India's capabilities in steering global efforts towards enhancement of global maritime security."[53] The outcome document emerging from the debate, as also other policy proclamations by India, needs to be acted upon. Doing that at a regional and global level will require a WoG approach led by the MEA.

Foreign Policy: Regional Approaches

India's foreign policy vision also lays focus on specific geographical areas within the wider IOR, including in the promotion of security cooperation. These include the 'Act East' and 'Act Far East' policy, the 'Neighbourhood First' and the 'Act West' policies. These contemporary region-specific approaches intimately interplay with India's maritime policies thereby setting the contours of the scope, degree, and nature of engagements for maritime security cooperation, on bilateral and regional bases.

India's 'Neighbourhood First' policy *inter alia* focuses on the development of a regional framework for stability and prosperity, based on a consultative, non-reciprocal, and outcome-oriented approach, including in security.[54] The South Asia Association for Regional Cooperation (SAARC) and Bay of Bengal Initiative for Multi-Sectoral Technical and Economic Cooperation (BIMSTEC) are two of the important regional organisations for promotion of cooperation, including in security. More recently, the Colombo Security Conclave (CSC) has emerged as the most significant neighbourhood grouping for enhancing maritime security corporation in the immediate neighbourhood.

The 'Look East' policy, initiated in 1990, initially conceived as an economic initiative, has gained traction over the years. The scope of engagement has been widened and the policy has assumed a strategic dimension, and institutional mechanisms have been established for progressing cooperative endeavours.[55] In 2014, the Look East policy was upgraded to the 'Act East' policy and was formally enunciated in November 2014 at the 9th EAS held in Nay Pyi Taw, Myanmar.[56] The principles and objectives of the upgraded policy include the development of strategic partnerships with countries in the Asia-Pacific through continuous engagement at bilateral, regional, and multilateral levels.[57] Multilateral engagements on maritime security and related themes are undertaken through engagements with multilateral constructs, such as ASEAN, ASEAN Regional Forum (ARF), EAS, ASEAN Defence Ministers' Meeting Plus (ADMM+), BIMSTEC, etc.[58] In 2019, the Act East policy was further complemented by an 'Act Far East" policy expanding India's economic engagement with Russian Far East.[59] Westward, India has also articulated an 'Act West' policy; however, the exact dimensions of the security aspects, especially from a maritime security perspective, are still unclear.[60]

INDIAN NAVY'S APPROACH

> *In today's world, naval diplomacy has a crucial role to play because as a means of 'engagement' it can materially help shape the international environment, and contain, resolve or prevent conflict.*
>
> —Geoffery Till[61]

Historical Overview: 1975-2021

Broadly, larger navies which have the necessary capabilities, also include the diplomatic role as part of the triad (or quartet) of roles, the others being the military and constabulary roles. With a growing Navy, by the 1990s there was a realisation within the Indian Navy that "as a rising world power having the potential for a larger regional role in the years ahead."[62] Accordingly, it was anticipated that that there would be enhanced engagement with Extra-Regional navies, such as those of Russia, UK, US, and with navies of Indian Ocean Countries, including France, through exercises.[63]

With the end of the Cold War in 1991, and the emergence of unipolar world with the US as a sole superpower, India reappraised her role in the new world order, and it was concluded that "India could no longer be considered as a marginal and benign presence and that it could play a stabilizing role in West Asia, South Asia and South East Asia."[64] Important facets of India's reorientation included redefining relationships with major powers, the 'Look East Policy,' and the recognition to forge closer relationships with IOR nations.[65] India also liberalised its economy at that time, which meant that the Indian economy also began to grow rapidly thereafter, and economic growth can result in enhanced military spending.[66]

At about the same time there was an orchestrated international campaign, to project the expanding Indian Navy as a threat to smaller littorals.[67] To dispel the misconceptions, it was decided to "dispel these misapprehensions by letting other navies interact with India's Navy during joint naval exercises at sea."[68] India expanded its engagements with the US and other countries, through talks and other engagements, such as exercises, MILAN interactions in line with the 'Look East Policy', International Fleet Review (IFR), etc.[69] India's position was that in a new world order, "adversarial postures ought to be shed and countries of the Indian Ocean Region should come closer for mutual benefit."[70]

These developments happened also in the backdrop of coming into force of UNCLOS (1994), which established a new rules-based maritime order, and increasing recognition of wider dimensions to security (non-traditional threats), including in the maritime domain.[71] The growing attention towards the nascent concept of maritime security, and specific issues such as maritime terrorism and transnational organised crime, also created a favourable environment for furthering the Indian Navy's constructive engagements.[72] In other words, the 1990s were significant foundational years, which reflected the confluence of growing political will and economic growth, and a navy in transition. On hedging against the likelihood of an assertive China, the Indian Navy's official history highlights the need for India to emerge as a strong power with economic linkages with ASEAN.[73]

At the turn of the 21st century the Indian Navy began to consolidate on the progress made, and 'maritime diplomacy' was recognised as a means to achieve the broader ends of good order at sea and maritime security.[74] In backdrop of the '9/11' incident, the concept of 'maritime security' began to find a mention in UN documents, and over the early years of the 21st century, as the concept of maritime security evolved and was increasingly recognised, so did India's approach to international cooperation for maritime security.

The official history of the Indian Navy for the period 2001-2010, driven by the transformation of the Indian Navy to blue water force, reflected it its title *Blue Waters Ahoy!* notes: *The first decade of the twenty-first century was transformational in many ways. This was also a decade in which the Navy's outreach increased significantly. Numerous bilateral exercises were initiated and the Navy collaborated with a number of regional and extra-regional navies. The Indian Ocean Naval Symposium (IONS) [in 2008] was constituted and the Navy set about to assume its role as the 'net security provider' in the Indian Ocean Region.*[75] Organisationally, in September 2005, the Directorate of Foreign Cooperation (DFC), was established as the single-point of contact at the Integrated Headquarters of Ministry of Defence (Navy) for all foreign cooperation issues, including policy, material, training and operational, as also the creation of a new Flag-rank post to oversee the functioning, that of the Assistant Chief of the Naval Staff (Foreign Cooperation and Transformation) which was in February 2006 rechristened as the Assistant Chief of the Naval Staff (Foreign Cooperation and Intelligence) [ACNS (FCI)].[76]

The second decade of the 21st century began with the articulation of the mandate of the Indian Navy to be net security provider to nations in the IOR. As highlighted earlier, this was followed with the SAGAR vision (2015), the 'Five S' vision (2018), and the IPOI (2019). Clearly, there was political will for a greater role on India for maritime security. This was also the time when China considerably increased its presence in the IOR, and of skirmishes and stand offs along the land borders, leading to a deterioration of relationship.[77] In the second decade of the 21st century, the Indian Navy exponentially ramped-up its engagements with partners and established several new partnerships, which continue to expand.[78] Expanding its engagements, two of the key developments in this period were the setting-up of the IFC-IOR and the establishment of the Goa Maritime Conclave (GMC).[79] In the absence of any amplifications, the subtitle of the Indian Navy's official history, *Signalling Power and Partnerships,* perhaps focuses on the expanding maritime partnerships which the Indian Navy was forging in line with its vision of being a 'preferred security partner.'

In short, the Indian Navy's cooperative engagements have, from modest beginning in the early 1990s, gained significant traction over the subsequent decades. Global and regional developments, national interests, developing economy, political will, capacity and capabilities of a growing Indian Navy, were some of the major factors that converged at different periods have contributed to giving effect to the national vision for an enhanced role of India in maritime security.

Doctrinal and Strategic Articulations

The *Indian Maritime Doctrine* (2004) included the diplomatic role as one of the roles of the Indian Navy. It defined the diplomatic role as the "use of maritime forces as a diplomatic instrument in support of political objectives and foreign policy."[80] Its missions under the diplomatic role include maritime diplomacy, developing healthy partnerships, gaining confidence of IOR littorals to meet contingencies, providing assistance, contributions to UN peacekeeping forces, and interoperability with multinational forces. The doctrine also lists naval diplomacy as a peacetime task, and predicted that the "tasks will assume greater importance as the global focus shifts from geo-strategic concerns to geo-economic dictates.'[81] It briefly touches upon a range of activities as part of the role: 'showing the flag' in foreign ports; assistance to foreign countries in crises; deterrence, coercion, and power projection; as well as showcasing Indian culture and progress.[82] As examples of naval diplomacy the doctrine cites Operation CACTUS (1988),[83] International Fleet Review (2001), seaward security to African Union Summit in Mozambique (2003), and regional response to Tsunami (2004) as examples. Notably, the Indian Navy had also taken part in peacekeeping operations in Sri Lanka (1987-90) and Somalia (1993-94). Notwithstanding the fact that the doctrine was published in a policy vacuum, and at a time when naval reach and engagements were relatively limited, the doctrine did foretell that the diplomatic role would grow. Moreover, the concept of maritime security was just emerging at that time.

The *Indian Maritime Doctrine* (2009) further dilated on the diplomatic role and stated that the larger purpose of the role is "to favourably shape the maritime environment in the furtherance of national interests, in consonance with foreign policy and national security objectives."[84] It emphasised that navies lean toward the diplomatic roles primarily on two counts, the first being the fact that the presence (or absence) of navies in or off certain areas signals national intent and commitment, and the second, the inherent attributes of maritime forces offer a range of ways for furthering foreign policy goals. The doctrine also detailed specific *objectives*, *missions*, and *tasks* for the Indian Navy, in the diplomatic role. Importantly, the concepts related to net security, the Indo-Pacific, and maritime security were taking shape around this time. In particular, the doctrine articulates fresh missions as: (1) constructive maritime engagement; (2) maritime assistance and support; (3) presence; (4) peace support operations. The expanded scope of 'tasks' now included overseas deployments, technical and logistic support, training, Coordinated Patrol (CORPAT), bilateral exercises, NEO, peacekeeping (and associated operations), 'Out-of-Area' Contingencies (OOAC) operations, and also activities under the IONS programme.[85] The 2009 doctrine provided greater granularity on the diplomatic role of the navy, alignment with national policy and foreign perspectives, including widening the missions, objectives and tasks, and importantly, included not only promotion of regional stability, but also global objectives. It appears that the broadened scope was based on the Indian Navy's own engagements since the 2004 doctrine such as in evacuations from Lebanon (2004), anti-piracy operations off the Horn of Africa/Gulf of Aden (2008), and the expanding scope of bilateral exercises/CORPAT with friendly countries, etc. In 2015, the doctrine was updated; however, it did not change the Indian Navy's fundamental approach to the diplomatic role.

In 2015, the *Indian Maritime Security Strategy* laid out the roadmap for shaping a favourable and positive maritime environment, quintessentially driven by cooperative endeavours. The strategy included several activities, which were not limited to just the diplomatic role, but also incorporated other doctrinal roles.[86] The 2015 strategy further expanded the task-list for its diplomatic role/task of shaping the environment in consonance with the vision of being a 'net maritime security provider' in the region, and was pragmatically based on experience, ongoing efforts, and on the desire to shape the environment. The usage of the term 'security provider' in the maritime context is not limited to India; in 2022, the EU has also used the term 'maritime security provider.'[87] The actions envisaged for shaping the environment include presence and rapid response, maritime engagements, capacity-building, regional MDA, maritime security operations, and strategic communications. The inclusion of maritime security operations and MDA in 2015 marked the direct assimilation of maritime security related activities and tasks into the naval strategy. The articulation of the SAGAR doctrine (2015), the continued presence HoA/GOA since 2008, the terrorist attacks on Mumbai '26/11', and the vision to be a 'net security provider' were some of the factors which could have contributed to the shift. The activities for 'net maritime security' under each action are tabulated below:

Table 2.1: Activities for 'Net Maritime Security'

Sl. No.	Action	Activities/Tasks
1.	Presence and Rapid Response	• Presence and Surveillance Missions (PSM) • Patrols • Overseas Deployments (OSDs)
2.	Maritime Engagement	• Port Visits/Showing the flag/Hosting foreign warships • Personnel exchange • Staff talks • Exercises • Maritime assistance (relief supplies, medical, diving, hydrographic, etc.) • Operational interactions • High-level strategic Interactions
3.	Capacity Building	• Technical Cooperation • Training Cooperation • Hydrographic Cooperation
4.	Regional MDA	• Coastal radar systems • White-shipping information exchange
5.	Maritime Security Operations	• Exclusive Economic Zone (EEZ) surveillance and patrols • CORPAT • Counter Infiltration • Anti-piracy/anti-poaching/anti-trafficking operations • HADR operations • NEO • Maritime Interdiction Operations (MIO) • Peace Support Operations (PSO) • Maritime SAR (M-SAR)

Notwithstanding the wide scope of activities and the inter-linkages between the multiple naval roles, many of the tasks associated with the strategy, directly or indirectly contribute towards building interoperability and furthering practical maritime security cooperation.

Practically, the Indian Navy has also been used as means to project soft power. For example, as part of the International Day of Yoga (IDY) celebrations in 2023, the Indian Navy created an 'Ocean Ring of Yoga,' with the deployment of 11 warships overseas.[88] Further, eight IN ships were concurrently deployed to seven foreign ports in six continents, to commemorate 75 years of India's Independence and hoist the National Flag, as part of AKAM celebrations.[89]

Shifting Paradigm: Signalling Partnerships

While India has positioned itself as a net security provider in the IOR, in 2019, the Raksha Mantri lauding the Indian Navy's foreign cooperation initiatives, stated that these initiatives had not only strengthened maritime security, but also transformed the Indian Navy into a 'preferred partner' for engagement in the IOR.[90] Subsequent press releases on India's humanitarian assistance efforts to assist Friendly Foreign Countries (FFCs) during the COVID pandemic reiterated India's position as a 'dependable partner' and the Indian Navy as a 'preferred security partner and first responder.'[91] In February 2021, the Chief of the Naval Staff (CNS) addressing a seminar at *Aero India 2021* on the theme 'Collective Maritime Competence towards SAGAR,' stated: "… the concept of security and growth for all in the region remains crucial since it emphasises an inclusive and engaged ecosystem for partnership in the maritime domain and India's emphasis has been on partnering as equals to create an inclusive framework rather than a prohibitive elitist one and in this the Indian Navy truly believes that each one amongst us in the IOR is an equal and critical partner in the business of keeping the seas safe and secure."[92] Towards the end of 2021, the President, Shri Ram Nath Kovind, also used the term 'preferred security partner' when he said that "the Indian Navy is looked upon by our maritime neighbours as a preferred security partner in the IOR."[93]

It therefore appears that in the late 2010s, India's efforts towards strengthening maritime security cooperation focused on an inclusive approach to building partnerships amongst equals, rather than an exclusive self-driven approach. Outside alliances, 'partnerships' are the preferred/dependable mode of maritime security cooperation between like-minded nations. Strategic partnerships, based on convergence of interests, can not only provide increased flexibility and latitude, but can also deliver.[94] It has been opined that formal alliances are not necessary for a solid relationship.[95] As is in the case of India's articulation, the term 'partnership' is often prefixed with an adjective emphasising a particular facet of the partnership by other countries as well;

for example the EU seeks to increase EU capacity as a "reliable partner and a maritime security provider."[96]

Broadly, India's approach to security is not based on military alliances, but that of an equal partnership in all mechanisms that it is part of.[97] Interestingly, in May 2023, a U.S. House Select Committee recommended strengthening the 'NATO-Plus' framework by including India.[98] The rationale for the recommendation is essentially to win the strategic competition with China.[99] However, as per media reports, the EAM rejected the idea as the "NATO template does not apply to India."[100] It has also been reported that Iran is also forming a naval alliance comprising Saudi Arabia, three Gulf States, as also India and Pakistan.[101] While the details of the alliance have not been revealed, India's approach to such an alliance is likely to be no different.[102]

Collective Maritime Competence

In 2019, the CNS, Admiral Karambir Singh, highlighting the need for nations to work together, underscored the Indian Navy's belief in 'collective military competency' as no one nation has all the capacities or competencies to deal with all the challenges.[103] Subsequently in December 2020, he brought out that the India Navy's engagements with friendly-foreign countries aims at building collective maritime competence."[104] The concept of 'collective maritime competence' was later described by the CNS at the Aero India 2021.[105]

The CNS described the 'collective maritime competence' as the ability to "collectively promote maritime interests in the global commons by collaborating with like-minded nations to build capacities and deepen linkages." The CNS said that the core idea behind the concept was shared professionalism [competence] in cooperative efforts [collective] in the maritime domain. The reasons for the idea, the CNS expounded, was that the threats were transnational, that safe and secure seas were in the interest of all nations, and finally, no single nation has the resources to harness all the opportunities or to address all the challenges. The CNS also reiterated that each nation has unique capabilities that could be harnessed and synergised to develop greater collective resilience and response. The CNS said that two important ways to achieve collective maritime competence were first, frequent engagements and exercises for enhancing interoperability, and second, greater information-sharing for developing MDA. The CNS also highlighted that trust can only be developed through committed long-term engagements; conversely, *ad hoc* fleeting engagements could hardly contribute to developing trust.

Collective competence engenders collective action, and in times of resource constraints and growing challenges, collective action therefore becomes a strategic necessity. However, despite the platitudes, outside treaty alliances, collective actions come with little or no assurance. The Defence Secretary, in 2021, also reiterated the Indian Navy's position as a 'preferred security partner,' but with a small variation; he stated that the aim was to eventually become a 'dependable maritime neighbour.'[106] Notably, in maritime terms, a 'maritime neighbourhood' is not always limited to the contiguous neighbourhood.

Maritime Security Cooperation: Central Lines of Effort

Towards effectuating India's strategy and policy for advancing maritime security cooperation, especially in the Indo-Pacific, in December 2020, writing in the *Indian Naval Despatch*, the Indian Navy's flagship journal, the CNS articulated the Indian Navy's approach. He articulated three lines of effort:[107]

> *First*, collaboration and cooperation towards comprehensive maritime security, including in operations, MDA, countering non-traditional threats, etc. He also articulated his vision of developing the Indian Navy as a maritime information hub in the IOR.
>
> *Second*, forging regional solutions to regional problems through initiatives such as MILAN, IONS, Goa Maritime Conclave (GMC), Indo-Pacific Regional Dialogue (IPRD), etc, as well as developing the Indian Navy as a 'first responder' and 'preferred security partner.'
>
> *Third*, enhancing reach and sustenance through Operational Turn Around (OTR)/agreements, and logistic support arrangements.

In August 2021, the CNS, Admiral Karambir Singh, while addressing the United Services Institute (USI) on *Transforming the Indian Navy to be a Key Maritime Force in the Indo-Pacific*, described five lines of effort in the wider context of the Indo-Pacific, including domestic imperatives:[108]

> *First*, collaboration and cooperation with like-minded nations for comprehensive maritime security. He highlighted efforts at building collective maritime competence through frameworks such as IONS,

GMC, etc. He cited the IONS HADR Guidelines, and highlighted the importance of developing interoperability through coordinated operations with regional navies

Second, the readiness to operate in the 'competition continuum' by leveraging the Indian Navy's foreign cooperation efforts and leveraging its geographic advantage.

Third, building MDA and understanding of the environment through national MDA, IFC-IOR, and through persistent surveillance, not only by ships (mission-based deployment), but also by Long Range Maritime Patrol (LRMP), High Altitude Long Endurance (HALE), and satellites.

Fourth, coordination of efforts across Government of India (GoI) stakeholders by breaking silos in the maritime domain, such as through the proposed National Maritime Security Coordinator (NMSC),[109] and the need to develop 'integrated maritime capability' to allow response across different situations.

Fifth, effective long-term perspective planning with due consideration to force capabilities, and force multipliers, such as unmanned systems, networking, space, and cyberspace, etc. with a focus on indigenisation.

Broadly, the lines of effort described by the CNS for promoting cooperation, which can be broadly termed as 'constructive engagements,' involve strengthening partnerships with friendly countries, enhancing MDA, and enhancing reach and sustenance through agreements. Furthermore, integrating national efforts, and at the service-level, force planning and capability development, are also imperatives. It is no surprise, therefore, that the focus of priorities to shape the environment are particularly on enhanced maritime engagements, such as through the IONS construct; operational coordination and exercises with likeminded navies towards developing interoperability; cooperation in MDA for developing deeper understanding; and, expanding reach and sustenance through logistic and OTR agreements.

It is instructive to note that the cooperative efforts are largely in the realm of *capability enhancements*, rather than building of capacity. The segregation of MDA as a standalone line of effort, and the focus on persistent surveillance through aerospace assets marks an important shift in the approach to ISR. Further, the need to streamline the overall maritime security governance architecture is a vital pathway, as hitherto, the need for a single-point agency was largely viewed from a domestic perspective (coastal security), and not from a wider geostrategic perspective.

The public articulations of the CNS, which grow on, and further amplify the Indian Navy's own doctrinal articulations, provides overarching guidance, and focus to the naval staff in the implementation of foreign and maritime security cooperation efforts. While the approach to the Indo-Pacific is significantly influenced by persistent Chinese presence in the IOR, as the CNS clarified, the focus of the approach is on 'comprehensive' maritime security, which, in other words, also includes the entire spectrum of maritime security threats.

As the preponderant maritime security agency of India, the Indian Navy's articulations reflect the executive-level manifestation of India's own conceptual, political, and policy framework. The Indian Navy, since the mid-1990s, has progressively consolidated its own approach to its diplomatic role, in line with the approach of the GoI; In pursuit of becoming a security provider, a first responder, a preferred and dependable partner, the key features of India's contemporary approach to maritime security cooperation is based on building partnerships, enhancing capabilities, developing collective competence, and where possible capacity building.

THE COAST GUARD'S APPROACH

The Coast Guard is primarily responsible for security and for maritime law enforcement in the maritime zones of India; in other words, its primary responsibility is in those areas over which India exercises jurisdiction. However, as per its mandate and charter, the Coast Guard envisages its 'international operations' role, as primarily that of furthering India's adherence to its international obligations in the Indian maritime zones, and to develop and strengthen cooperation with regional coast guard/equivalents, such as for SAR, marine environmental and protection.[110] Progressively, as the capacity of the Coast Guard has grown, especially after the '26/11' incident, so have its international engagements. 'International Cooperation' in the context of the Coast Guard is achieved primarily through overseas deployment of ships, high-level meetings with foreign maritime law enforcement agencies, MOUs and exercises with regional, and even extra-regional partners, and joint maritime surveillance in foreign EEZ, such as in Maldives.[111] In addition, the Coast

Guard has also trained foreign personnel, both in India and abroad, and has supported capacity building, such as by providing Interceptor Boats (IBs) to Mozambique.[112] In 2020-21, a series of incidents, MV *Wakashi's* oil spill (2020), MT *New Diamond's* fire and oil spill (2020), MV *X-Press Pearl* fire (2021) burnished the image of the Coast Guard as a regional first responder to maritime casualties at sea, such as fire and pollution response.[113]

Since 2006, the Coast Guard has signed Memorandums of Understanding (MOUs)/Memorandum of Cooperation with coast guard/equivalent agencies of four of India's seven maritime neighbours, with countries afar in West and East Asia, and one regional organisation viz. South Asia Co-operative Environment Programme (SACEP). Presently, the Coast Guard has MOUs/ with Bangladesh (2015), Indonesia (2020), Japan (2014), Korea (2006), Oman (2016), Pakistan (2016), Sri Lanka (2018) and Vietnam (2015).[114] Some of the broad areas of cooperation under the MOU include law enforcement; suppression and prevention of crimes such as piracy, armed robbery illegal trafficking in arms and drugs, smuggling, illegal migration; SAR; pollution response; information exchange; capacity-building; High Level Meeting (HLM); ship visits, etc.[115] Under the MOU with Pakistan, a communication link has been established with the Pakistan Maritime Security Agency (PMSA).[116] While the MOUs are reflective of closer engagement with specific coast guards, and indicative of a mutual intent for deeper collaboration, the Coast Guard also engages with other coast guard agencies. In addition, Coast Guard ships have also undertaken exercises with a number of foreign maritime security/maritime law enforcement agencies, such as those of Australian Border Force, Bangladesh Coast Guard, Cambodia Navy, Japan Coast Guard, Korea Coast Guard, Malaysia Maritime Enforcement Agency, Maldives National Defence Force, UAE Coast Guard, and US Coast Guard.[117]

Overall, there is scope for widening engagement of the Coast Guard, for progressing bilateral and multilateral engagements in accordance with its mandated functional areas of responsibility, especially in the contiguous maritime neighbourhood. For example, the US Indo-Pacific strategy envisions a wider role of the US Coast Guard in bolstering capabilities of its partners.[118] Likewise, ARF too has been working on mechanisms for enhancing cooperation amongst Maritime Law Enforcement Agencies (MLEA).[119] Australian scholars such as Sam Bateman and David Brewster have advocated a wider role of the

Coast Guard in maritime security.[120] Ironically, Australia itself does not have a coast guard of its own. Likewise, similar sentiments have also been expressed in India for a wider role of the Coast Guard, including by the Raksha Mantri (Defence Minister).[121] In other words, there is wide support for greater participation of coast guards in maritime security, focused on non-military maritime security challenges, albeit in accordance with national laws and policy. The Coast Guard's proven capabilities to act as a first responder in certain situations at sea, such as for oil pollution response and SAR, provides national policy-makers another means to play a greater role in promoting regional maritime safety and security.

In addition to the Coast Guard, almost all national agencies engaged in law enforcement/investigation/security, such as the Directorate of Revenue Intelligence (DRI) and the Narcotics Control Bureau (NCB) (for smuggling and drug enforcement), engage with partner agencies on an international, regional, and bilateral basis. Strengthening overall maritime security cooperation also needs enhanced maritime cooperation by other law enforcement/investigation agencies.

Having covered the Indian approach to cooperation, including contemporary national policies driving maritime security cooperation, as well as the approaches of the Indian Navy and Coast Guard over the past three decades, the next chapter focuses on the mechanisms for maritime security cooperation.

NOTES

1 Kautilya, *The Arthashastra,* trans. and ed. L.N. Rangarajan (Penguin), 568.

2 Bipandeep Sharma, "'De-Securitising the Arctic' Climate Change: An Indian Perspective," *India Quarterly* 77, no. 4 (2021): 622-641, https://journals.sagepub.com/doi/abs/10.1177/09749284211047721.

3 Ministry of Defence, "Aero India 2021: IOR Seminar Building Collective Maritime Competence Towards Security and Growth for All In The Region (SAGAR)," Press Information Bureau, 04 February 2021, https://pib.gov.in/Pressreleaseshare.aspx?PRID=1695245, accessed on 20 August 2023.

4 Mahesh Kumar Sachdev, "Indian Diplomacy through Ages," Ministry of External Affairs, Government of India, Distinguished Lectures Details, 12 November 2014, https://mea.gov.in/distinguished-lectures-detail.htm?174, accessed on 20 August 2023.

5 Sachdev, "Indian Diplomacy through Ages."

6 Sachdev, "Indian Diplomacy through Ages."

7 Kautilya, *The Arthashastra*, 511.

8 Kautilya, *The Arthashastra*, 511.
9 Kautilya, *The Arthashastra*, 528-30.
10 Constitution of India, Article 51, https://www.mea.gov.in/Images/pdf1/Part4.pdf,
11 Constitution of India, Article 37.
12 Constitution of India, Article 51.
13 Constitution of India, Article 51.
14 Times News Network, "Quad a 'small clique' intended to target China, says Beijing," *Times of India,* May 13, 2021, https://timesofindia.indiatimes.com/world/china/quad-a-small-clique-intended-to-target-china-says-beijing/articleshow/82593815.cms, accessed on 12 March 2022.
15 "External Affairs Minister's speech at the 4th Ramnath Goenka Lecture, 2019," Ministry of External Affairs, 14 November 2019, https://www.mea.gov.in/Speeches-Statements.htm?dtl/32038, accessed on 12 January 2022.
16 S. Jaishankar, "9 Years, 1 Big Footprint," *Times of India*, May 30, 2023, https://timesofindia.indiatimes.com/blogs/toi-edit-page/9-years-1-big-footprint/, accessed on 20 August 2023.
17 Jaishankar, "9 Years, 1 Big Footprint."
18 Jaishankar, "9 Years, 1 Big Footprint."
19 *Panchsheel* (1954) refers to the five principles of mutual respect for each other's territorial integrity and sovereignty; mutual non-aggression; mutual non-interference; equality and co-operation for mutual benefit, and peaceful co-existence. The objectives of the non-alignment movement include, amongst others, non-adherence to multilateral military pacts and the independence of countries from great power rivalries; non-interference in internal affairs and peaceful coexistence among all nations; rejection of the use or threat of use of force; strengthening of the UN; and restructuring of international cooperation "History and Evolution of the Non-Aligned Movement," Ministry of External Affairs, 22 August 2012, https://mea.gov.in/in-focus-article.htm?20349/History+and+ Evolution + of+NonAligned+Movement, accessed on 12 January 2022.
20 "External Affairs Minister's speech at the 4th Ramnath Goenka Lecture, 2019," Ministry of External Affairs, 14 November 2019, https://www.mea.gov.in/Speeches-Statements.htm?dtl/32038; Vijay Gokhale, "Why Taiwan Strait Matters to India." *Times of India*, 26 June 2023, https://timesofindia.indiatimes.com/blogs/toi-edit-page/why-taiwan-strait-matters-to-india/, accessed on 20 August 2023.
21 Ministry of Defence, "India Stands for Open & Rule-Based Maritime Borders in Indo-Pacific: Raksha Mantri during 18th Heads of Asian Coast Guard Agencies Meeting in New Delhi," Press Information Bureau, 15 October 2022, https://pib.gov.in/PressReleasePage.aspx?PRID=1868008, accessed on 20 August 2023.
22 Ministry of Defence, "Indian Navy-Net Security Provider to Island Nations in IOR: Antony," Press Information Bureau, 12 October 2011, https://pib.gov.in/newsite/printrelease.aspx?relid=76590, accessed on 09 February 2021.
23 "PM's speech at the foundation stone laying ceremony for the Indian National Defence University at Gurgaon," Former Prime Ministers of India, https://archivepmo.nic.in/drmanmohansingh/speech-details.php?nodeid=1316, accessed on 09 February 2021.
24 Integrated Headquarters of Ministry of Defence (Navy), *Ensuring Secure Seas: India's Maritime Security Strategy*, 80.

While the primary areas of interest are restricted to the IOR, the secondary areas of interest are fare wider.

25 Integrated Headquarters of Ministry of Defence (Navy), *Ensuring Secure Seas*, 80.

26 Integrated Headquarters of Ministry of Defence (Navy), *Ensuring Secure Seas*, 80.

27 Integrated Headquarters of Ministry of Defence (Navy), *Ensuring Secure Seas*, 80

28 Integrated Headquarters of Ministry of Defence (Navy), *Ensuring Secure Seas*, 81.

29 The White House, *Indo-Pacific Strategy of the United States* (2020), 13, https://www.whitehouse.gov/wp-content/uploads/2022/02/U.S.-Indo-Pacific-Strategy.pdf, accessed on 09 March 2022.

30 Ministry of External Affairs, *Annual Report 2020-21*, 148, http://www.mea.gov.in/Uploads/PublicationDocs/33569_MEA_annual_Report.pdf, accessed on 20 August 2023.

31 Jaishankar, *The India Way: Strategies for an Uncertain World*, 185.

32 Jaishankar, *The India Way: Strategies for an Uncertain World*, 185-86.

33 Jaishankar, *The India Way: Strategies for an Uncertain World*, 185-86.

34 Ministry of Defence, "Raksha Mantri's keynote address at IOR Defence Ministers' Conclave stresses on Prime Minister's 'Five S' vision to tackle global challenges," Press Information Bureau, February 04, 2021,

35 Jaishankar, *The India Way: Strategies for an Uncertain World*, 186-87.

36 Jaishankar, *The India Way: Strategies for an Uncertain World*, 102.

37 Jaishankar, *The India Way: Strategies for an Uncertain World*, 102.

38 Jaishankar, *The India Way: Strategies for an Uncertain World*, 102.

39 Prime Minister's Office, "Text of Prime Minister's Keynote Address at Shangri La Dialogue," Press Information Bureau, 01 June 2018, https://pib.gov.in/newsite/PrintRelease.aspx?relid=179711, accessed on 20 August 2023.

40 Rahul Roy-Chaudhury, "Modi spells out free, open, inclusive Indo-Pacific policy," International Institute of Strategic Studies, 07 August 2018, https://www.iiss.org/blogs/analysis/2018/08/modi-free-open-inclusive, accessed on 03 January 2022.

41 Roy-Chaudhury, "Modi spells out free, open, inclusive Indo-Pacific policy."

42 Ministry of External Affairs, *Annual Report 2020-21*, 148.

43 Ministry of External Affairs, *Annual Report 2020-21*, 148.

44 Ministry of External Affairs, *Annual Report 2020-21*, 148.

45 Aneedrisha Hazarika, "Fleshing out The Maritime Security Pillar of The India's Indo-Pacific Oceans' Initiative," *DEFSTRAT* 14, no. 5 (Nov–Dec 2020), 27, https://www.defstrat.com/magazine_articles/fleshing-out-the-maritime-security-pillar-of-the-indias-indo-pacific-oceans-initiative/.

46 Ministry of External Affairs, *Annual Report 2020-21*, 148.

47 "English translation of Prime Minister's remarks at the UNSC High-Level Open Debate on "Enhancing Maritime Security: A Case for International Cooperation" (09 August 2021)," Ministry of External Affairs, https://www.mea.gov.in/Speeches-Statements.htm?dtl/34151/English_tra, accessed on 16 August 2021. The translation on the MEA website is an approximate translation; origin remarks were delivered in Hindi.

48 UN Security Council, "Presidential Statement", Statement by the President of the Security Council, S/PRST/2021/15 (09 August 2021), https://undocs.org/S/PRST/2021/15.

49 UN Security Council, "Presidential Statement."

50 Harsh V. Pant, "Lessons in new ways to lead," Observer research Foundation, 16 August 2021, https://www.orfonline.org/research/lessons-in-new-ways-to-lead/, accessed on 21 August 2021.

51 Sachin Parashar, "Want India on board, important its vote on Ukraine matches its words: French Envoy," *The Times of India*, 08 March 2022, http://timesofindia.indiatimes.com/articleshow/90083658.cms?utm_source=contentofinterest&utm_medium=text&utm_campaign=cppst, accessed on 11 March 2022.

52 Kanwal Sibal, "View: Putin's presence in UN debate on maritime security underlines India's strategic autonomy," *Economic Times*, 16 August 2021, https://economictimes.indiatimes.com/news/india/putins-presence-in-un-debate-on-maritime-security-underlines-indias-strategic-autonomy/articleshow/85354251.cms, accessed on 21 August 2021.

53 Debasis Bhattacharya, "India's focus on enhancing maritime security as the UNSC president: Leadership envisioning a global roadmap," Observer Research Foundation, 26 August 2021, https://www.orfonline.org/expert-speak/indias-focus-on-enhancing-maritime-security-as-the-unsc-president/, accessed on 06 September 2021.

54 "Unstarred Question No.3692: Neighbourhood First Policy," Rajya Sabha, 25 July 2019, https://mea.gov.in/rajya-sabha.htm?dtl/31673/QUESTION+NO3692+NEIGHBOUR HOOD+FIRST+POLICY, accessed on 06 January 2022

55 "Unstarred Question No. 312: Look East And Act East Policy," Lok Sabha, 16 March 2016, https://mea.gov.in/lok-sabha.htm?dtl/26554/QUESTION_NO_3121_ LOOK _EAST_AND_ACT_EAST_POLICY, accessed on 06 January 2022; Sanjay Baru, "The sprouting of the 'Look West' policy," *The Hindu*, 19 August 2015, https://www.thehindu.com/opinion/lead/sanjaya-baru-writes-the-sprouting-of-the-look-west-policy/article7554403.ece, accessed on 06 January 2022.

56 "India-ASEAN Relations," Ministry of External Affairs, August 2018, https://mea.gov.in/aseanindia/20-years.htm , accessed on 08 January 2022.

57 "Unstarred Question No. 312: Look East and Act East Policy."

58 "Unstarred Question No. 312: Look East and Act East Policy."

59 "Prime Minister's Virtual-Address at Eastern Economic Forum 2021," Ministry of External Affairs, 23 September 2021, https://mea.gov.in/Speeches-Statements.htm?dtl/34216/prime+ministers+virtualaddress+at+eastern+economic+forum+2021, accessed on 12 January 2022.

60 Ministry of External Affairs, *Annual Report 2020-21*, 18.

61 Geoffrey Till, *Seapower: A Guide for the Twenty-First Century* (Oxford: Routledge, 2004), 285, https://doi.org/10.1604/978071468436Second Edition.

62 Gulab Mohanlal Hiranandani, *Transition to Eminence: The Indian Navy 1976-1990* (Lancer, 2005), https://www.indiannavy.nic.in/sites/default/files/Transition-to-Eminence-07Apr16.pdf

63 Hiranandani, *Transition to Eminence.*

64 Gulab Mohanlal Hiranandani, *Transition to Guardianship: The Indian Navy 1991–2000* (Lancer, 2009), 27 and 31.

65 Hiranandani, *Transition to Guardianship*, 31.

66 Oana Ramona Lobont, Oana Ramona Glont, Leonardo Badea, and Sorana Vatavu,

"Correlation of military expenditures and economic growth: lessons for Romania," *Quality & Quantity* 53 (2019): 2957-2968, https://link.springer.com/article/10.1007/s11135-019-00910-9#Sec5.

67 Hiranandani, *Transition to Guardianship*, 31.

68 Hiranandani, *Transition to Guardianship*, 27.

69 Hiranandani, *Transition to Guardianship*, 31; in 1991-92, exercises were held with navies from Australia, France, US, UK, followed by navies from Oman and Singapore in 1993.

70 Hiranandani, *Transition to Guardianship*, 31.

71 Sam Bateman, "Managing Maritime Affairs: The Contribution of Maritime Security Forces," in Jo Inge Bekkevold and Geoffrey Till, eds., *International Order at Sea: How it is Challenged; How it is Maintained* (London: Palgrave Macmillan, 2016), 261.

72 Hiranandani, *Transition to Guardianship*, 31.

73 Hiranandani, *Transition to Guardianship*, 31.

74 Anup Singh, *Blue Waters Ahoy!: The Indian Navy 2001–2010* (2018), 130.

75 Chief of the Naval Staff, foreword to *Blue Waters Ahoy!*, by Anup Singh, ix.

76 Anup Singh, *Blue Waters Ahoy!*, 313.

77 "'State Of Border Still Abnormal": S Jaishankar On Ties With China," NDTV.com, 28 June 2023, https://www.ndtv.com/india-news/state-of-border-still-abnormal-s-jaishankar-on-ties-with-china-4161512, accessed on 20 August 2023.

78 M. Doraibabu and Amrut Dilip Godbole, *A Decade of Transformation: The Indian Navy, 2011-21* (Gurugram: Harper Collins, 2023), 37.

79 Doraibabu and Godbole, *A Decade of Transformation: The Indian Navy, 2011-21*, 37.

80 Integrated Headquarters of Ministry of Defence (Navy), *Indian Maritime Doctrine* (New Delhi: 2004), 93.

81 Integrated Headquarters of Ministry of Defence (Navy), *Indian Maritime Doctrine*, 110.

82 Integrated Headquarters of Ministry of Defence (Navy), *Indian Maritime Doctrine*, 23-24.

83 Intervention in Maldives in response to a coup.

84 Integrated Headquarters of Ministry of Defence (Navy), *Indian Maritime Doctrine* (2015), 107.

85 Integrated Headquarters of Ministry of Defence (Navy), *Indian Maritime Doctrine* (2015), 108.

86 Integrated Headquarters of Ministry of Defence (Navy), *Ensuring Secure Seas*, 11.

87 "Coordinated Maritime Presences: Council extends implementation in the Gulf of Guinea for two years and establishes a new Maritime Area of Interest in the North-Western Indian Ocean," European Council, 21 February 2022, https://www.consilium.europa.eu/en/press/press-releases/2022/02/21/coordinated-maritime-presences-council-extends-implementation-in-the-gulf-of-guinea-for-2-years-and-establishes-a-new-concept-in-the-north-west-indian-ocean/, accessed on 09 March 2022.

88 Ministry of Defence, "Indian Navy - Ocean Ring of Yoga International Day of Yoga (IDY 23)," Press Information Bureau, 20 June 2023, https://pib.gov.in/PressReleseDetail.aspx?PRID=1933722, accessed on 20 August 2023.

89 Ministry of Defence, "Ministry of Defence – Year End Review 2022," https://pib.gov.in/PressReleasePage.aspx?PRID=1884353, accessed on 20 August 2023.

90 Ministry of Defence, "Raksha Mantri Shri Rajnath Singh lauds indigenisation efforts of

Navy in safeguarding maritime security," Press Information Bureau, 22 October 2019, https://pib.gov.in/Pressreleaseshare.aspx?PRID=1588745, accessed on 20 August 2023.

91 Ministry of Defence, "Mission SAGAR III - INS Kiltan Arrives at Ho Chi Minh City," Press Information Bureau, 25 December 2019, https://pib.gov.in/Pressreleaseshare.aspx?PRID=1588745, accessed on 20 August 2023.

92 Indian Navy "IOR Seminar 1," YouTube, 04 February 2021, https://www.youtube.com/watch?v=X1OPrhuYVao, accessed on 09 February 2021.

93 "Address by the President of India, Shri Ram Nath Kovind on the Occasion of Presentation of the President's Standard to 22nd Missile Vessel Squadron," 08 December 2021, https://presidentofindia.nic.in/speeches-detail.htm?887, accessed on 12 January 2022.

94 Editorial, "Friends and benefit," *Times of India*, 22 June 2023, https://timesofindia.indiatimes.com/blogs/toi-editorials/friends-and-benefits/, accessed 20, 2023.

95 Editorial, "Friends and benefits."

96 "Coordinated Maritime Presences," European Council.

97 Dipanjan Roy Chaudhury. "India Chooses Wider Partnerships, Not Military Pacts in Indian Ocean Region." *The Economic Times*, June 07, 2023, https://economictimes.indiatimes.com/news/india/india-choses-wider-partnerships-not-military-pacts-in-indian-ocean-region/articleshow/100802661.cms?from=mdr, 20 August 2023.

98 "India Should Refuse America's 'NATO Plus' Bait," *The Hindu*, 03 July 2023, https://www.thehindu.com/opinion/op-ed/india-should-refuse-americas-nato-plus-bait/article67038238.ece, accessed on 20 August 2023.

99 "Not South or North, but Global Equator," *Economic Times,* 28 May 2023, https://economictimes.indiatimes.com/opinion/et-editorial/not-south-or-north-but-global-equator/articleshow/100574343.cms?from=mdr, accessed on 20 August 2023.

100 "India Should Refuse America's 'NATO Plus' Bait."

101 "Middle East Play: Iran's New Naval Alliance May Be Ambitious, but India Should Be Wary of China's Growing Influence in the Region." *Times of India,* June 5, 2023, https://timesofindia.indiatimes.com/blogs/toi-editorials/middle-east-play-irans-new-naval-alliance-may-be-ambitious-but-india-should-be-wary-of-chinas-growing-influence-in-the-region/, accessed on 20 August 2023

102 "Middle East Play," Times of India Blog.

103 Asian News International, "Indian Navy believes in 'collective military competency': Admiral Karambir Singh," *Business Standard,* 18 October 2019, https://www.business-standard.com/multimedia/video-gallery/general/indian-navy-believes-in-collective-military-competency-admiral-karambir-singh-92758.htm, accessed on 09 February 2021.

104 Asian News International, "Prepared to face both COVID-19, Chinese challenge on LAC: Navy chief," *Business World*, 03 December 2020, http://www.businessworld.in/article/Prepared-to-face-both-COVID-19-Chinese-challenge-on-LAC-Navy-chief/03-12-2020-349540/, accessed on 09 February 2021,

105 "IOR Seminar-1," YouTube, posted by Indian Navy.

106 Ministry of Defence, "Aero India 2021: IOR Seminar Building."

107 Karambir Singh, "Dynamics of Security in the Indo-Pacific," *Indian Naval Despatch* 1, no. 1 (Winter 2020): 4-5.

108 "Transforming the Indian Navy to be a key Maritime Force in the Indo-Pacific," Talk by the Chief of the Naval Staff, Admiral Karambir Singh at the United Services Institute,

New Delhi, 27 August 2021.

109 The National Maritime Security Coordinator was instituted by the Government of India in February 2022.

110 "International Operations," Indian Coast Guard, https://www.indiancoastguard.gov.in/International_Co_Operation.aspx?ID=343, accessed on 01 January 2022.

111 Ministry of Defence, *Annual Report 2018-19*, 51-54, https://www.mod.gov.in/dod/sites/default/files/MoDAR2018.pdf, accessed on 01 January 2022; Ministry of Defence,"Year End Review – 2020 Ministry of Defence," https://pib.gov.in/PressReleseDetail. aspx?PRID=1685437, accessed on 01 January 2022.

112 Ministry of Defence, *Annual Report 2018-19*, 51-54,

113 Indian Coast Guard (@IndiaCoastGuard), Twitter, 30 December 2021, https://twitter.com/IndiaCoastGuard/status/1476516762548006912, accessed on 01 January 2022.

114 "Memorandum of Understanding," Indian Coast Guard, https://www.indian coastguard.gov.in/content/1732_3_MoU.aspx, accessed on 13 January 2021; Ministry of Defence, "Signing of Agreements with other Countries," Press Information Bureau, 05 February 2018, https://pib.gov.in/PressReleaseIframePage.aspx?PRID =1519147, accessed on 13 January 2021; "Signing of MOU between Indian Coast Guard and Indonesia Coast Guard," Indian Coast Guard, accessed on 13 January 2021, https://www.indian coastguard.gov.in/WriteReadData/Tender/202007080953389212753 PRESS_BRIEF.pdf

115 "Signing of MOU between Indian Coast Guard and Indonesia Coast Guard," Indian Coast Guard; "Memorandum of Understanding between the Coast Guard of the Republic Of India and the Coast Guard of the Democratic Socialist Republic of Sri Lanka for the establishment of a Collaborative Relationship to Combat Transnational Illegal Activities at Sea and develop Regional Co-Operation Between The Indian Coast Guard And The Sri Lanka Coast Guard," https://www.mea.gov.in/Portal/LegalTreatiesDoc/LK18B3322.pdf, accessed on 13 January 2021.

116 "Memorandum of Understanding," Indian Coast Guard.

117 Ministry of Defence. "Ministry of Defence – Year End Review 2022," https://www.mod.gov.in/gallery/indian-coast-guard

118 The White House, *Indo-Pacific Strategy of the United States* (2020), 13.

119 "Second ARF Workshop on Enhancing Regional Maritime Law Enforcement Cooperation," ASEAN Regional Forum, https://aseanregionalforum.asean.org/wp-content/uploads/2019/01/ANNEX-24-10th-ISM-on-MS.pdf, accessed on 10 March 2022.

120 Sawan, "Problems and prospects of maritime security cooperation in the Indian Ocean Region."

121 Ministry of Defence, "Maritime Preparedness in Ever-Changing Global Situation Must to Safeguard National Interest: Raksha Mantri at 39th Commanders' Conference of Indian Coast Guard," Press Information Bureau, May 30, 2022, https://pib.gov.in/PressReleasePage.aspx?PRID=1829428, accessed on 20 August 2023.

3

Cooperation Mechanisms

Maritime security cooperation is undertaken using different formats for engagements – multilateral, plurilateral, bilateral, and through regional organisations. Multilateralism, as a concept, refers to the "process of organising relations between groups of three or more states." Multilateralism is principally associated with the events after World War II which led to the creation of the UN and other multilateral constructs.[1] The UN, which is the most representative international body, is considered as the utmost expression of multilateralism.[2] From a security perspective, NATO, and from a trade perspective, the World Trade Organization (WTO), are also representative of the principles of multilateralism viz. indivisibility of interests, diffused reciprocity, and dispute settlement mechanisms.[3] A specific variation of multilateralism, which is increasingly gaining traction, is that of 'plurilateralism,' which, in the context of the WTO, refers to trade and investment negotiations between three or more countries, but fewer than all WTO members.[4] Increasingly, the benefits of multilateralism are under question, and plurilateralism, is increasingly proliferating into other domains of cooperation, including in the ways in which maritime security architectures are being operationalised. The principal advantage of plurilateral frameworks is that they are a flexible, pragmatic, and issue-focused grouping of likeminded nations.[5] Speaking at a panel discussion at the Raisina dialogue in April 2021,

India's EAM highlighted that multilateralism is not delivering, therefore, requiring groups of countries [plurilateral groupings] to work together:[6]

> To my mind, we need plurilateralism, because if you look at multilateralism, which is the highest end of it, it's not delivering the way it used to ... So my point is that, in a sense, there is a sort of vacuum which has emerged, where multilateralism has fallen short, powers are not what they used to be, bilateral delivery is not what it used to be. So it requires countries which are comfortable with each other, who see merit in working with each other and who, frankly, will make the world a better place by working together, come together ... As a broad case, I think the world is moving towards groups of countries who are looking to work together, you can call them whatever coalition of the enthusiastic, the convergence, the willing, pick your region, pick your combination, but I think that's where the world is moving.

Chapter VII (Action with Respect to Threats to the Peace, Breaches of the Peace, and Acts of Aggression) of the Charter of the United Nations and Statute of the International Court of Justice authorises action by the UN Security Council to manage threats to global peace and security. The UN Security Council could take economic, diplomatic, or military measures to restore international peace and security, including by naval forces. The UN Security Council can, therefore, call upon Member States to deploy their armed forces, including navies, to enforce blockades, or undertake other operations to restore international peace and security. Notably, the seas are not only a means to maintain peace and order, but also a medium where international peace and security may be disturbed.

From its inception, the UN has been involved in addressing maritime security challenges.[7] While in the period 1946-2007 resolutions related to maritime security were adopted at an average of once every 20 months, between 2008-18 resolutions were being adopted at an average of one every two and half months, which is almost eight times more than earlier.[8] Broadly, the resolutions pertained to counter-proliferation, non-proliferation of WMD, counter-piracy, and countering trafficking-in-persons/migrant smuggling.[9] The increasing engagement of the Security Council to address threats to peace and security in the maritime domain is viewed as a positive development; however, there are concerns that the Council may be diluting principles enshrined in

UNCLOS, such as by providing certain temporary exemptions, and about its inability to handle inter-state disputes.[10] The August 2021 UN Security Council debate, has been described as path-breaking by some scholars, as proposals were made for new governing structures for maritime security, regionally by Prime Minister Modi, and within the UN, by President Putin.[11] Such efforts should go beyond India's tenure as president of the Council, and the success of the debate should spur greater vibrancy in steering the discourse on maritime security in other international, regional and multilateral forums, which directly or indirectly have an impact on maritime security, including reforming of regional and global structures for maritime security.

One most notable contemporary examples of maritime security cooperation, under the aegis of the UN, involving India, is that of the India Navy's engagement as part of the international anti-piracy naval effort in the Gulf of Aden. Following a request from the Transitional Federal Government (TFG) of Somalia for international assistance to counter the surge in piracy and armed robbery, UN Security Council Resolution 1851 (2008) of December 2008, acting under Chapter VII of the UN Charter, called on States and organisations to actively participate in countering piracy and armed robbery off Somalia's coast by "deploying naval vessels and military aircraft, and through seizure and disposing boats and arms used in the commission of those crimes."[12] The resolution had been renewed annually till it lapsed in 2022, and since 2008, Indian Navy ships were deployed off the Horn of Africa/Gulf of Aden in pursuance of the resolution. It is also worthwhile to note that the Indian Navy deployments began a few months prior to the adoption of UN Security Council Resolution 1851.

REGIONAL COOPERATION

With the end of the Second World War, there was an urge amongst States to pursue peace and security. States, however, realised that importance of regional cooperation to address regional issues. This realisation, became the basis of regionalism. The roots of regionalism, therefore, lay in the belief that there are common regional interests which could be 'most efficiently and effectively promoted by the close and continuing cooperation within a regional framework.' This has led to the evolution of a number of regional organisations, including in South Asia, and such organisations continue to form; however, regionalism is not always associated with geographical contiguity. Acknowledging the relevance of regional arrangements for international security, Chapter VIII of the United Nations Charter provides the basis for the involvement of regional arrangements or agencies for the maintenance of international peace and security consistent with the 'purposes and principles of the (UN).'[13] Likewise, UNCLOS also promotes regional cooperation, such as between States bordering enclosed or semi enclosed areas. India has, in fact, taken a proactive role in the creation of several regional organisations, such as IORA and IONS, and is either a member or an observer in almost all regional organisations in India's areas of maritime interest. Some regional constructs are discussed in the following paragraphs.

SAARC. The South Asian Association for Regional Cooperation (SAARC), established in 1985, comprises eight member states: Afghanistan, Bangladesh, Bhutan, India, Maldives, Nepal, Pakistan, and Sri Lanka.[14] The fact that four of the eight members are maritime nations, fringing the Arabian Sea and the Bay of Bengal, underlines the maritime potential of the organisation. Under SAARC, several initiatives were taken to further security cooperation, in transnational crime, such as terrorism, drug trafficking, and cybercrime, including through development of a regional architecture.[15] Considering the emerging threats from the sea in South Asia, including the upsurge of piracy and the heinous attack on Mumbai in 2008 by terrorists using the sea-route, in the late 2000s, SAARC made efforts towards developing a regional cooperative response to maritime security. The SAARC Ministerial Declaration on Cooperation in Combating Terrorism in 2009 reiterated the commitment of States to share expertise and information about terrorists bearing in mind the threats posed to maritime and coastal security and to share information regarding investigation and prosecution of terrorist acts.[16] However, there has been little progress under SAARC on security cooperation, including on maritime security on account of the difficult India-Pakistan relationship which has had an adverse impact on SAARC.[17] Notwithstanding the lack of progress, overall, India remains committed to SAARC.[18]

BIMSTEC. The Bay of Bengal Initiative for Multi-Sectoral Technical and Economic Cooperation (BIMSTEC), set up in 1997, is a sub-regional organisation comprising seven countries in the Bay of Bengal littoral: Bangladesh, Bhutan, India, Nepal, Sri Lanka, and two from Southeast Asia, Myanmar, and Thailand.[19] Unlike SAARC, the majority of BIMSTEC are maritime nations. While it was initially established as an economic block, over time, the 'sectors' of cooperation were expanded to include security (counter-terrorism) in 2008.[20] The National Security Agencies (NSAs) of BIMSTEC nations, highlighting the importance of recognising the Bay of Bengal as common security space, have agreed to collectively deal with challenges in the Bay of Bengal.[21] Progressively, cooperation in security has expanded to include maritime security cooperation as well.

The BIMSTEC Convention on Cooperation in Combating International Terrorism, Transnational Organised Crime and Illicit Drug Trafficking was signed in Nay Pyi Taw in 2009.[22] India leads the counter-terrorism and transnational crime 'sector' of BIMSTEC that comprises six sub-groups focused on specific aspects of transnational crime.[23] The NSAs of BIMSTEC nations, prior to the outbreak of the COVID pandemic, met annually between 2017 and 2019 and underscored, amongst others, the need for a common legal and institutional framework as well as information sharing for addressing common security threats, along with greater dialogue at the Track 1.5 level amongst think tanks.[24] In 2019, the IFC-IOR hosted a coastal security workshop for the seven BIMSTEC countries.[25] Despite its efforts at strengthening maritime security cooperation, indicators point to little tangible progress; however, considering that some of the challenges are shared sub-regional challenges, such as those related to natural disasters, marine environment protection, drug trafficking, etc, the maritime security cooperation agenda deserves renewed attention.[26]

ASEAN. India's relationship with ASEAN is a key pillar of India's foreign policy, and in 2012, the ASEAN-India partnership was upgraded into a Strategic Partnership.[27] Political-security cooperation has emerged as a 'key and emerging' pillar of India-ASEAN relationships on account of growing challenges to security, both traditional and non-traditional.[28] Accordingly, responses are being crafted which rely on coordination, cooperation and multilevel experience sharing.[29] The 'Delhi Declaration' (2018) reaffirmed the commitment of India and ASEAN to work on regional and international security issues, including on maritime safety and security.[30] Specifically, the declaration mentions cooperation in prevention and management of accidents and incidents at sea, cooperation in SAR, cooperation between research institutions, and collaboration in maritime education, research, development, and innovation. The 2021-25 Action Plan (2020) echoes similar sentiments, and also includes counter-piracy and information sharing as areas for cooperation.[31] India is an active participant in several regional ASEAN led forums like the Asia-Europe Meeting (ASEM), EAS, ARF, ADMM+, and the Expanded ASEAN Maritime Forum (EAMF), including leadership roles in some working groups.[32] These forums facilitate dialogue across a range of issues, such as UNCLOS, fisheries, maritime law enforcement, etc. The 'Delhi Dialogue' is an annual Track 1.5 for discussing politico-security and economic issues between ASEAN and India.[33] While the intentions are well articulated and progress has indeed been made, both with ASEAN and bilaterally with ASEAN countries, a more granular plan and strategy would do well for meaningful progress.

IORA. The Indian Ocean Rim Association (IORA), established in 1997, is a regional organisation focused on strengthening regional cooperation and sustainable development in the IOR.[34] It comprises 23 member states and 10 dialogue partners.[35] Its priority areas include interrelated areas of Maritime Safety and Security (MSS), fisheries management, and blue economy.[36] Notwithstanding, IORA, however, makes a distinction between safety and security.[37] In addition to a declaration on maritime security cooperation, IORA activities in maritime security and safety under the aegis of the Working Group on MSS (WGMSS) has included development of an action plan (2017-21) and preparation of a blue print for maritime safety and security.[38] The IORA also holds an annual Track 1.5 engagement in the form of the 'Indian Ocean Dialogue,' an event which has been hosted multiple times by India.[39] Overall, IORA seeks to develop on existing national, regional, and multilateral measures for promoting maritime safety and security.[40] Considering the plethora of mechanisms, and limited resources, this approach is perhaps a pragmatic one. Accordingly, plans are reported to devolve around capacity building, SAR, development of a centre for excellence, and strengthening of surveillance and information sharing.[41] However, like other regional organisations, the delivery here too appears to be muted. A study in 2021 recommended that a prioritised agenda for IORA could include SAR, port security and governance, blue economy, fisheries management, and counter terrorism.[42] India has already developed capabilities in some of the priority areas, such as SAR and counter-terrorism, and is consolidating its approach to some others, such as blue economy. Therefore, India, in consonance with its policy of SAGAR, can contribute to the priority areas of IORA. The potential for harmonisation of efforts between IORA and IONS is discussed later.

ReCAAP. Regional Cooperation Agreement on Combating Piracy and Armed Robbery against Ships in Asia (ReCAAP), an inter-governmental organisation, is the primary mechanisms for combating piracy and armed robbery in Asia, including for coordination of operational response.[43] India, along with Japan and Singapore, were instrumental in the conclusion of this agreement. The three pillars of the agreement are information sharing, capacity building, and mutual legal assistance.[44] A secure web-based Information Network System (IFN) facilitates information exchange between focal points and ReCAAP ISC. Notably, the procedures promulgated by the International Maritime Organisation (IMO) for reporting piracy and armed robbery incorporate the ReCAAP mechanism for Asia. The Director General Coast Guard (DGCG) is the Indian 'Governor' in the Governing Council of the ReCAAP Information Sharing Centre (ISC), and Maritime Rescue Coordination Centre (MRCC), Mumbai is the ReCAAP focal point in India.[45] The Coast Guard has hosted meetings and workshops under the ReCAAP agreement in India.[46] While national agencies are responsible for handling piracy reports in accordance with domestic procedures, the focal point—MRCC (Mumbai) in India's case—is required to coordinate responses and submit reports to ReCAAP ISC. The principal limitation of the ReCAAP agreement is that its mandate is restricted to piracy and armed robbery. In August 2021, the MEA announced the election of Director General, Coast Guard, Mr K Natarajan as the Executive Director of ISC, Singapore.[47] In April 2022, Mr Natrajan assumed the appointment of the Executive Director of the ISC, and became the first Indian to do so. The election of Mr K Natarajan is another example of India's growing engagement in regional and international bodies, including for maritime security. Such efforts need to be consolidated further, including at the working level.

PLURILATERAL COOPERATION

Increasingly, as discussed earlier, India's approach to foreign affairs is seeing a shift towards plurilateral structures (also used often interchangeably with minilaterals). The rise of China is seen as the reason for the growth of such arrangements.[48] Some of the plurilateral mechanisms are discussed in subsequent paragraphs.

Quadrilateral Cooperation

The concept of a Quadrilateral Security Dialogue (QSD), also known as the QUAD—between Australia, India, Japan, and the US—which was conceptualised in 2007 lost traction a few years later only to be revived in 2017 with renewed focus and vigour. The unprecedented rise of China as a common challenge to the four countries, along with the narrative about the Indo-Pacific as one continuum are perhaps the main reasons for the resurgence of the QUAD. Of the four QUAD countries, India shares a disputed land border with China, and Japan has an ongoing dispute with China over the Senkaku/Diaoyu islands in the East China Sea. Between 2017 and 2018, officials of the QUAD countries consultatively determined the areas of cooperation, including on maritime security. Since the reconvening of the QUAD in 2017, it has gained immense attention, and engagements under the arrangement have been elevated to the highest levels and the scope expanded significantly to include the COVID-19 pandemic, climate change, cyber security, etc.[49] The security manifestations of the QUAD are exemplified in the MALABAR exercise. This is perhaps the most complex naval exercise that India undertakes with any navy (or group of navies). The MALABAR naval exercise, which originally began as a bilateral exercise between India and the United States in 1992, expanded to include the other members of the QUAD: Japan, in 2017 and Australia, in 2020 (Australia also took part in 2007 along with Singapore).[50]

The QUAD has been described as 'partnership for global good' with a positive and constructive agenda on a range of contemporary issues, and as one of the ways to address strategic competition and geopolitical challenges in the Indo-Pacific region.[51] The Indian EAM has also described the QUAD, an arrangement bereft of any formal mandate or structure, as a "21st century way of responding to a more diversified, dispersed world."[52] Considering the wide swath of activities undertaken under the aegis of the QUAD, and the high levels of cooperation between the four navies, this partnership has significant potential to expand maritime security cooperation, albeit focused on higher-level naval engagements. Notably, the US Indo-Pacific strategic lists flexible partnerships, including with ASEAN, India, the QUAD and Europe, as a 'strategic means' to meet the 'strategic end' of advancing a free and open Indo-Pacific.[53] The spin-off is that engagements under the QUAD framework can also be leveraged in a host of situations, such as the Tsunami of 2004 demonstrated when Australia, India, Japan, and US formed a "core group" to respond jointly.[54]

Trilateral Cooperation

As a 'sub-region' in South Asia, NSA-level trilateral meetings on trilateral maritime security cooperation, later renamed as the Colombo Security Conclave (CSC), have been held between India, Maldives and Sri Lanka since 2011; Mauritius joined the conclave as a member at the fifth meeting in 2022.[55] At the second meeting in 2013, it was agreed to enhance cooperation in three categories of activities: first, enhancing MDA under the aegis of IMO-mandated systems such as Long Rang Identification and Tracking (LRIT) and Automatic Identification System (AIS); second, training and capacity building in MDA, SAR, and oil pollution response; and third, joint activities, such as exercises, information exchange on illegal activities, oil response contingency plan, and cooperation in legal and policy issues related to piracy.[56] Till early 2022, five meetings had been held in India (2014), in Maldives (2011 and 2022), in Sri Lanka (2013 and 2020). In addition, Mauritius and Seychelles attended the third meeting as guests in 2014, and Bangladesh and Seychelles at the fifth meeting in 2022 as observers. Deputy NSAs of the three countries have also met for "sustained engagement and implementation of the discussion of the NSA level meetings."[57] According to the joint statement issued after the fourth meeting in November 2020, "past deliberation and outcomes have helped the three countries in improving close cooperation in maritime security in the region."[58] At the fourth meeting, it was agreed to strengthen cooperation in MDA, HADR, joint exercises, capacity building, marine pollution, and in protection of underwater heritage.[59] It was also agreed to improve sharing of intelligence and expand the scope of discussions to include terrorism, extremism, drugs, arms and human trafficking, money laundering and effect of climate change on maritime environment.[60] At the fifth meeting, the NSAs identified five key areas (pillars) for cooperation: (1) maritime safety and security; (2) countering terrorism and radicalisation; (3) combating trafficking and transnational organised crime; (4) cyber security and protection of critical infrastructure and technology; and (5) HADR.[61] Despite the expansion of the areas of security cooperation, considering that most participants are island states, the principal maritime dimension of the construct is unlikely to be diluted.

The trilateral meetings on maritime security at the level of the NSA underscores the importance the three countries attach to sub-regional cooperation in maritime security. The trilateral is perhaps the only institutionalised political-level maritime security regional grouping in which India is a participant. Ironically, within India's domestic structures, there is no maritime security forum which is politically led. Strengthening of sub-regional cooperation, including through measures such as MDA, information- and intelligence-sharing, strengthens maritime security in the proximate and critical immediate neighbourhood. The development of the CSC, under the aegis of the trilateral gives the forum an operational arm and the means to actualise the visions of the trilateral. Some of the activities which have been undertaken under the aegis of the CSC include maritime law workshops, a coastal security conference, Table-Top Exercises (TTX), and focused operations.[62] Considering the failure of SAARC in security cooperation, and the modest progress of BIMSTEC, the trilateral initiative is particularly important for regional maritime security.

The maiden India-France-Australia Senior Officials' Trilateral Dialogue was held virtually in September 2020.[63] The discussions, led by the Indian Foreign Secretary, focused on geostrategic challenges and cooperation in the Indo-Pacific, cooperation in the global commons, and potential areas for practical cooperation, including through regional organisations, such as ASEAN, IORA, and the Indian Ocean Commission (IOC).[64] The references to the maritime global commons and to the Indo-Pacific are indicative of the maritime orientation of the trilateral dialogue. Furthermore, the broader aims of the dialogue are not achievable without maritime security. The annual meetings are held with the objective of building on the shared strong bilateral relations and synergising strengths to "ensure a peaceful, secure, prosperous, and rules-based Indo-Pacific.[65] In May 2021, at the ministerial dialogue, the ministers agreed to deepen cooperation on maritime safety and security in the Indo-Pacific region.[66] A tangible outcome of the trilateral has been an information sharing workshop at the IFC-IOR and the deployment of liaison officers to the IFC-IOR.

Unlike the India-Maldives-Sri Lanka trilateral that is in the immediate neighbourhood and has an exclusive focus on maritime security, this trilateral is a linkage between important regional players in different reaches of the IOR, and has a wider remit. An analyst in 2020 opined that 'this trilateral is here to stay."[67] However, with the straining of relations between France and Australia after Australia called off a submarine deal with France, and the creation of the AUKUS alliance, there have been questions of the future of this trilateral. In general, while this reflects the uncertainties associated with plurilaterals, the possibilities of such events should not prevent such engagements which are increasingly gaining traction to meet contemporary challenges. Multiple plurilateral arrangements can also be an instrument to hedge against unpredictability.

India, Japan, and the US have held trilateral summit meetings between the Prime Ministers of India and Japan and the President of the United States in the context of the challenges in the Indo-Pacific, including in maritime security cooperation.[68] The leaders have met twice in 2018 and in 2019. Similarly, the Australia-India-Japan trilateral dialogue has "stressed the need for greater collaboration on maritime security and domain awareness and disaster response capabilities."[69] Senior officials from Australia, India, and Indonesia have had annual dialogues between 2017 and 2019 focused on the Indo-Pacific and related maritime issues.[70] The Australia-India-Indonesia trilateral, unlike some others, is considered as a partnership amongst regional 'middle powers' that can possibly better protect middle power interests, rather than those of global powers.[71] In addition, some of the other trilateral initiatives which are being considered or have been initiated include India-Italy-Japan trilateral.[72] In addition, a Track 2 level India-Japan-Russia trilateral has also been launched with a focus on the Russian Far East.[73]

BILATERAL COOPERATION

Since the end of the Cold War, India has signed 'strategic partnership' agreements with more than 35 countries.[74] Some partnerships have been upgraded to 'Comprehensive Strategic Partnership,' and the partnership with the US is defined as 'Comprehensive Global Strategic Partnership.'[75] The upgrading of relations to 'strategic' is often a recognition of the progress already made, and not merely a futuristic vision.[76] In addition, adjectives such as 'special and privileged' [Russia] and 'Green' [Denmark] have also been used to describe certain relationships reflecting an ordering within the broad framework of strategic partnerships.[77] While the term 'strategic partnership' has not been defined, typically, a strategic partnership reflects a commitment to a privileged and enduring relationship, often with a focus on defence and security.[78] Strategic partnerships, also considered as alternatives to alliances, reflects a long-term engagement in areas of mutual interest, across multiple areas of cooperation, including, economic, political, defence, and security.[79] Consequently, even amongst strategic partners, there is diversity in the scope and level of engagement.[80] As such, 21st century organisations are increasingly showing a tendency to move away from formal structures to more informal arrangements.

India's strategic partnerships with maritime nations/groupings, include, ASEAN, Australia, Brazil, China, EU, France, Germany, Indonesia, Iran, Israel, Malaysia, Mauritius, Nigeria, Oman, Russia, Saudi Arabia, Seychelles, Singapore, South Africa, South Korea, Japan, UAE, UK, US, and Vietnam.[81] These maritime nations reflect a majority of the countries with which India has strategic partnerships. The importance of partnerships can be gauged by the fact that the 2022 US Indo-Pacific strategy prioritises the US network of security alliances and importantly, partnerships as the "greatest asymmetric strength," and two of its ten lines of effort to achieve its strategic aims focus on India and the QUAD.[82]

An overview of India's bilateral maritime security cooperation efforts, based on Shishir Upadhyaya's exhaustive work on the issue is annexed at **Annexure B**. Broadly, he concludes that India has established 'close' security relations with most of the countries in the IOR.[83] He has categorised the 'level' of bilateral cooperation into three distinct levels as tabulated below, with Level 3 being the lowest and Level 1 the highest level of cooperation. However, within the broad categorisation, there will remain inherent variations in the scope and depth of engagement even between countries in the same grouping. The table below provides a short overview, as updated, of the overall bilateral maritime security relationship, region-wise. The table has been correlated with the foreign policy, broad geographical groups, and respective divisions responsible in MEA in square brackets; strategic partners are indicated in bold font.

Table 3.1: Region-wise Maritime Security Cooperation

Level/Region-FP[84]	Level 3	Level 2	Level 1
1. South Asia/ *NeighbourhoodFirst/*	Maldives, Sri Lanka [IOR]	Bangladesh/ [BM]	Pakistan [PAI]
Act East/ Immediate Neighbourhood	[BIMSTEC & SAARC Division][85]		
2. East Africa-IO Island states *Sagar, Island/ Extended Neighbours*	Egypt, Madagascar, **Mauritius**, Mozambique, **Seychelles**, **South Africa** [E&SA/IOR]	Kenya, Tanzania [E&SA/IOR]	Comoros, Djibouti, Somalia,Sudan [WANA/IOR]
3. E/SE Asia-Australia/ *Act East Extended IOR Neighbours*	**Indonesia**, Myanmar, **Singapore**, Thailand, **Vietnam** [BM/Oceania/Southern]	**Australia**, **Malaysia**, Thailand [Southern]	Cambodia, Timor Leste [Southern]
5. West Asia *Think West Extended IOR neighbour*	**Israel**, Kuwait, **Oman**, Qatar [Gulf/PAI]	**Iran**, Iraq, Tunisia, Kuwait, **UAE** [Gulf/WANA]	Bahrain, Yemen, **Saudi Arabia** [Gulf/WANA]
Specific Issues: D&ISA/Indo-Pacific Division			

Source: Shishir Upadhyaya.

Despite India's close bilateral relationships with most IOR countries, Shishir Upadhyaya argues that the bilateral approach is wasteful (and unsustainable) in the long term considering the quantum of effort required, the possibility of not living up to the expectations of partner countries, and the challenge from rising Chinese influence.[86] He also further argues that forging strong ties is no guarantee for support in perpetuity, and recommends a strategy that "leverages own means rather than dependency of foreign relations that could change over time."[87] While there are fundamental truths in the arguments with respect to military threats, the focus of his thesis, non-military threats are contextually a different paradigm with different dynamics. For example, the Indian Navy's mission-based deployments, such as in the Gulf of Aden (anti-piracy) and in the Persian Gulf (maritime threats) over several years, have been logistically sustained primarily on account of India's bilateral engagements with regional countries. As India expands its presence to play a wider role, so will its need for distant support, for which, oftentimes, bilateral agreements will remain the mainstay till regional constructs and other groupings develop the requisite international institutional framework, if at all one can be developed. However, the argument still has merit as cooperative endeavours in any form need to be balanced with other competitive imperatives. Nations can ill afford supporting maritime security in distant waters by compromising own maritime security. In short, despite the urge to expand maritime security cooperation there are inherent limitations which merit consideration.

In addition to regional countries, India shares strong naval ties with naval forces of extra-regional countries, and with France, a resident Indian Ocean power with territory in the Indian Ocean. Over the years, these ties have also progressively intensified. The Indian Navy has strong historical ties with the Royal Navy from which it emerged post-independence, and several extra-regional powers, particularly Russia, have contributed to the growth of the Indian Navy to one of the largest and modern navies in the world; France, Israel, and UK being other major defence partners.[88] In more contemporary times, the US has emerged as a major partner in defence and maritime security cooperation. Policy pronouncements by the US unambiguously support India's vision of being a security provider in the Indian Ocean.[89] However, in the context of the withdrawal of the US from Afghanistan in 2021, concerns have been raised about the reliability of the US as a partner, which, like any other country, is driven by its own interests.[90] The US challenge to India's position on military manoeuvres in Indian EEZ is an example of differences that may get amplified if not managed; India abstaining from voting against Russia in UN bodies after Russian invasion of Ukraine is another example of differences. India is also developing partnerships with Japan and Vietnam. Overall, Shishir Upadhyaya has concluded that India's maritime security cooperation with some of the major extra-regional powers "clearly point to a hedging strategy aimed at balancing China."[91] While surely the 'China factor' is a major determinant in the maritime space, it surely is not just about China; it is also, amongst others, about ensuring alternative sources of military hardware and strategic hedging. From a maritime security cooperation partnership, the India-

Japan-US engagement, with Australia, under the QUAD framework, *inter alia* to counter the growing Chinese threat in the Indo-Pacific, has political support and therefore has the greatest potential, at least for now.

THEMATIC COOPERATION

In addition to regional cooperation for maritime security there is also a need for international cooperation on thematic issues related to maritime security, such as maritime crime and environmental protection. Some of the areas of thematic cooperation for maritime security are discussed in this section.

Maritime Crime

The Global Maritime Crime Programme (GMCP), a programme under the aegis of the UNODC, supports member states in developing capacity for tackling maritime crimes across the word.[92] Multiple teams of the GMCP are engaged in related activities across India's areas of maritime interest. The core activities of the GMCP are focused on maritime law enforcement, crime detection and interdiction, investigation, prosecution, detention, and importantly regional cooperation; thematically, the GMCP also focuses on submarine cable protection, fishery crimes, and counter terrorism.[93] Capacity building is undertaken through embedded mentorship, training programmes, developing of prosecutor networks, etc.[94] Importantly, the focus of the GMCP is on law enforcement and other activities associated with providing a legal finish to maritime crime, an area that often does not get adequate focus.[95] The GMCP also runs associated programmes such as the Indian Ocean Forum for Maritime Crime (IOFMC), and its subordinate programmes, such as the Southern Route Partnership (SRP). The UNODC operates a regional programme for South Asia (2018-21), which has been extended till 2023, that focuses *inter alia* on countering transnational organised crime, drugs, terrorism, and crime prevention and criminal justice.[96]

The engagement of Indian maritime security agencies with the UNODC, a UN office, has been relatively modest through workshops and participation in meetings and conferences. Consequently, there is scope for expanding engagement with UNODC.[97] Considering the vast linkages of the UNODC, and the wide remit of the GMCP, strengthening linkages could facilitate dissemination of global best practices to Indian law enforcement, maritime, investigative and prosecution agencies. Further, India could also be a contributor to activities under the UNDOC GMCP, like other countries/ regional groupings, such as the EU and Japan.

International Maritime Policing

The International Criminal Police Organization (INTERPOL) is an inter-governmental organisation that connects the police agencies of 195 member states.[98] INTERPOL also works on maritime crimes with local, regional, and international stakeholders including regional and international organisations, countries, maritime security agencies, and naval forces, as well as private industry bodies to improve maritime governance and security.[99] The primary areas of work relate to information exchange through the Global Maritime Security Database, capability enhancement of MLEA and judicial services through regionally focused programmes, and building international and cross-sectoral partnerships.[100]

India has been a member of the INTERPOL since 1949, and the Central Bureau of Investigation (CBI) which is the designated 'National Central Bureau' is the national Point of Contact (POC) for INTERPOL.[101] The CBI is "one of the relatively more active members of INTERPOL," and has hosted several INTERPOL events, including on anti-piracy. Several directors and officials of the CBI have also served in the Executive Committee of the INTERPOL.[102] Domestically, the CBI, as the National Central Bureau, is also the coordinating authority with states for all matters related to the INTERPOL, and in the context of maritime security, with all coastal States. Considering the CBI's high seas mandate and the transnational nature of maritime crimes, such as piracy and drug trafficking, strengthening domestic capabilities, particularly in maritime investigations and prosecution, through regular interactions and participation in INTERPOL's activities is also a maritime security imperative. India could also support activities of the INTERPOL, especially in South Asia.

Coordinated Economic Border Management

The World Customs Organisation (WCO), established in 1952, has 183 members, who together process about 98 per cent of global trade, most of which is carried through the sea routes.[103] India joined the WCO in 1971 and has acceded to several conventions and has bilateral Customs Mutual Administrative Assistance Agreements with several countries.[104] The concept of 'Coordinated Border Management' (CBM) focuses on coordinating domestic and international border controls to balance trade facilitation on one hand, and to ensure regulatory compliance on the other.[105] For example, the WCO has worked with the UNODC on a UNODC-WCO Container Control Programme (CCP) to improve supply chain security and related risk management activities.[106] In India, the Indian Customs exercises customs border control, and has taken measures towards improving supply chain security and risk management, with more being planned. In 2017, the CBIC established a Directorate of International Customs (DIC) to assist the CBIC in international matters.[107] The National Academy of Customs, Indirect Taxes, and Narcotics (NACIN) is also accredited with the WCO, and other international bodies as an "important institution of capacity building."[108] Overall, strengthening customs border control mechanisms through enhanced international cooperation and participation in international activities can also contribute to strengthening overall maritime security. Notably, the UK *National Strategy for Maritime Security* (2022), considers maritime security as an extension of the homeland or 'UK border.'[109]

Marine Environmental Protection

The South Asia Co-operative Environment Programme (SACEP), an inter-governmental organisation, was set up in 1982 with the objective of promoting and supporting protection, management, and enhancement of the environment in South Asia.[110] SACEP adopted the action plan for the South Asian Seas Programme (SASP) in 1995 to assist members in the protection of the environment.[111] One of the priority areas of the SASP is the development of a regional oil and chemical spill contingency plan. The plan aims to establish cooperative mechanisms for coordination of oil pollution response in South Asia.[112] *Inter alia,* these include designation of national authorities, setting-up of information exchange mechanisms, capacity building, such as by conduct of meetings and training activities, and risk assessment.[113]

India signed an MOU with SACEP on 'Co-operation on the Response to Oil Spill and Chemical Pollution in the South Asia Seas Region' on 12 May 2018.[114] The Coast Guard is the national authority under the SACEP MOU, as also the 'Competent National Authority' and 'National Operational Contact' for implementation of the Regional Oil Contingency Plan for South Asia, which has been developed jointly with the IMO. Further, Indian MRCCs have been designated as emergency response centres.[115] Under the MOU, parties have agreed to cooperate individually, and jointly, to respond to pollution incidents in line with the principles of the regional plan. In recent years, the SACEP has also been operationalised in response to oil pollution incidents off the Sri Lanka coast, such as the MT *New Diamond* incident (2020) involving fire onboard the tanker off the Sri Lankan coast.

SECTORAL COOPERATION

The '1000-ship navy' concept, defined by the US Navy's Chief of Naval Operations (CNO) Admiral Mike Mullen as "a global maritime partnership that unites maritime forces, port operators, commercial shippers, and international, governmental and non-governmental agencies to address mutual concerns" stressed on the need for cross-sectoral integration for maritime security.[116] In hindsight, the nomenclature ('*1000 ship navy*') with its naval focus was perhaps a misnomer. While the concept could not be actualised in the global context, in India, soon after the '26/11' incident, it was realised that cross-sectoral integration was a necessity, and a unifying framework integrating various maritime sectors such as ports, shipping, fisheries, offshore, as also the community, was set up to address contemporary maritime security challenges such as terrorism. Internationally, the counter-piracy efforts off Somalia are a fine example of a multi-pronged operational approach to tackle maritime security challenges involving international naval forces and the global shipping industry, complemented by other measures, such as capacity building for maritime security and for criminal justice. The establishment of inclusive mechanisms for anti-piracy, such as the Contact Group on Piracy off the Coast of Somalia (CGPCS) and the SHADE, exemplify the necessity for cross-sectoral approach to maritime security. While these measures surely contribute to suppression of maritime insecurity, eradication requires addressing root causes which invariably lie ashore. Maritime security cooperation, therefore, cannot be an exclusive grouping of maritime security agencies, but an inclusive mechanism involving all stakeholders who can contribute, as also those who are affected by maritime insecurity. Maritime security cooperative groupings/

regional bodies working on maritime security, therefore, need to engage with key stakeholders, such as the shipping sector. This section discusses some of the major maritime sectors.

Shipping

The International Maritime Organization (IMO), a UN specialised agency, has a mandate for safety and security of international shipping, including development of the international regulatory framework through the Maritime Security Committee (MSC) and other committees.[117] Its notable work in maritime security includes, amongst others, the development of the International Ship and Port Facility Security (ISPS) Code, under the International Convention for the Safety of Life at Sea, 1974 (SOLAS Convention), and the Suppression of Unlawful Acts against the Safety of Maritime Navigation (SUA) treaties.[118] Amendments to the SOLAS convention to include provisions for implementation of LRIT and AIS have also facilitated greater MDA, and thereby maritime security itself. Its work in response to piracy situations in some parts of the world include the development of the Djibouti Code of Conduct (DCoC) and the Yaoundé Code of Conduct in East Africa and West Africa respectively; the development of suitable shipping guidance, including for Best Management Practices (BMP), armed security, and for investigation of piratical incidents; maintenance of a global information repository through the Global Integrated Shipping Information System (GISIS); and other capacity building initiatives, particularly in the western IOR.[119]

India is one of the earliest members of the IMO and joined the organisation in 1959. India has been a member of the IMO Council under Category "B" almost continuously with a small break.[120] More recently, India won elections to the IMO council for two-year terms in 2017 and 2021. The IMO provides an important avenue to engage with the international shipping community, including on maritime security. Some of the areas of engagement steered by India under the aegis of the IMO include regulation of private security in the shipping industry and information sharing through the IFC-IOR.[121] A more active role for India in the IMO, and more specifically in the MSC, could buttress India's leadership credentials in maritime security, especially in the shipping industry.

In July 2004, the ISPS Code—a mandatory international code—was included in Chapter XI-2 [Special measures to enhance maritime security] of the International Convention for the Safety of Life at Sea (SOLAS) 1974 SOLAS's. The aim of the Code is to ensure that applicable ocean-going ships and port facilities implement the highest standards of security. The ISPS code contains mandatory security-related requirements for governments, port authorities, and shipping companies, as also guidelines on how the mandated requirements are to be met.

The IMO has defined Port State Control (PSC), a responsibility of port States, as the inspection of foreign ships in national ports to verify compliance with international regulations promulgated by the IMO *inter alia* for maintenance, operations and manning of ships engaged on international routes.[122] While the primary responsibility for compliance with IMO requirements is that of the Flag State, IMO conventions provide for inspection of ships by the Port State when ships visit a foreign port.[123] PSC, therefore, provides a backup to the Flag State for ensuring regulatory compliance, as also a 'safety net,' to prevent substandard ships from endangering safety and security. Overall, PSC is applicable to 14 IMO conventions, which *inter alia* include SOLAS, the International Convention for the Prevention of Pollution from Ships (MARPOL), and the International Convention on Standards of Training, Certification and Watchkeeping for Seafarers (STCW), including for security training of crew.[124] Towards enhancing efficiency, and precluding unnecessary delays in PSC inspections, inspections by Port States are coordinated through regional agreements, such as the Indian Ocean Memorandum of Understanding on PSC (IOMOU) which is headquartered in Goa.[125]

The IOMOU, which is the regional MOU for PSC in the IOR, has 20 member states.[126] In accordance with its international commitments to identify and eliminate sub-standard shipping and domestic legislation, India undertakes PSC inspections, and publishes the results in an annual report.[127] An assessment of PSC in India by comparing it to some of the most active MOUs in the world, which includes the US PSC regime, the Paris MOU, and the Tokyo MOU in 2018, revealed lower inspection rate, lesser focus on security-related inspections [ISPS Code], and lower detection rates of ISPS-related deficiencies.[128] Therefore, there is scope for strengthening implementation of the IOMOU by India. Further, as the membership of the IOMOU is limited to 20 countries, expanding the scope of the IOUMOU to include all IOR littoral countries and further strengthening of the IOMOU, particularly by India, can contributing to safer and more secure seas in the region.

Fisheries

Illegal, Unreported, Unregulated (IUU) fishing, a transnational crime, is recognised as one of the principal threats to maritime security, necessitating regional/international cooperation. The International Cooperation division in the DoF is responsible for multilateral and bilateral cooperation on fisheries, including with the FAO and Regional Fisheries Management Organisations (RFMOs).[129] RFMOs *inter alia* manage and monitor fishing in designated regional areas.[130] While India is a member of the Bay of Bengal Programme Inter-Governmental Organisation (BOBP-IGO), the Indian Ocean Tuna Commission (IOTC) and the Asia-Pacific Fishery Commission (APFIC), the other important RFMOs in the IOR of which India is not a member, include the Commission for the Conservation of Southern Bluefin Tuna (CCSBT) and the Southern Indian Ocean Fisheries Agreement (SIOFA).[131] Overall, it has been assessed that there are gaps in the governance mechanisms for regional fisheries management, such as in spatial coverage, species covered, and in the enforcement of Conservation and Management Measures (CMM) adopted by RFMOs.[132] Further, there has also been a need to harmonise efforts between RFMOs.[133] The capacity of any RFMO is a function of the capacities of individual member states; in other words, unless capacities of individual states are strengthened, regional fisheries management is unlikely to be effective.[134] Therefore, there is a need for strengthening regional capacity.

In addition to RFMOs, Regional Fisheries Bodies (RFB), which provide voluntary guidelines and minimum standards, also influence management of fishery resources in the Indian Ocean.[135] Fisheries related issues are also discussed at several multilateral forums such as in ASEAN and other ASEAN-led initiatives, BIMSTEC, IORA, SAARC, etc. For strengthening bilateral cooperation in the fisheries sector, India has concluded MOUs with five countries (Bangladesh, Iceland, Morocco, Norway, Vietnam [two MOUs]) and set up Joint Working Groups (JWGs) with four countries (Bangladesh, Iceland, Norway, and Sri Lanka).[136] An assessment by BOB-IGO indicates that overall the status of implementation of management measures and laws is inadequate.[137] Therefore, there is scope for strengthening international engagements in fisheries management, multilaterally and bilaterally.

The IOTC, of which India is a member, is an RFMO responsible for the management of tuna and tuna-like species in the Indian Ocean.[138] *Inter alia,* the IOTC monitors compliance with promulgated CMM, and notably also maintains a list of authorised, active, and IUU fishing vessels. The availability of the list of fishing vessels, including blacklisted ones, is a useful resource for maritime security agencies.[139] In addition to meeting regional CMM, there is also a need to meet other regional requirements. For example, the EU through its 'carding system' prevents import of fish from countries that do not meet EU standards of fisheries management.[140] As India is amongst the largest exporters of fish, non-compliance with international standards could potentially have an adverse impact on the economics of the fisheries sector and the well-being of the fishing community.

BOBP-IGO, headquartered in Chennai, is a regional advisory body focused on sustainable coastal fisheries development and management amongst the countries adjoining the Bay of Bengal.[141] The programme, instituted in 2003, evolved from the FAO's Bay of Bengal Programme which was started in 1979. Eight countries of the Bay of Bengal region are party to the project; while Bangladesh, India, Maldives, and Sri Lanka are contracting States, Indonesia, Malaysia, Myanmar, and Thailand are cooperating parties of the project. In addition, in the Bay of Bengal, the Bay of Bengal Large Marine Ecosystem (BOBLME) project works on issues related to sustainable exploitation of resources, protection of critical habitats such as mangroves, coral reefs, sea grass, and pollution.[142] The project aims at strengthening governance, improving resource management, and expanding knowledge.[143]

At the bilateral level, illegal fishing has significant implications not only for fisher safety and security, but also for bilateral relationships. With Sri Lanka, multi-level engagements have been instituted at the levels of security agencies, government officials, and importantly amongst political leaders as well to address fisheries-related issues. Such forums for engagement ensure that fisheries-related issues, which are often emotive, are addressed through dialogue.

The Meenakumari Report (2014) on India's deep-sea fishing policy had recognised that "fisheries is set in a globalised world," and the multidimensional linkages of the sector to diverse issues such as safety and security, environment, and biodiversity conservation.[144] The National Policy on Marine Fisheries (2017) rightly envisages a leadership role for India in the management of marine resources by active participation in regional and international bodies.[145] Further, considering shared ecosystems with neighbouring countries and the presence of migratory and straddling fish stock, the policy also states that the government will foster strong regional cooperation not only for conservation, but also for fisher safety and security.[146] The draft National Fisheries Policy (2020) also echoes similar sentiments.[147] Considering the wide realisation of IUU fishing as a threat to maritime security, strengthening international cooperation in fisheries CMM would not only promote sustainable fisheries, but also maritime security. Specifically, these could include expansion in the engagements across RFMOs and RFBs in the IOR, taking on leadership and management roles in international/regional bodies, widening engagements with maritime neighbours, and fostering sensitisation in the fisheries sector. Such engagements would also need robust cross-sectoral engagements at the domestic level, including with maritime security agencies.

TRACK 1.5/2 ENGAGEMENTS

One of the ways to continue and sustain dialogue, such as on maritime security cooperation, is through 'multi-track diplomacy,' with alternative channels complementing the official channels.[148] Track 1.5 engagements, involving both government officials and others, and Track 2 engagements, involving unofficial channels, such as think tanks, are relatively unencumbered by the official line on issues, and can therefore facilitate more frank and open discussions, especially on issues that may be sensitive. The output from such engagements can however flow into the policymaking process and help in better decision-making. Dialogues through informal channels, such as Track 1.5 and 2, can also lay the foundation for dialogue and interaction between governments.

Reportedly, India has over 600 think tanks, and is ranked third after the US and China. There is, therefore, little doubt that think tanks in India can play a key role not only in advancing the academic discourse on maritime security, but also in shaping maritime security policies, not only domestically, but also on a regional and international basis. The Raisina Dialogue, organised by the Observer Research Foundation (ORF) in collaboration with the MEA, and the IPRD, organised by the NMF in collaboration with the Indian Navy are examples of increasing convergence between Track 1 and Track 1.5/2 organisations to facilitate dialogue on pressing contemporary challenges.

Some Indian think tanks focused on maritime issues, include the Pune-based Indian Maritime Foundation (IMF) and the Maritime Research Centre (MRC), and the New Delhi-based NMF. The NMF, India's foremost maritime think tank, includes, amongst its research objectives, suggesting maritime Confidence-Building Measures (CBMs) and enhancing maritime cooperation to achieve a stable security environment in the Indo-Pacific Region. Towards achieving this, and other objectives, which broadly encompass all issues 'maritime,' albeit with a focus on holistic maritime security, the NMF has partnerships, through MOUs, with 26 think tanks from across the world. The NMF conducts regular events with partners on wide ranging maritime issues, including amongst others, geopolitics, maritime security, MDA, climate change, blue economy, maritime laws (Public International Maritime Law), etc.[149] In addition, the NMF also participates in events across the world on maritime issues. The increasing use of the virtual medium during the COVID pandemic has facilitated even greater global interactions.

For a maritime country the size of India, with significant maritime interests, the NMF is, however, a leanly staffed organisation with the research faculty comprising both service officers (Indian Navy and Coast Guard) and civilian faculty.[150] Consequently, only limited expertise can be available at any given time with the institution, precluding a broad cross-cutting interdisciplinary approach to issues maritime; this is also the case elsewhere Strengthening academic discourse in maritime security in India is an indisputable imperative, and therefore, strengthening of maritime think tanks, and the maritime component of other think tanks is an imperative.

While the NMF is a dedicated maritime think tank, other think tanks too are involved in maritime issues, including maritime security cooperation. Think tanks contribute to shaping the contours for maritime security cooperation, therefore, embedding Track 1.5/2 engagements in institutional multilateral or bilateral engagements, where necessary/possible, is perhaps a useful way for enriching multilateral/bilateral dialogue. Also, as several countries are yet to adopt a Track 1.5/2 approach to maritime dialogues, to facilitate such dialogues, established think tanks in India could also contribute to the development of similar organisations in other countries for sustained multi-track dialogue.

This chapter focused on the details on how India progress maritime security cooperation across multiple formats, such as regional, plurilateral, and bilateral cooperation. The chapter also delved into the various dimensions of thematic cooperation, such as for maritime crime, policing, SAR, environmental protection, as also sectoral cooperation across maritime sectors, such as shipping and fisheries. The chapter also highlighted the role of Track 1.5 and Track 2 engagements to further maritime security cooperation. The next chapter focuses on aspects of operational cooperation.

NOTES

1 James Scot, "Multilateralism," *Encyclopaedia Britannica*, https://www.britannica.com/, accessed on 04 January 2022.

2 United Nations, 'International Day of Multilateralism and Diplomacy, 24 April," https://www.un.org/en/observances/Multilateralism-for-Peace-day, accessed on 04 January 2022,

3 James Scot, "Multilateralism."

4 Naoise McDonagh, "Is plurilateralism making the WTO an institutional zombie?," Institute for International Trade (University of Adelaide), https://iit.adelaide.edu.au/news/list/2021/02/23/is-plurilateralism-making-the-wto-an-institutional-zombie, accessed on 04 January 2022.

5 Swaran Singh, "India's Pursuit of Plurilateralism," Diplomatist, 22 December 2022, https://diplomatist.com/2022/12/22/indias-pursuit-of-plurilateralism/, accessed on 20 August 2023.

6 "External Affairs Minister participates in a panel discussion at the Raisina Dialogue 2021- "Crimson Tide, Blue Geometries: New Partnerships for the Indo-Pacific" (14-04-2021)," Ministry of External Affairs, https://www.mea.gov.in/interviews.htm?dtl/33806, accessed on 04 January 2022.

7 Brian Wilson, "The Turtle Bay Pivot."

8 Brian Wilson, "The Turtle Bay Pivot," 41-42.

9 Brian Wilson, "The Turtle Bay Pivot," 1.

10 Brian Wilson, "The Turtle Bay Pivot," 1; Bueger, "Does Maritime Security Require a New United Nations Structure?"

11 Press Trust of India, "India ensured concerns of all 15 UNSC members taken on board on outcome documents from signature Presidency events: Ambassador Tirumurti," *The Economic Times*, 24 August 2021, https://economictimes.indiatimes.com/news/defence/india-ensured-concerns-of-all-15-unsc-members-taken-on-board-on-outcome-documents-from-signature-presidency-events-ambassador-tirumurti/articleshow/85584418.cms?utm_source=contentofinterest&utm_medium=text&utm_campaign=cppst, accessed on 06 September 2021.

12 UN Security Council, "Security Council Authorizes States To Use Land-Based Operations

In Somalia, As Part Of Fight Against Piracy Off Coast, Unanimously Adopting 1851 (2008)," Press Release, 16 December 2008, https://www.un.org/press/en/2008/sc9541.doc.htm, accessed on 10 March 2022.

13 Charter of the United Nations, Articles 52-54, https://www.un.org/en/about-us/un-charter/chapter-8.

14 "About SAARC ," South Asian Association for Regional Cooperation, https://www.saarc-sec.org/index.php/about-saarc/about-saarc, accessed on 07 January 2022.

15 "Education, Security & Culture," South Asian Association for Regional Cooperation, , https://www.saarc-sec.org/index.php/areas-of-cooperation/education-security-culture, accessed on 11 April 2021.

16 South Asian Association for Regional Cooperation, "SAARC Ministerial Declaration on Cooperation in Combating Terrorism (2009)," https://www.iri.edu.ar/publicaciones_iri/anuario/cd%20Anuario%202010/Asia/SAARC/SAARC%20Declaration%20Coopera tion %20 in%20Combating%20Terrorism.pdf, accessed on 12 January 2022.

17 Achal Malhotra, "India's Foreign Policy: Current priorities and relevance of SAARC," Ministry of External Affairs, 08 October 2018, https://mea.gov.in/distinguished-lectures-detail.htm?766, accessed on 11 March 2022.

18 Malhotra, "India's Foreign Policy: Current priorities and relevance of SAARC."

19 "About BIMSTEC," Bay of Bengal Initiative for Multi-Sectoral Technical and Economic Cooperation, https://bimstec.org/?page_id=189, accessed on 12 January 2022.

20 About BIMSTEC," Bay of Bengal Initiative for Multi-Sectoral Technical and Economic Cooperation.

21 "Keynote address by Secretary (East) at the BIMSTEC Coastal Security Workshop (20 November 2019)," Ministry of External Affairs, 2022, https://www.mea.gov.in/Speeches-Statements.htm?dtl/32068/Keynote_address_by_Secretary_, accessed on 12 January 2022.

22 "BIMSTEC Convention on Cooperation in Combating International Terrorism, Transnational Organised Crime And Illicit Drug Trafficking," Ministry of External Affairs, https://mea.gov.in/bilateral-documents.htm?dtl/5070/BIMSTEC+Convention+on+Co operation+in+Combating+International+Terrorism+Transnational+Organised+Crime+ And+Illicit+Drug+Trafficking, accessed on 11 April 2011.

23 "Counter-Terrorism and Transnational Crime," Bay of Bengal Initiative for Multi-Sectoral Technical and Economic Cooperation, https://bimstec.org/?page_id=288, accessed on 11 April 2011. The sub-groups include those on narcotics, intelligence sharing, law enforcement, terror financing and money laundering, human trafficking, and countering radicalisation and terrorism.

24 "Counter-Terrorism and Transnational Crime," Bay of Bengal Initiative for Multi-Sectoral Technical and Economic Cooperation.

25 "Coastal Security Workshop for BIMSTEC Countries," Bay of Bengal Initiative for Multi-Sectoral Technical and Economic Cooperation, https://bimstec.org/?event=coastal-security-workshop-for-bimstec-countries, accessed on 12 January 2022.

26 Gurpreet S. Khurana, "BIMSTEC and Maritime Security; Issues, Imperatives, and Way Ahead," National Maritime Foundation, 16 November 2018, https://maritimeindia.org/bimstec-and-maritime-security-issues-imperatives-and-way-ahead/, accessed on 07 January 2022.

27 "India-ASEAN Relations," Ministry of External Affairs.
28 "India-ASEAN Relations," Ministry of External Affairs.
29 "India-ASEAN Relations," Ministry of External Affairs.
30 "Delhi Declaration of the ASEAN-India Commemorative Summit to Mark the 25th Anniversary of ASEAN-India Dialogue Relations," Association of South East Asian Nations,
31 "Plan of Action to Implement the ASEAN-India Partnership For Peace, Progress And Shared Prosperity (2021-25), Association of South East Asian Nations, https://asean.org/asean2020/wp-content/uploads/2021/03/11.-ASEAN-India-POA-2021-2025-Final.pdf, accessed on 12 January 2022.
32 "India-ASEAN Relations," Ministry of External Affairs.
33 "India-ASEAN Relations," Ministry of External Affairs.
34 "Home," Indian Ocean Rim Association, https://www.iora.int/en, accessed on 12 January 2022.
35 "Home," Indian Ocean Rim Association.
36 "Home," Indian Ocean Rim Association.
37 Maritime security includes elements of international peace and security, sovereignty/territorial integrity/political independence, security from crimes at sea, security of resources and environmental security; while Maritime safety is concerned with training (both technical and personnel), transport, construction and equipment related issues, assistance in distress situations, etc. Source: Indian Ocean Regional Organisation; https://www.iora.int/en/priorities-focus-areas/maritime-safety-and-security.
38 "Maritime Safety and Security,' Indian Ocean Regional Association, https://www.iora.int/en/priorities-focus-areas/maritime-safety-and-security, accessed on 08 January 2021.
39 "Maritime Safety and Security," Indian Ocean Regional Association.
40 "Maritime Safety and Security," Indian Ocean Regional Association.
41 Rahul Roy-Chaudhury, "Strengthening maritime cooperation and security in the Indian Ocean," International Institute of Security Studies, 06 September 2018, https://www.iiss.org/blogs/analysis/2018/09/maritime-cooperation-indian-ocean, accessed on 12 January 2021.
42 Stable Seas, *Challenges and Solutions for Maritime Security in the Indian Ocean*, 3.
43 "Press Release,' Indian Coast Guard, https://indiancoastguard.gov.in/WriteReadData/Tender/201712121250146665957Press_Release.pdf, accessed on 13 January 2021.
44 "Press Release," Indian Coast Guard.
45 "Press Release," Indian Coast Guard; "ReCAAP Focal Points," ReCAAP, https://www.recaap.org/focal-points, accessed on 13 January 2021.
46 "Press Release,' Indian Coast Guard; "Singapore to host the ReCAAP ISC for another five years," Marine and Port Authority Singapore, https://www.mpa.gov.sg/web/portal/home/media-centre/news-releases/detail/db79671b-9c98-4747-86da-3d3861ee88e5, accessed on 13 January 2021.
47 "Election of Mr. K. Natarajan as next Executive Director of ReCAAP," Ministry of External Affairs, Press Release, 05 August 2021, https://www.mea.gov.in/press-releases.htm?dtl/34138/Election_of_Mr_K_Natarajan_as_next_Executive_Director_of_ReCAAP, accessed on 18 August 2021.
48 Rajeswari Pillai Rajgopalan, "Rise of the Minilaterals: Examining the India-France-

Australia Trilateral," *The Diplomat*, 17 September 2020, https://thediplomat.com/2020/09/rise-of-the-minilaterals-examining-the-india-france-australia-trilateral/, accessed on 12 January 2022.

49 "Fact Sheet: Quad Leaders' Summit," Ministry of External Affairs, 24 September 2021, https://www.mea.gov.in/bilateral-documents.htm?dtl/34319/Fact+Sheet+Quad+Leaders+Summit, accessed on 12 January 2022.

50 "Question No. 2411: Features of Quadrilateral Security Dialogue," Rajya Sabha, January 03, 2018, https://mea.gov.in/rajya-sabha.htm?dtl/30869/question+no2411+features+of+quadrilateral+security+dialogue, accessed on 12 January 2022.

51 "Foreign Secretary's Remarks on 'Quad and Future of the Indo-Pacific' at the 5th India-US Forum," Ministry of External Affairs, 02 December 2021, https://www.mea.gov.in/Speeches-Statements.htm?dtl/34571/Foreign_Secretarys_Remarks_on_Quad_and_Future _of_the_IndoPacific_at_the_5th_IndiaUS_Forum, accessed on 12 January 2022,

52 Press Trust of India, "Don't slip into the 'lazy analogy' of referring Quad as Asian NATO: EAM Jaishankar," *The New Indian Express*, 20 February 2022, https://www.newindianexpress.com/world/2022/feb/20/dont-slip-into-the-lazy-analogy-of-referring-quad-as-asian-nato-eam-jaishankar-2421719.html, accessed on 20 February 2022.

53 The White House, *Indo-Pacific Strategy of the United States* (2020), 10.

54 Indo-Asian News Service, "From 2004 tsunami to Covid-19 pandemic: A timeline of Quad elevation," *Business Standard*, 23 September 2022, https://www.business-standard.com/article/international/from-2004-tsunami-to-covid-19-pandemic-a-timeline-of-quad-elevation-121092300168_1.html, accessed on 12 January 2022.

55 "4th NSA Level Meeting on Trilateral Maritime Security Cooperation," Ministry of External Affairs, 26 November 2020, https://www.mea.gov.in/press-releases.htm?dtl/33238/4th+NSA+Level+Meeting+on+Trilateral+Maritime+Security+Cooperation, accessed on 17 January 2021; "Joint Press Statement of the 5th NSA Level Meeting of the Colombo Security Conclave held on 09–10 March 2022, in Maldives," Ministry of External Affairs, Press Release, 10 March 2022, https://mea.gov.in/press-releases.htm?dtl/34943/Joint+Press+Statement+of+the+5th+NSA+Level+Meeting+of+the+Colombo+Security+ Conclave+held+on+09++10+March+2022+in+Maldives, accessed on 13 March 2022.

56 "NSA level meeting on trilateral Maritime Security Cooperation between India, Sri Lanka and Maldives," Ministry of External Affairs, 06 March 2014, https://www.mea.gov.in/in-focus-article.htm?23037/NSA+level+meeting+on+trilateral+ Maritime+ Security+Cooperation+between+India+Sri+Lanka+and+Maldives, accessed on 17 January 2021.

57 "Joint Press Statement," Ministry of Defence, Sri Lanka, 28 November 2020, http://www.defence.lk/Article/view_article/2654, accessed on 17 January 2021.

58 "Joint Press Statement," Ministry of Defence, Sri Lanka.

59 "Joint Press Statement," Ministry of Defence, Sri Lanka.

60 "Joint Press Statement," Ministry of Defence, Sri Lanka.

61 Ministry of External Affairs, "Joint Press Statement of the 5th NSA Level Meeting of the Colombo Security Conclave held on 09–10 March 2022, in Maldives," Press Release, 10 March 2022, https://mea.gov.in/press-releases.htm?dtl/34943/Joint+Press+Statement+of+the+5th+NSA+Level+Meeting+of+the+Colombo+Security+Conclave+held+on+ 09++10+March+2022+in+Maldives, accessed on 20 August 2023.

62 Ministry of Defence. "Indian Coast Guard Region (North East) Organises 4th Table Top Exercise in Kolkata under Colombo Security Conclave to Discuss Maritime Challenges in Indian Ocean Region," Press Information Bureau, 15 March 2023, https://pib.gov.in/PressReleaseIframePage.aspx?PRID=1907141, accessed on 20 August 2023.; Ministry of Defence, "Colombo Security Conclave Focused Operation Between Maldives and Sri Lanka," 28 November 2021. pib.gov.in/PressReleaseIframe Page.aspx?PRID=1775797, accessed on 20 August 2023; Press Trust of India, "Gujarat: RRU Holds Maritime Law Workshop, Several Nations Take Part." The Print, 13 April 2023, https://theprint.in/india/gujarat-rru-holds-maritime-law-workshop-several-nations-take-part/1517146/ accessed on 20 August 2023; Press Information Bureau. "Coastal Security Conference (CoSC) under the Aegis of Colombo Security Conclave Inaugurated," 01 December 2022, https://pib.gov.in/PressReleasePage.aspx?PRID=1880373, accessed on 20 August 2023

63 "1st Senior Officials' India-France-Australia Trilateral Dialogue." Ministry of External Affairs, 09 September 2020, https://www.mea.gov.in/press-releases.htm?dtl/32950/1st+Senior+Officials+IndiaFranceAustralia+Trilateral+Dialogue, accessed on 17 January 2021.

64 "1st Senior Officials' India-France-Australia Trilateral Dialogue." Ministry of External Affairs.

65 "1st Senior Officials' India-France-Australia Trilateral Dialogue." Ministry of External Affairs.

66 Ministry of External Affairs, *India-France-Australia Joint Statement on the occasion of the Trilateral Ministerial Dialogue (May 04, 2021)*, https://mea.gov.in/bilateral-documents.htm?dtl/33845/IndiaFranceAustralia+Joint+Statement+on+the+occasion+ of+the+Trilateral+Ministerial+Dialogue+May+04+2021, accessed on 12 January 2022.

67 Rajeswari Pillai Rajgopalan, "Rise of the Minilaterals: Examining the India-France-Australia Trilateral."

68 "Japan-U.S.-India Summit Meeting," Ministry of Foreign Affairs Japan, https://www.mofa.go.jp/s_sa/sw/page3e_001038.html, accessed on 12 January 2022.

69 "4th India-Australia-Japan Trilateral Dialogue (13 December 2017)," Ministry of External Affairs, https://mea.gov.in/press-releases.htm?dtl/29176/4th_IndiaAustraliaJapan_Trilateral_Dialogue_December_13_2017, accessed on 12 January 2022.

70 "Third India-Australia-Indonesia Trilateral Senior Officials' Dialogue," Department of Foreign Affairs and Trade, Australia, https://www.dfat.gov.au/news/media/Pages/third-india-australia-indonesia-trilateral-senior-officials-dialogue, accessed on 12 January 2022.

71 Jagganath Panda, "The Australia-India-Indonesia Trilateral: Fostering Maritime Cooperation between Middle Powers," National Bureau of Asian Research, 23 April 2021. https://idsa.in/system/files/news/all-map-nbr-analysis-min.pdf, accessed on 12 January 2022.

72 Dipanjan Roy Chaudhury, "India launches new trilateral with Italy and Japan for Indo-Pacific stability," *The Economic Times*, June 18, 2021, https://economictimes.indiatimes.com/news/india/india-launches-new-trilateral-with-italy-and-japan-for-indo-pacific-stability/articleshow/83624187.cms?utm_source=contentofinterest &utm_medium=text&utm_campaign=cppst, accessed on 12 January 2022.

73 Dipanjan Roy-Chaudhury, "India-Russia-Japan Trilateral: Focus on Resource Rich

Russian Far-East & Russian Arctic Regions," *The Economic Times*, January 30, 2021, https://economictimes.indiatimes.com/news/politics-and-nation/india-russia-japan-trilateral-focus-on-resource-rich-russian-far-east-russian-arctic-regions/articleshow/80596403.cms, accessed on 20 August 2023.

74 Rakesh Sood, "Why France is a reliable strategic partner for India," Observer Research Foundation, January 20, 2020. https://www.orfonline.org/research/why-france-is-a-reliable-strategic-partner-for-india-60480/, accessed on 12 January 2022.

75 Ministry of External Affairs, "Joint Statement: Vision and Principles for India-U.S. Comprehensive Global Strategic Partnership," Press Release, 25 February 2020, https://mea.gov.in/bilateral-documents.htm?dtl/32421/Joint_Statement_Vision_and_ Principles _ for_IndiaUS_Comprehensive_Global_Strategic_Partnership, accessed on 11 October 2021.

76 Inputs from a closed-door meeting at the National Maritime Foundation.

77 Ministry of External Affairs, *Annual Report 2020-21*, 12 and 20, https://www.mea.gov.in/Uploads/PublicationDocs/33569_MEA_annual_Report.pdf.

78 Tran Viet Thai "Strategic partnership: a framework of foreign relations in the age of globalization," Vietnam Law and Legal Forum, 01 October 2013, https://vietnamlawmagazine.vn/strategic-partnership-a-framework-of-foreign-relations-in-the-age-of-globalization-3437.html, accessed on 11 October 2021.

79 Institute of Defence Studies and Analyses, "Ask and Expert," https://idsa.in/askanexpert/What-is-the-function-of-strategic-partnerships, accessed on 11 October 2021.

80 Ankit Panda, "Why Does India Have So Many 'Strategic Partners' and No Allies?" *The Diplomat*, 23 November 2013. https://thediplomat.com/2013/11/why-does-india-have-so-many-strategic-partners-and-no-allies/, accessed on 20 August 2023.

81 Ian Hall, "Multialignment and Indian Foreign Policy under Narendra Modi," *The Round Table* 105, no. 3 (May 2016): 271-286, https://doi.org/10.1080/00358533.2016.1180760, accessed on 20 August 2023.

82 The White House, *Indo-Pacific Strategy of the United States* (2020), 12,

83 Upadhyay, "Maritime Security Cooperation in the Indian Ocean Region," 283.

84 FP: Foreign Policy.

85 BIMSTEC: Bay of Bengal Initiative for Multi-Sectoral Technical and Economic Cooperation; SAARC: South Asian Association for Regional Cooperation; E&SA: East and South Asia; E&SA: East and South Africa; IOR: Indian Ocean Region; WANA: West Africa and North Africa; PAI: Pakistan, Afghanistan, Iran.

86 Upadhyaya, "Maritime Security Cooperation in the Indian Ocean Region," iv-v, 297-98.

87 Upadhyaya, "Maritime Security Cooperation in the Indian Ocean Region," 298.

88 Upadhyaya, "Maritime Security Cooperation in the Indian Ocean Region," 225.

89 Upadhyaya, "Maritime Security Cooperation in the Indian Ocean Region," 283.

90 Swaminathan Anklesaria Aiyar, "Lessons for India from Af retreat: US is an undependable ally," *Times of India*, 29 August 2021.

91 Upadhyaya, "Maritime Security Cooperation in the Indian Ocean Region," 283.

92 "Maritime Crime," United Nations Office on Drugs and Crime, https://www.unodc.org/unodc/en/piracy/index.html, accessed on 06 January 2022.

93 United Nations Office on Drugs and Crime, *Global Maritime Crime Programme: Briefing*

Package, https://www.unodc.org/documents/Maritime_crime/UNODC-GMCP_Briefing_Package.pdf, accessed on 06 January 2022.

94 "GMCP #1: Global Maritime Crime Programme," United Nations Office on Drugs and Crime, https://youtu.be/Lvkf6R-SSoo, accessed on 06 January 2022.

95 United Nations Office on Drugs and Crime, *Global Maritime Crime Programme: Briefing Package,*

96 United Nations Office on Drugs and Crime, *Promoting the Rule of Law and Countering Drugs and Crime in South Asia: Regional Programme for South Asia 2018-21* (2018), 9, https://www.unodc.org/documents/southasia//Promoting_the_Rule_of_Law_ Final_Rev.pdf , accessed on 12 January 2022; United Nations Office on Drugs and Crime, "Regional Programme for South Asia (2018-June 2023)," https://www.unodc.org/southasia/en/topics/frontpage/2009/regional-programme-for-south-asia-2018-2021.html, accessed on 20 August 2023.

97 United Nations Office on Drugs and Crime South Asia, *ODYSSEY; Special Newsletter from UNODC South Asia* (October 2021), https://www.unodc.org/documents/southasia//Newsletter/2021/UNODC_South_Asia_Newsletter_Odyssey_October_2021.html, accessed on 06 January 2022.

98 "What is INTERPOL?" International Criminal Police Organization, https://www.interpol.int/en/Who-we-are/What-is-INTERPOL, accessed on 07 January 2022.

99 "Maritime Crimes," International Criminal Police Organization, https://www.interpol.int/en/Crimes/Maritime-crime/The-issues, accessed on 12 January 2022.

100 "Maritime Crimes," International Criminal Police Organization.

101 "INTERPOL," Central Bureau of Investigation, https://cbi.gov.in/National-Central-Bureau-Interpol-New-Delhi, accessed on 12 January 2022.

102 "INTERPOL," Central Bureau of Investigation.

103 "Discover the WCO," World Customs Organisation, http://www.wcoomd.org/en/about-us/what-is-the-wco/discover-the-wco.aspx, accessed on 12 January 2022.

104 "International Cooperation," Department of Revenue Intelligence, https://dor.gov.in/preventionofmoneylaundering/international-cooperation, accessed 12 January 2022.

105 Coordinated Border Management (CBM) refers to the coordinated approach by border control agencies, both domestic and international, in the context of seeking greater efficiencies in managing trade and travel flows, while maintaining a balance with compliance requirements.

106 "UNODC-WCO Container Control Programme," https://www.unodc.org/unodc/en/ccp/index.html, accessed on 12 January 2022.

107 Ministry of Finance, Office Memorandum A-11013/20/2017-Ad.IV, 11 July 2017, https://www.cbic.gov.in/resources//htdocs-cbec/deptt_offcr/administrative-wing/admn-wing-circ/dic.pdf, accessed on 07 January 2022.

108 "International Cooperation & Training," National Academy of Customs, Indirect Taxes, and Narcotics, https://nacin.gov.in/page/ict, accessed on 12 January 2022.

109 Government of UK, *National Strategy for Maritime Security*, August 2022, 28. https://assets.publishing.service.gov.uk/government/uploads/system/uploads/attachment_data/file/1100525/national-strategy-for-maritime-security-web-version.pdf, accessed on 20 August 2023.

110 "About Us," South Asia Co-operative Environment Programme, http://www.sacep.org/

about-us, accessed on 14 January 2021.

111 "South Asian Seas Programme - Action Plan," South Asia Co-operative Environment Programme, http://www.sacep.org/programmes/south-asian-seas/action-plan, accessed on 14 January 2021.

112 SMDP Anura Jayatilake, 'South Asian Seas Programme," Presentation at the South Asia Co-operative Environment Programme, https://wedocs.unep.org/bitstream/handle/20.500.11822/11088/south_asian_seas_programme-a._jayatilake_-sacep.pdf?sequence=1&isAllowed=y, accessed on 14 January 2021.

113 SMDP Anura Jayatilake, 'South Asian Seas Programme."

114 "SASP Milestone," South Asia Co-operative Environment Programme, http://www.sacep.org/programmes/south-asian-seas/sasp-milestones, accessed on 14 January 2021.

115 Cabinet Secretariat, "Cabinet approves MoU between India and South Asia Cooperative Environment Programme for Co-operation on the response to Oil and Chemical Pollution in the South Asian Seas Region," Press Information Bureau, 28 March 2018, https://pib.gov.in/PressReleasePage.aspx?PRID=1526894, accessed on 13 January 2021.

116 Khurana, "Thousand-Ship Navy."

117 "Maritime Security and Piracy," International Maritime Organisation, http://www.imo.org/en/OurWork/MSAS/Pages/PortStateControl.aspx, accessed on 26 January 2021.

118 International Maritime Organisation. "Maritime Security," https://www.imo.org/en/OurWork/Security/Pages/GuideMaritimeSecurityDefault.aspx, accessed on 20 August 2023.

119 Code of Conduct concerning the Repression of Piracy and Armed Robbery against Ships in the Western Indian Ocean and the Gulf of Aden (Djibouti Code of Conduct) and Code of Conduct concerning the Repression of Piracy, Armed Robbery against Ships, and Illicit Maritime Activity in West and Central Africa in the Gulf of Guinea region of West Africa (Yaoundé Code).

120 Ministry of Shipping, "India re-elected as Member of International Maritime Council for two years (2018-19)," Press Information Bureau, 02 December 2017, https://pib.gov.in/newsite/printrelease.aspx?relid=174057, accessed on 06 January 2022.

121 Author was personally engaged in the process with the DG Shipping; Sidhant Sibal, "UK deputes officer to India's information fusion centre," WION, 22 June 2022, https://www.wionews.com/india-news/uk-deputes-officer-to-indias-information-fusion-centre-393203, accessed on 06 January 2022.

122 "Port State Control," International Maritime Organisation, http://www.imo.org/en/OurWork/MSAS/Pages/PortStateControl.aspx, accessed on 26 January 2021.

123 Port State Control," International Maritime Organisation.

124 "Port State Control Division (CG-CVC-2)," United States Coast Guard, https://www.dco.uscg.mil/Our-Organization/Assistant-Commandant-for-Prevention-Policy-CG-5P/Inspections-Compliance-CG-5PC-/Commercial-Vessel-Compliance/Foreign-Offshore-Compliance-Division/Port-State-Control/Annual-Reports/, accessed on 26 January 2021.

125 Port State Control," International Maritime Organisation.

126 Directorate General of Shipping, *Annual Report on Port State Control (PSC) and Flag*

State Implementation (FSI) 2017, https://www.dgshipping.gov.in/WriteReadData/userfiles/file/Annual%20Report%202017.pdf [Site has moved]

127 Directorate General of Shipping, *Annual Report on Port State Control (PSC)*

128 Collated by the author.

129 Department of Fisheries, "International Cooperation," https://dof.gov.in/international-cooperation, accessed on 01 January 2022.

130 Food and Agriculture Organization, "Regional fisheries management organizations and deep-sea fisheries, https://www.fao.org/fishery/en/topic/166304/en, accessed on 01 January 2022;

131 R. Jeyabaskaran, "Fisheries Management – An Indian Perspective" PowerPoint presentation at Online Workshop on Fisheries Issue, November 07, 2021; R. Jeyabaskaran, "Fisheries Management as a Geostrategic Issue in the Indian Ocean," PowerPoint Presentation at an Online Workshop on Fisheries Issue, November 01, 2021.

132 Johnny Louys, "Sustainable Fisheries Development and IUU Fishing," IORA Capacity Building Workshop, Indian Council of World Affairs, January 29, 2021.

133 Louys, "Sustainable Fisheries Development and IUU Fishing"

134 Yugaraj Yadava, "Bay of Bengal Project Inter-Governmental Organisation." https://www.bobpigo.org/pages/view/bobp, accessed on 20 August 2023.

135 R. Jeyabaskaran, "Fisheries Management as a Geostrategic Issue in the Indian Ocean." These include the Southwest Indian Ocean Fisheries Commission (SWIOFC), Regional Commission for Fisheries (RECOFI), Asia-Pacific Fishery Commission. (APFIC), and the Southeast Fisheries Development Centre (SEAFDEC). India is a member of the APFIC.

136 Department of Animal Husbandry, Dairying and Fisheries, *Annual Report 2018-19*, 139-40, https://dahd.nic.in/sites/default/filess/Annual%20Report_0.pdf, accessed on 01 January 2022.

137 Yadava, "Bay of Bengal Project Inter-Governmental Organisation."

138 "Home," Indian Ocean Tuna Commission, https://www.iotc.org/, accessed on 01 January 2022.

139 "Vessels,' Indian Ocean Tuna Commission, https://www.iotc.org/vessels, accessed on 01 January 2022.

140 "EU Carding Decisions," IUU Watch, http://www.iuuwatch.eu/map-of-eu-carding-decisions/, accessed on 01 February 2020.

141 Yadava, "Bay of Bengal Project Inter-Governmental Organisation," accessed on 31 January 2021.

142 "Bay of Bengal Large Marine Ecosystem Project," Bay of Bengal Large Marine Ecosystem Project https://www.boblme.org/About_BOBLME_Brochure_2011.pdf, accessed on 31 January 2021.

143 "Bay of Bengal Large Marine Ecosystem Project."

144 Meenakumari Bharathiamma, *Report of the Expert Committee constituted for Comprehensive Review of the Deep Sea fishing Policy and Guidelines*, 102-104, https://www.researchgate.net/publication/322821544_Report_of_the_Expert_Committee_constituted_for_Comprehensive_Review_ of_the_Deep_Sea_fishing_Policy_and_Guidelines/citation/download, accessed on 29 December 2020.

145 Ministry of Agriculture And Farmers Welfare, *National Policy on Marine Fisheries, 2017*,

20, https://dahd.nic.in/news/notification-national-policy-marine-fisheries-2017, accessed on 01 January 2021.

146 Ministry of Agriculture and Farmers Welfare, *National Policy on Marine Fisheries, 2017*, 21.

147 "National Fisheries Policy, 2020, Sixth Draft for Consideration, 30 December 2020," National Fisheries Development Board, 36-37, http://nfdb.gov.in/PDF/Policy/english.pdf, accessed on 03 March 2021.

148 Jennifer Staats, "A Primer on Multi-track Diplomacy: How Does it Work?," United States Institute of Peace, 31 July 2019. https://www.usip.org/publications/2019/07/primer-multi-track-diplomacy-how-does-it-work, accessed on 13 January 2022.

149 "The Foundation," National Maritime Foundation, https://maritimeindia.org/the-foundation/#toggle-id-4, accessed on 02 January 2022.

150 The author was on study leave at the NMF from Aug 20-Aug22.

4

Operational Cooperation

The willingness to shoulder greater responsibility must continue.

—S Jaishankar[1]

Operational cooperation amongst maritime security agencies is one of the more tangible products of maritime security cooperative efforts. It is reflective of 'walking-the-talk' on maritime security cooperation, and reflects practical manifestations of higher-level engagements. Typically, operational cooperation extends across a range of operational functions. These include *inter alia* participation in maritime security operations, operational coordination, intelligence and information sharing, logistic support, etc. A study by Stable Seas, a Non-Governmental Organisation (NGO), highlighted that in comparison to the global average, countries in the IOR are relatively better placed in terms of maritime capacity and capabilities.[2] However, while some countries such as Australia and India already have relatively robust capabilities, others, such as Somalia and Yemen, are in the process of developing maritime security capabilities. Consequently, cooperative efforts can contribute to bridging the capacity-capability gap between regional countries. As such, the transnational nature of many of the maritime security challenges necessitates cooperative endeavours. Cooperative mechanisms established in the Gulf of Aden and in the Sulu-Celebes Seas to counter armed robbery/piracy are examples of such efforts. Cooperation in oil pollution response, HADR, NEO are other significant examples of cooperation amongst maritime security agencies. The Indian Navy and the Coast Guard, amongst the largest in the world and definitely the largest in the region, have a major part to play in bridging this gap. This chapter focuses on the operational aspects of maritime security.

REGIONAL OPERATIONAL COORDINATION

IONS

The Indian Ocean Naval Symposium (IONS) is a regional forum wherein the heads of designated maritime security agencies responsible for maritime security in the IOR meet to "promote measures and mechanisms for constructive engagement that bear upon issues of regional maritime security and cooperation in the maritime domain."[3] IONS comprises 24 member countries and eight observer countries, with rotational leadership amongst the four sub-regional grouping of countries viz. South Asia; West Asia; East Africa; and the South East Asia and Australian littoral. The forum, which is voluntary and consensus driven, focuses on multilateral solutions to maritime security issues in the IOR.[4] IONS has constituted three IONS Working Groups (IWG) on Humanitarian Assistance & Disaster Relief (HADR), maritime security, and information sharing and interoperability.[5] As of 2022, India was a chair/co-chair in all the three working groups.[6] In addition to the work being pursued under the three IWGs, hydrography, salvage, submarine-rescue, SAR, and marine meteorology have been identified as some of the other areas of possible cooperation.[7]

The broad activities under the forum include a biennial Conclave of Chiefs and preparatory workshops, IONS commemorative events, workshops under the IWGs, and an essay competition. Bangladesh conducted the first operational exercise on SAR in 2017, the IONS Multilateral Maritime SAR Exercise (IMMSAREX) and a second operational exercise on anti-piracy coordinated by Iran was planned, but did not materialise in view of the COVID-19 pandemic.[8] However, IMMSAREX was followed up with Indian Ocean Naval Symposium (IONS) Maritime Exercise 2022 (IMEX-22) which was hosted by India off the coast of Goa in 2022 and saw the participation of 16 of the 25 members.[9] IMEX-22, in particular, focused on building interoperability in HADR. In addition to the operational exercises, the other main accomplishment of IONS has been the adoption of the IONS Guidelines on HADR (2019) and the WPNS Code of Unalerted Encounters Sea (CUES).[10] During the COVID-19 pandemic, the Indian Navy also shared its own guidelines for ships, submarines and shore establishments, and other innovations, with IONS nations.[11] It is essential for maritime security agencies to keep their personnel safe from health risks to enable them to effectively discharge their maritime security roles at sea, a form of force-protection, and therefore, such efforts also contribute towards promoting regional maritime security.

The two important features of IONS are, one, it is an operationally focused naval construct, and two, it encompasses a wider participation than IORA which is the other IOR-focused forum. This fact points to a wider recognition of the forum amongst littoral states of the IOR; however, it still does not represent all the states of the IOR.[12] Overall, while some scholars have rued the slow pace of progress, others have expressed satisfaction at the reasonable progress by the forum.[13] Some of the problems that have been identified with IONS include: the large size and wide diversity of the grouping; the lack of direct political involvement in the institutional structure which itself is not permanent; decision-making by consensus; lack of resources and funds; and practical issues, such as those related to quick turnaround of personnel, wide variance in the level of engagements [*inter se* protocol], the relative higher restraints of service protocols, and the lack of secure channels for communication.[14] The problems faced with IONS are likely to be faced by any large operational construct and are emblematic of large constructs; reportedly similar challenges have been faced by the Western Pacific Naval Symposium (WPNS), a much older organisation.[15] As the problems and challenges have been identified, the need is to address them pragmatically and in a prioritised manner, through an inclusive and participative approach.

Towards strengthening IONS, a greater and more active role for India has been recommended, without being an overbearing partner.[16] *Inter alia* some areas of engagement have been identified as: funding for capacity building; training and secretarial support, hosting/supporting IONS-led exercises; and strategic communication in the branding of IONS. While indeed there is a vision, and scope, doing so will need to be balanced with a host of other engagements that India pursues with others bilaterally and multilaterally. Plurilateral engagements by the Indian Navy could also be effectively leveraged to foster IONS objectives, on the lines of the Coast Guard, which fosters the SACEP objectives, in its regional outreach to countries in South Asia. Further, India could in partnership with other larger navies of the construct prioritise and collectively support capacity building efforts, with India in the lead, if the need be.

India has played an important role in the development of both IORA and IONS, two of the main multilateral mechanisms for maritime cooperation in the Indian Ocean.[17] The role of IONS is widely considered complementary to that of IORA, as it provides an operational (executive) dimension to the IORA, which is essentially a regional organisation. However, despite IORA's pronouncements on collaborating with IONS (Perth Communiqué of 2014 and Padung Communiqué of 2015), an assessment in 2021 brought out that both the organisations are working Independent of each other.[18] *Prima facie* issues precluding greater alignment are, the wide remit of IORA's activities, a possible lack of leadership on the part of the IORA despite being better positioned to take the lead, insecurity within IONS regarding its loss of autonomy, and finally, dissimilar membership between both the organisations.[19] Practical measures, therefore, need to be taken to give effect to the intent for greater collaboration.

The convergence between the UN-mandated CGPCS and the military-led voluntary SHADE forum (along with the industry focused MIEVOM forum [Maritime Information Exchange Vessel Operators Meeting]) in the counter-piracy efforts off the Gulf of Aden is perhaps an example to look at for developing synergies between political-level groupings and military-groupings. The first step would be for IONS WGs to proactively take a more meaningful role in IORA in line with IORA's objectives; the rest will likely follow. IONS HADR Guidelines if also adopted by IORA, would reflect progress, albeit a modest one.

WPNS

The Western Pacific Naval Symposium (WPNS) includes navies whose countries border the western Pacific Ocean. The WPNS, inaugurated in 1988, is a forum for leaders of regional navies to meet to discuss cooperative initiatives. Under the WPNS, member countries meet biennially to discuss regional and global maritime issues. Currently, WPNS membership stands at 21 members and six observers, including India. One of the major successes of the WPNS has been in the development of the CUES which was later adopted by the IONS. The WPNS and IONS together provide the Indian Navy with a pan Indo-Pacific membership of 'executive-level' bodies. In addition to biennial meetings, the Indian Navy has also participated in WPNS multilateral exercises.[20]

HACGAM

The Heads of Asian Coast Guard Agencies Meeting (HACGAM), set up in 2004, includes coast guard agencies of Asia, and other stakeholders as associate members and observers.[21] Overall, it comprises 23 countries and two international organisations.[22] In 2022 the Indian Coast Guard hosted the 18th HACGAM at New Delhi, which witnessed the participation of 18 coast guard agencies and two international organisations.[23] HACGAM aims at the "construction and development of capabilities in coast guard organisations for the Asian region through working-level discussion on overall maritime safety, security and environment protection issues."[24] Following the objectives, the meetings focus largely on coast guard functions, such as SAR, marine environmental protection, suppression of unlawful acts, counter-piracy, capacity building and information exchange. HAGCM, in addition to promoting safe and secure maritime environment and cleaner seas, is also a means of developing trust and fostering cooperation.[25] The HACGAM forum comprises HLM and Working-level Meetings (WLMs). The DGCG, being the head of the Coast Guard, is the Indian representative to the meeting. HACGAM, *de facto*, is complementary to the IONS initiative, and a greater role of the Coast Guard would only burnish India's credentials as a leading player across the maritime safety and security spectrum. In 2022, India hosted the 18th HACGAM meeting in coordination with the HACGAM secretariat.[26]

CSC: Focused Operations

In 2021, almost a decade after the initiation of the trilateral engagement, the CSC, took certain tangible operational initiatives in 2021. In March 2021, an operational secretariat was set up in the Sri Lankan Naval Headquarters.[27] Reportedly, going beyond the white shipping agreements, the secretariat would facilitates sharing of maritime intelligence.[28] In July 2021, the Indian Navy coordinated a two-day virtual anti-narcotics and SAR tabletop exercise (Exercise SHIELD) which saw the participation of the lead maritime agencies of all the three countries viz. the Indian Navy, the Maldives National Defence Force (MNDF), and the Sri Lankan Navy.[29] The exercise *inter alia* had a primary emphasis on improving trilateral cooperation for maritime security. This included efforts to enhance collective awareness, share best practices and procedures for countering transnational maritime crimes, provide mutual assistance for SAR, and facilitate the exchange of intelligence and information. Subsequently, in November 2021, the three agencies undertook a 'focused operation' in the EEZs of the three countries with broadly similar aims as the tabletop exercise, reflecting the 'operationalisation' of the conclave.[30]

Smaller engagements, in the 'minilateral' and plurilateral formats, especially amongst maritime neighbours, have a special significance, and strategic importance. Considering the deep ties that India shares with some of its neighbours, such engagements also have immense potential, not only for meeting the specific objectives of the engagements, but also as building blocks for strengthening and widening cooperative endeavours, for bridging the gap between bilateral and larger sub-regional/regional engagements, and importantly, promoting safety and security of the proximate neighbourhood where the imperatives for cooperation are highest. Despite the slow start, there can be little doubt that the scope and complexity of such exercises can be progressively expanded in accordance with vision for engagement; and that such engagements between maritime neighbours can be an exemplar for maritime security cooperation elsewhere.

MARITIME ENGAGEMENTS

Maritime security forces engage with each other bilaterally and multilaterally by a number of ways. These include meetings, talks, dialogues, as well as operational engagements between ships, submarines, and aircraft, such as participation in exercises and events, including fleet reviews and defence expos, etc. In particular, 'high-level maritime strategic interactions' conducted by way of high-level visits, delegation visits, and dialogues, have been seen as ways to improve strategic communication, share perspectives, review engagements, shape policy, and also to facilitate persuasion and dissuasion.[31] Some of these are discussed in succeeding paragraphs.

Staff Talks/Executive Steering Meetings

Staff Talks, also termed navy-to-navy staff talks or service-level staff talks, are institutionalised bilateral meetings between naval staff on an annual/biennial basis aimed at consolidating and enhancing bilateral engagements. Typically, the agenda for the talks include conduct of exercises; sharing of best practices; finalising schedule for HLM, Key Leader Engagements (KLE) and other activities; reviewing and progressing activities in identified areas for cooperation, such as in operations, information exchange, Meteorological and Oceanographic (METOC), training, education, technical cooperation, medical, etc., and also identifying areas for furthering bilateral and regional/ multilateral cooperation, such as IONS-related activities.[32] These meetings, depending on the level of cooperation, are normally co-chaired from the Indian side by the Assistant Chief of the Naval Staff (Foreign Cooperation) or the Principal Director (Foreign Cooperation), officers of the rank of Rear Admiral and Commodore respectively.

The Indian Navy holds Staff Talks with about 20 navies.[33] This includes Australia, Bangladesh, France, Indonesia, Israel, Japan, Maldives, Malaysia, Myanmar, Oman, Russia, Singapore, South Africa, South Korea, Sri Lanka, Thailand, UAE, and Vietnam.[34] The staff talks are foundational institutional mechanisms to foster bilateral naval cooperation, and it is not a mere coincidence that high levels of naval cooperation have already been achieved with several of the countries with which the Indian Navy holds Staff Talks.

With major partners, such as the UK and the US, staff talks are referred to as Executive Steering Group (ESG) meetings.[35] The ESG is described as the primary mechanism for enhancing cooperation between two navies.[36] In a two-tier structure, talks are held at the level of a Defence Consultative Group (DCG) and Military Sub Group(s) (MSG). The ESG with US takes place at the level of the Deputy Chief of the Naval Staff (DCNS) from the Indian side and the Commander of the US Navy Seventh Fleet, both of whom are three-star officers of the rank of Vice Admiral. Considering India's comprehensive strategic partnerships with both the US and the UK, high-level participation in the ESG reflects the upper end of navy-to-navy staff engagement, with potentially strategic implications.

Leader Engagements

'Key Leader Engagements' (KLE) have been described by the US Joint Forces as engagements of military leaders with foreign audiences that have defined objectives, such as policy change, supporting joint force objectives, etc.[37] These engagements are used to shape and influence foreign leaders, and may also be targeted at religious/tribal leaders, leading academics, etc, and can also applied to a range of operational situations. These engagements can also give direction cooperative endeavours. More generically, KLE are focused engagements between military leaders with specific aims. KLE are also undertaken as part of other high-level engagements, including at the delegation level, as also on the sidelines of larger international events. In India the Coast Guard uses the term HLM to describe bilateral meetings at the apex level with foreign partners to discuss issues of mutual concerns, generally under the terms of an MOU.[38]

Leadership Engagements normally include visits overseas by the naval/ defence leadership and hosting of leaders from foreign navies in India; but could also include engagements elsewhere. The countries visited by naval/ defence leadership, and the timing of such visits can often have an underlying strategic message, and could be timed with important events, or as a build-up to important events. Increasingly, visiting leaders also hold discussions with non-naval military leaders, such as the CDS, bureaucrats, such as the Foreign Secretary, and leading think tanks. The personality of individual leaders, and their vision, as well as the personal rapport between leaders can significantly influence the nature and scope of present and future engagements. While in the past such engagements were largely limited to physical engagements, the increasing use of the virtual medium, driven by the COVID pandemic, has emerged as an alternative to physical engagements. As KLE are leadership-led engagements, outcomes from KLE reflect a 'top-down' approach to security cooperation, in contrast to staff talks, which are a 'bottom-up' approach. Both are, therefore, complementary mechanisms to progress similar objectives.

Dialogues

Since 2017, the Indian Navy hosts two main dialogues: the Indo-Pacific Regional Dialogue (IPRD) and the Goa Maritime Conclave (GMC). The IPRD and the GMC can be distinguished from each other based on the nature of discussions, the levels of participation, and the target audience. The IPRD is categorised as a dialogue at the 'strategic' level, while the GMC is largely a dialogue at the 'strategic-operational' level.[39] These dialogues also complement the MILAN engagement which could be categorised as an engagement in the 'operational-tactical' level.

Indo-Pacific Regional Dialogue. The IPRD is an annual, apex-level maritime focused international conference of the Indian Navy, with the NMF as the knowledge partner. The idea of an IPRD was first conceptualised in 2018 with the inaugural edition held in 2018. The IPRD has been held every year since, barring 2020, wherein the event had to be cancelled in the early stages of the COVID pandemic; in 2021, the event was conducted in the online format. The theme for the fourth edition of the IPRD in 2022 was "Operationalising the Indo-Pacific Oceans Initiative (IPOI) Programme."

Each edition of the IPRD aims to review the prevailing geopolitics within the Indo-Pacific and identify opportunities and challenges arising from geopolitical developments. Since inception, the event has grown with an expanding milieu for discussions. The speakers, representing a wide cross-section of maritime stakeholders, include a host of senior, eminent thinkers, academics, professionals, and military leaders from India and abroad.

Goa Maritime Conclave. The GMC is a biennial meeting of naval leaders (chiefs of navies/heads of maritime forces) conducted by Naval War College (NWC), Goa. The maiden conclave was held in 2017 and was inaugurated by the then Raksha Mantri, Shrimati Nirmala Sitharaman.[40] The conclave is positioned by the Indian Navy as a "multinational platform to harness the collective wisdom of practitioners of maritime security and the academia towards garnering outcome oriented maritime thought."[41] The GMC aims to bring together like-minded nations to evolve and formulate collective responses to emerging challenges in the maritime domain.[42] The GMC, unlike the IPRD, being a navy-centric dialogue at the strategic-operations level, focuses specifically on maritime security and maritime security cooperation. In addition to the naval leadership, senior officials from the Indian government also participate in the GMC. The GMC is preceded by working-level deliberations at the Goa Maritime Symposium (GMS).[43]

Operational Engagements

Maritime Border Engagements. While India shares its maritime borders with seven maritime neighbours, institutional mechanisms for engagement at the level of maritime security agencies have been institutionalised with Sri Lanka and Pakistan to address issues related to respective borders. With Sri Lanka, respective local naval and coast guard commanders hold annual meetings to foster mutual understanding and facilitate maritime security coordination.[44] The agenda for the meetings include issues related to patrolling, fishers, information sharing, prevention of crime, such as smuggling, etc.[45] In addition, a hotline has also been established between the coast guards for information exchange, particularly in respect of fishers who routinely transgress respective maritime boundaries.[46] At a sub-regional level, the bilateral arrangement between Indian and Sri Lanka has been further complemented with the establishment of CSC.

With Pakistan, the provisions of a 2005 MOU between Indian and Pakistan for the establishment of a communication link between the Coast Guard and the Pakistan Maritime Security Agency (PMSA), provide the contours of engagement between the two agencies.[47] The MOU, which came into effect in 2006, was extended in 2016 for a period of five years till 2021.[48] While the Director Generals of the two agencies met in 2016 and 2018, as per media reports, the meeting in 2019 was called off. In the earlier meetings, issues related to marine environment pollution response, SAR, and importantly, humane treatment and early release of fishers and their boats have been discussed.[49] In addition, a communication link has also been established under the MOU between the two agencies. The need for dedicated communication channels outside the normal diplomatic channel emerges from special circumstances, and specific challenges. Should a need arise, communication links could also be set up with other maritime neighbours with whom India shares maritime boundaries.

Exercises. Institutionalisation of bilateral exercises by the Indian Navy began in the early 1990s. While the number of such exercises grew in the first decade of the 21st century, the second decade saw an exponential surge, perhaps reflecting the growing international willingness to cooperate for maritime security, and possibly also because of the increasing heft of the Indian Navy in the IOR. In terms of numbers, between 2015 and 2020, the number of exercises grew four-fold from 15 to more than 30.[50]

Figure 4.1: Institutionalised Bilateral Exercises

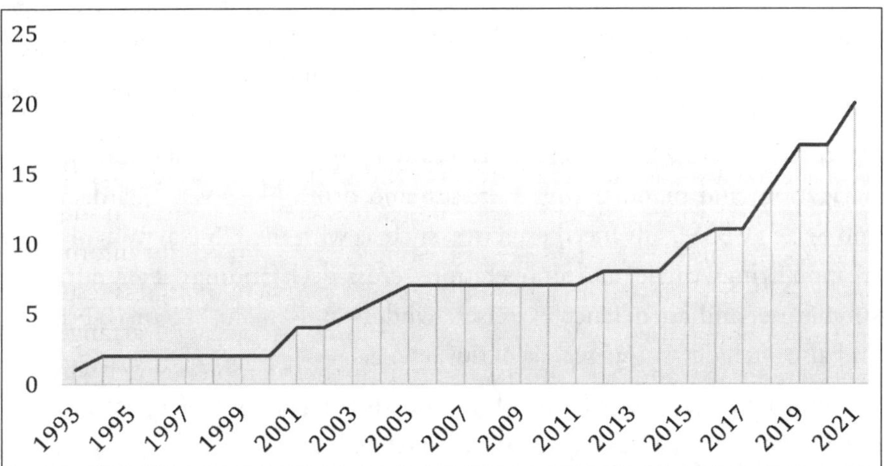

Increasingly, exercises are being undertaken not only within the IOR but also in distant waters. Exercises reflect the practical manifestations of maritime security cooperation, and are one of the important deliverables. The broad aims of exercises include developing interoperability at one end, and fostering mutual trust, understanding, respect, and friendship at the other.[51] Exercises also contribute to projection of capabilities, and facilitate benchmarking, honing of skills, and the adoption of best practices.[52] Further, exercises reflect shared interests and a mutual commitment to a rules-based order, and give effect to foreign policy.[53] Importantly, the aims and objectives of exercises cannot be achieved through 'one-off' engagements, but need to be developed through a sustained long-term approach. A dynamic environment only further adds to the imperatives for regular exercises.

Exercises by the Indian Navy are conducted in three broad formats: Passage Exercises (PASSEX), occasional exercises, and institutional exercises. PASSEX are opportune exercises; occasional exercises are those which are either held occasionally, or periodic exercises in which the Indian Navy's participation is occasional; and, 'institutionalised' exercises are those that are conducted regularly with a navy, or a group of navies. Lately, it appears that the term Maritime Partnership Exercise (MPX) has gained traction over PASSEX. MPX has been described as exercises "with friendly foreign naval units on opportune occasions to enhance interoperability and imbibe best practices.[54] In the first 10 months of 2022, the Indian Navy undertook 47 MPX with 28 countries from across the globe.[55] Another way of categorisation of naval exercises, depending on the number of agencies taking part, is as a bilateral exercise, or as a multilateral exercise.[56] The scope of exercises also varies significantly, from 'basic' exercises to 'advanced' exercises, terms which can be subjectively interpreted. While basic exercises typically involve fundamental seamanship, navigation, and manoeuvring exercises, and drills, like Visit, Board, Search and Seize (VBSS), advanced exercises, such as with the US Navy, involve live weapon firings, carrier and air operations, cross-deck landings of aircraft, anti-submarine, and air defence exercises, Underway Replenishment (UNREP), and also include 'war-at-sea' scenarios, etc.

In June 2021, the IAF joined the Indian Navy in exercising with the US Navy Carrier Strike Group (CSG).[57] The IAF assets that took part in the exercise included fighters, Airborne Warning and Control System (AWACS), Airborne Early Warning and Control (AEW&C), and air-to-air refuelling aircraft. This marks a new paradigm in air operations at sea, and with the proposed setting up of the Maritime Theatre Command (MTC) it is likely that jointness will only grow further. In addition to naval exercises, the Indian Navy also takes part in tri-service exercises with foreign countries, which also provide an avenue for furthering the objectives of maritime security cooperation. As evinced by Op CACTUS, a tri-service intervention in Maldives in 1988 in response to an attempted coup, future scenarios may also necessity rapid deployment of integrated capabilities to handle 'out-of-area contingencies.' A list of Indian naval and tri-service exercises, country-wise and year-wise, as collated from multiple resources is placed at **Annexure C**.

Exercise MALABAR is an exemplar of progressive enhancement of the scope and scale of exercises over three decades (starting 1992) with 27 editions till 2023. The exercise, which began as a bilateral exercise, was later, driven by geopolitical developments, upgraded to a multilateral exercise with the inclusion of Japan and Australia.[58] The exercise is held not only in the Indian Ocean, but also the Pacific Ocean, thereby encompassing the wider Indo-Pacific. The progression of the exercise can be gauged from the participation of aircraft carriers in the exercise: in 2005, two aircraft carriers from India and US took part, followed by three CSG in 2007 (one from India and two from US), and three aircraft carriers in 2017 (one each from India, Japan, and US). In 2019, Japan conducted the exercise for the first time, and in 2023, the exercise was hosted by the first time by Australia.[59] In a similar vein, bilaterally, the scale and scope of the Singapore-India Maritime Bilateral Exercise (SIMBEX) exercise—the Indian Navy's 'longest uninterrupted bilateral exercise' which began in 1994—has also witnessed an expansion engendering greater interoperability.[60] Owing to the pandemic, SIMBEX 2021 was planned without any physical interaction as an 'at-sea only' exercise.[61]

While navies may not routinely operate with each other, exercises provide an opportunity for navies to train together to operate together, should the need arise. In a democratic country where bureaucratic processes are seen as problematic and protracted, such exercises also mean that the administrative machinery is collectively geared to respond to crises when the timelines for processes need to be compressed. Admiral Karambir Singh, in a talk at the USI, emphasised the need to expand the conceptual scope of 'interoperability'—the ability to operate in conjunction with each other—to 'inter-changeability,' wherein one partner navy can fill-in for another.[62] Naval deployments in the GoA for anti-piracy missions is an example when a ship from one navy can be interchangeably used with that of another navy in specific situations, for example when force-flows are affected.

Sceptics may, however, argue on the benefits from increasing the number of exercises, which while pursuing the Indian Navy's diplomatic role, may need to be traded-off with other naval roles and tasks. However, as India seeks a greater role for itself in the maritime space, in line with its foreign policy, it must be prepared to work with multiple partners in different parts of the Indo-Pacific, across a range of possible threats. Such exercises therefore need to be expanded to other navies/equivalents through a planned and customised approach aimed at maximising interaction and leveraging opportunities, and available resources, and, as stated by the CNS, moving beyond building interoperability.

Overall, while the progress is laudable, and spin-offs many, there is no substitute for actual operational experience. National policy so far has been averse to participation in operations outside the UN framework precluding vital operational experience of taking part in and leading multinational naval task forces. Consequently, when opportunities arise, maritime security agencies must lean towards leveraging opportunities for operations, rather than exercises; however, till then, exercises remain the best substitute.

In addition to the Indian Navy, the Coast Guard also exercises with foreign partners per its remit. Since 1991, the Coast Guard has been holding a biennial exercise with the Maldives National Defence Force Coast Guard (MNDF-CG), Exercise DOSTI.[63] In 2012, Sri Lanka also joined the exercise, and the exercise in its present avatar is a trilateral exercise. The exercise aims to strengthen cooperation between respective agencies for SAR, Casualty Evacuation (CASEVAC), and combating piracy/armed robbery, marine pollution response.[64] Such exercises also contribute towards building interoperability for other maritime security operations as well, such as counter drug trafficking operations, etc. In 2021, two decades after the institutionalisation of the DOSTI exercise, the exercise has been complemented with a trilateral 'focused *operation*' under the CSC.[65] The Coast Guard has also held bilateral exercises with several other countries such as Bangladesh, Japan (SAHYOG-KAIJIN), Korea (SAHYOG–HYEOBLYEOG), Vietnam (SAHYOG-HOP TAC), and also conducts regional SAR Communication Exercise (SARCOMEX).[66] It is entirely conceivable that immediate maritime neighbours could be integrated as part of a regional framework for maritime security, through a regional exercise on the lines of India's national-level maritime security exercise, Exercise SEA VIGIL, which encompasses not only maritime security agencies, but also shore-based agencies, and other stakeholders.

IFR. An International Fleet Review (IFR) is essentially an international parade of naval ships, aircraft and submarines organised to promote goodwill, strengthen cooperation, and also to showcase organisational capabilities.[67] It is also a platform for professional exchanges and interaction on contemporary issues, such as maritime security; demonstration of capabilities, especially indigenous; and also presents an opportunity for exercises.[68] The Indian Navy has conducted two IFRs 15 years apart, at Mumbai in 2001 and at Visakhapatnam in 2016. The 2001 edition witnessed the participation of 30 navies with close to 90 ships, and the 2016 edition, witnessed participation by 50 navies with nearly 100 warships.[69] Indian naval units also participate in IFRs and defence/naval expositions organised overseas.

MILAN. MILAN (meeting), originally a forum for operational interaction between regional navies, conducted by the Indian Navy, has transformed itself to a multinational naval exercise.[70] The first MILAN, held in 1995 at Port Blair, witnessed the participation of four regional navies from Indonesia, Singapore, Sri Lanka, and Thailand. Over the years, the participation has grown significantly to include the wider IOR and extra-regional navies; beginning with four countries in 1995, 16 countries took part in 2018, and over 40 countries in 2022.[71] Likewise, the scale, complexity, and duration of the exercise have also been significantly enhanced. The 2022 edition, with the theme 'Camaraderie–Cohesion–Collaboration,' for example, also saw senior leadership from the four QUAD countries participating in the event, thereby transforming the event into a tool for strategic messaging as well.[72] In the years in which the IFR have been conducted, MILAN has not been held, considering the commonality of certain objectives between IFR and MILAN.[73]

A number of social and cultural activities are also being held with the aim of developing bonhomie, in addition to professional exchanges in the 'harbour phase' of the exercise, such as seminars, tabletop exercise, etc, and exercises at sea during the 'sea phase.' The themes of the seminar are carefully curated to reflect contemporary issues relevant to participating navies. In the 2018 edition, the theme was 'In pursuit of Maritime Good Order—Need for Comprehensive Information-Sharing Apparatus,' and in 2022 the theme was 'Harnessing Collective Maritime Competence through Collaboration.'[74] In 2018, twenty ships participated in the 'sea phase,' making it the largest multilateral exercise to be conducted in the Andaman Sea.[75] The 'sea phase' aims to enhance interoperability and exchanging best practices, such as for SAR, cross-deck flying, boarding operations, Medical Evacuation (MEDEVAC), etc.[76] In the 2022 edition, in addition to surface exercises, exercises in the sub-surface and air domains, and weapon firings were also included, indicating the growing confidence of navies to operate together at sea in all dimensions.

MILAN, unlike other exercises, works at two levels. In addition to building naval interoperability, it also provides an opportunity for leadership engagements and 'people-to-people' contact, essential prerequisites for building trust and confidence. The exercise also gives the Indian Navy real-time experience in the planning and conduct of large-scale multinational exercises, which is otherwise constrained by the fact that the Indian Navy is not a member of any naval alliance, such as NATO or EU Naval Force (EUNAVFOR). Considering the rapid growth of the exercise, it has been recommended that MILAN can be advanced as a regional forum for the promotion of maritime multilateralism at the operational level, and as a forum to exercise IONS Standard Operating Procedure (SOPs), such as on HADR.[77]

Considering resource constraints faced by security agencies globally, to support regional/multinational initiatives, leveraging and harmonising existing initiatives, led by individual navies, is perhaps a pragmatic way to move ahead for building multilateral/regional partnerships. While MILAN can indeed offer such a platform, subject to the acceptability of non-IONS navies taking part, India must also be open to other IONS navies to use similar platforms for progressing IONS-led initiatives.

While MILAN, since inception, was held in Port Blair, in 2023 the venue was shifted to Vishakhapatnam. According to a Ministry of Defence (MoD) press release, infrastructure requirements of a large naval gathering, led to shifting the event.[78] Taking into account the strategic importance of ANC, the expanded scope of the exercise beyond the Andaman Sea, and the learning value to the host Command, it may only be sensible to conduct the event on a rotational basis amongst operational naval commands and Headquarters, Andaman and Nicobar Command (HQANC).

OPERATIONAL DEPLOYMENTS: MISSION-BASED DEPLOYMENT

In 2017, the Indian Navy adopted 'Mission-based Deployment' philosophy with the aim of ensuring "a high degree of presence, visibility, and situational awareness in important maritime regions across the globe."[79] In 2020, the Raksha Mantri stated that the deployment of Indian warships is inspired by the vision of SAGAR.[80] The mission-deployed concept reflects the practical manifestation of the Prime Ministerial vision of SAGAR and the Indian Navy's own strategy for shaping the maritime environment. Accordingly, Indian naval ships are deployed across the IOR:

(1) Strait of Malacca (MALDEP),
(2) North Bay of Bengal (NORDEP),
(3) Andaman and Nicobar group of Islands (ANDEP),

(4) Persian Gulf (GULFDEP),
(5) Gulf of Aden (POGDEP),
(6) Off Maldives and Sri Lanka (CENTDEP), and
(7) South Indian Ocean off Mauritius, Seychelles, and Madagascar (IODEP).

These deployments also further other objectives, such as those of being a 'first responder' and 'preferred security provider,' and facilitate other areas of operational cooperation, such as in MDA, HA/DR, NEO, as well as capacity building/capability enhancement.[81] In 2021, a similar approach was adopted by the EU through the Coordinated Maritime Presences (CMP) approach which encompasses deployment of assets of EU Members States in identified maritime areas of interest.[82] The CMP which commenced in the Gulf of Guinea in 2021 was subsequently, in 2022, extended, and also expanded to include the North-Western Indian Ocean.[83]

As per a report in 2018, the philosophy entailed positioning of warships year-round on a 24/7 basis in the seven areas.[84] However, as per the Year End Review of the MoD for 2021, in 2021, seven deployments were undertaken as part of the philosophy in Malacca Straits [MALDEP], Dondra-Malacca[85] ISL [CENTDEP], Gulf of Aden [POGDEP], and beyond, in the Java Sea, and South China Sea.[86] The 2022 report, however, did not spell out the exact number of deployments.[87] It therefore appears that the philosophy has undergone a shift over the years, and now covers areas beyond the IOR, but perhaps with reduced frequency. Ship deployments are also complemented with deployment of LRMP aircraft. *De facto*, POGDEP, to counter piracy in the Horn of Africa, which began in 2008, and was continuing till 2022, had been the single longest unbroken deployment of Indian warships anywhere in the world.[88] Eleven years later, in 2019, Operation SANKALP was launched in 2019 in the Persian Gulf in the backdrop of deteriorating security situation.[89] In other words, two of the seven (about 30 per cent) deployments involve persistent presence by Indian warships in areas of interest to ensure safety and security of not only Indian shipping and Indian seafarers, but also vital ISLs.

Separately, it has also been assessed that the change in deployment pattern of IN ships coincided with a change in the deployment of People's Liberation Army (Navy) [PLA(N)] ships in the IOR.[90] While Abhijit Singh (September 2021) had argued that to counter the Chinese, such a posture must extend beyond the IOR, and into the Pacific, the MoD's official statement in December 2021 shows that the Indian Navy is just doing that – a creeping extension of the deployment areas into the wider Indo-Pacific.[91]

The IOR is not a homogenous entity, and both challenges and national interests are dynamic and constantly evolve. Maintaining ships with long sea-legs in distant areas on a 24/7 basis surely presents steep logistical challenges; this is further compounded by limited number of ships, competing requirements (including domestic and intra-service), budgetary considerations and other factors. However, such deployments provide an opportunity to develop familiarity and experience in operating in distant waters. Overall, such deployments need to be inherently flexible, and customised, calibrated, adjusted, and prioritised, not only as per the prevailing environment, but also in line the long-term vision. Regular re-assessments are therefore necessary bring in dynamism into the philosophy.

In addition to the Indian Navy, the Coast Guard, despite its primary domestic mandate, also undertakes deployments overseas in pursuance of its international cooperation agenda. This included 12 ships visiting 27 countries in 2018-19, six ships visiting 15 countries in 2019, and two ships visiting six countries in 2020.[92] In 2021, overseas deployment was undertaken only to Maldives for operational and exercise requirements.[93] However, in 2022 there were no overseas deployments.[94] The second half of the 2010-20 decade saw an upsurge in overseas deployment of the Coast Guard, and reflects another significant dimension of India's maritime security cooperation. Ideally, harmonisation of foreign cooperation effort, between maritime security agencies, would not only enable optimal utilisation of limited resources for diplomatic outreach with due consideration to domestic imperatives, but also prevent possible duplication.

MARITIME SECURITY AND SAFETY OPERATIONS

The US Department of Defence (DoD) has defined 'maritime security operations' as operations to "protect maritime sovereignty and resources and to counter maritime-related terrorism, weapons proliferation, transnational crime, piracy, environmental destruction, and illegal seaborne migration."[95] The definition is broad, and includes the multiple dimensions of maritime security, including sovereignty, that a state exercises over its territorial seas in accordance with UNCLOS, and activities to counter threats from terrorists and criminals, and to the environment. It is unclear from the definition, if 'protection of sovereignty' also includes armed conflict. On the other hand, safety operations at sea, such as HADR, SAR, focus on another dimension of maritime security viz. human security, and may also need to be undertaken by maritime security agencies in difficult situations, including during a conflict. As in the case of irregular human migration involving substandard vessels, issues of safety and human security can often conflate with maritime security. Some of the major international safety and security operations that the Indian Navy has taken part in is covered in subsequent paragraphs.

Naval Peacekeeping

Since independence, India has been committed to assisting the UN in the maintenance of international peace and security. Since the first deployment of Indian peacekeepers in 1950, India has been one of the largest contributors to UN Peacekeeping missions. As of August 2021, India had contributed over 2,50,000 troops in 49 missions and cumulatively was the single largest contributor to UN peacekeeping operations.[96] 174 Indian soldiers have also lost their lives in peacekeeping missions.[97] In addition to all three defence forces of the country, the CAPFs also contribute to UN peacekeeping efforts, including a Female Formed Police Unit (FFPU) in Liberia. India also provides training assistance to peacekeepers from round the globe. Under India's presidency of the UN Security Council in August 2021, peacekeeping was selected as one of the focus areas.[98] In a statement at the UN Security Council, the EAM highlighted that "peacekeeping continues to play a crucial role in India's vision of ensuring international peace and security."[99] At the meeting, he also highlighted the importance of technology for peacekeeping operations and announced the signing of an MOU between the GoI and the UN C4ISR Academy for Peace Operations (UNCAP) in this regard.[100]

The Indian Navy has taken part in two peacekeeping missions: the Indian Peace Keeping Force (IPKF) Operations (Sri Lanka, 1987-90) and Operation RESTORE HOPE (Somalia, 1993-94). In Sri Lanka, the Indian Navy was deployed primarily with the aim of inducting army units into Sri Lanka, and to sanitise offshore areas off Sri Lanka. Indian Navy's newly raised Special Force, the Indian Marine Special Force (IMSF)—later renamed as Marine

Commandos (MARCOs)—was also deployed to destroy militant assets in Sri Lanka. In Somalia, the primary aim of deploying Indian Navy units was to support UN humanitarian relief efforts. The experience of the UN-mandated mission in Somalia was a watershed and validated confidence of the Indian Navy to deploy units in far reaches of the IOR. Apart from being a demonstration of capability and a confidence builder, the operation heralded the start of an era when the Indian Navy could play a purposeful and productive part in international efforts in support of humanitarian/maritime security operations in the IOR; the Tsunami relief operations almost a decade later only reaffirmed this belief.

The reasons for the Indian Navy's absence from UN naval peacekeeping operations thereafter are unclear, barring one officer in the United Nations Assistance Mission in Somalia (UNSOM) since 2013.[101] However, in 2021, the Indian Navy, after a long hiatus, expressed its readiness to participate in the Maritime Task Force (MTF) as part of the UN Interim Force in Lebanon (UNIFIL), and it also appears that the Indian Navy was considering attaching a Military Advisor to the Permanent Mission of India (PMI) to the UN, New York.[102] Considering the wider role that India seeks to play in maritime security and in peacekeeping, under the UN umbrella, the Indian Navy could make a larger contribution to naval peacekeeping operations, and augment its presence in UN bodies engaged in maritime security, and relevant military bodies. As India is unlikely to be part of an alliance outside the UN framework in the foreseeable future, constabulary operations under the UN flag offers the Indian Navy perhaps the only opportunity to take part in integrated international maritime security operations within a multinational force structure. However, making a commitment would need to consider its overall force levels and other competing objectives.

Anti-Piracy

In addition to its engagement in ReCAAP, consequent to the rise of piracy off the Horn of Africa, India has been actively engaged in related anti-piracy cooperative mechanisms, such as the CGPCS and the SHADE. Pursuant to UN Security Council Resolution 1851, the CGPCS was created in January 2009.[103] The CGPCS as a voluntary, *ad hoc*, international forum was unique in that it brought together stakeholders, including industry bodies, non-government organisations, and academia, in the fight against piracy on one platform.[104] Its memberships included about 60 countries and 20 international organisations.[105] India has been an active member of the CGPCS, including in leadership roles, both at the plenary and in working group levels.[106] The highlight of the working of the CGPCS has been inclusivity and adaptability.

From an Indian perspective, the CGPCS played a crucial role in the 2015 revision of the piracy High Risk Area (HRA), which had been moved to the west coast of India, including Indian territorial seas, by the shipping industry in 2011. Consequent to the extension of the piracy HRA to the west coast of India, after extensive internal discussions amongst concerned ministries and agencies, a case for revision of the piracy HRA was taken up by India with the CGPCS.[107] The CGPCS, under EU presidency, worked with all stakeholders, primarily the shipping industry, to resolve the issue, and the HRA was revised in 2015, four years after it was extended.[108] The case for revision of the piracy HRA, which *de facto* was helmed by India, is a sterling example of how India's participation in international forums, can shape the discourse on maritime security issues. Notably, after the initial opposition from shipping industry bodies to revise the industry-promulgated HRA, the HRA continued to be periodically revised in line with the prevailing piracy situation till it was finally removed with effect from 01 January 23.[109] This validates India's position of revision of the piracy HRA based on empirical evidence. The success of the CGPCS (and SHADE) is representative of not only importance of *ad hoc* mechanisms in addressing specific localised challenges, but also of the need for a multi-pronged approach. Challenges also present themselves as opportunities, which aspiration powers, like India, need to leverage through some heavy lifting.

India is also part of the Shared Awareness and Deconfliction (SHADE) forum, a voluntary *ad hoc* forum for coordinating naval effort between task forces and independent naval deployers in the Gulf of Aden. The forum, like the CGPCS, is also open to all stakeholders.[110] Considering the wide variety of discussions at the SHADE forum, the proactive sharing of information and intelligence assessments, and its important inputs to the CGPCS in the case of the revision of the piracy HRA, it has been assessed that the Indian Navy has gained significantly from this engagement.[111] The success of the SHADE forum led to its replication in the Mediterranean in 2017 and in the Gulf of

Guinea in 2021, and has also previously been espoused to be used in South East Asia.[112] Similar forums could form a template for operational coordination in the future, and the utility of the forum to the Indian Navy once again demonstrates the need for active participation in international forums for both individual and collective benefit. Based on the experience gained, the Indian Navy could consider leading such forums, rather than leave it to extra regional task forces.

Subsequently in 2020, India also joined the Djibouti Code of Conduct/ Jeddah Amendment as an observer (DCOC/JA).[113] The DCoC/JA is an 18-member grouping of countries adjoining the Red Sea, Gulf of Aden, the east coast of Africa and island states in the western IOR. In West Africa, India is a full member of the G7++ Group of Friends of the Gulf of Guinea (FoGG), which was created in 2013 to support the maritime security architecture in West Africa, also known as the Yaoundé architecture.[114] Further, in August 2022 and September 2022, INS *Tarkash* undertook joint patrols in the Gulf of Guinea with the Nigerian Navy further expanding the Indian Navy's engagement in global anti-piracy effort to West Africa, at significantly extended ranges from India.[115] Put together, India has actively engaged in anti-piracy cooperation across the IOR, and beyond.

During the pandemic, India joined the US-led CMF based in Bahrain, as an Associate Partner.[116] The CMF, described as a multi-national naval partnership of 38 member States to promote security, stability and prosperity in 'international waters,' comprises three task forces focused on maritime security threats.[117] While the CMF is a flexible organisation without any fixed mandate, and contributions are voluntary, India's association with the CMF as an Associate Partner is reflective of India's readiness to engage with other maritime security partnerships, even outside the UN framework, to promote maritime security in the IOR.

Counter Drug-Trafficking

The UNODC, in its 2021 annual report stated that "fostering international cooperation remains a key objective for fighting the enduring problem of drug trafficking.[118] Regionally, the need to enhance international cooperation to counter drug trafficking has been highlighted at both bilateral/trilateral forums, and at BIMSTEC.[119] The *Smuggling in India Report 2020-21*, published annually by the DRI, has highlighted that there has been a significant increase in the seizure of heroin in the Arabian Sea in 2020-21 with major seizures in India from containerised cargo originating from Afghanistan.[120] In recent years, the increasing use of the Southern Route has led to increased operational coordination with Sri Lankan authorities resulting in major drug seizures.[121] In addition to operational coordination, as part of the international cooperation charter, the NCB has 27 bilateral agreements and 16 MOUs with other countries/organisations. Director General-level talks are also held with several countries, including Myanmar, Afghanistan, Sri Lanka, and Bangladesh.[122] Further, the NCB coordinates with various regional organisations for information and intelligence sharing to combat transnational drug trafficking.[123] Specifically, India is also a member of the Southern Route Partnership (SRP) framework under the Indian Ocean Forum on Maritime Crime (IOFMC).[124] Likewise, other Drug Law Enforcement Agencies (DLEA) in India, such as the Coast Guard, have established mechanisms for international coordination with foreign partners, which need to be widened and further strengthened.[125] In addition to agency-specific agreements, the IFC-IOR is particularly well suited for information sharing and trend analysis.[126] Mission-deployed Indian Navy can also contribute to international efforts at suppression of illicit trafficking in the high seas particularly along the Southern Route, and the Indian Navy has also been involved in some major seizures.[127] In 2022, the NCB had launched Operation SAMUDRAGUPTA to disrupt drug flows.[128] The operation also involved sharing of real time actionable intelligence with Sri Lanka and Maldives resulting in drug seizures by respective agencies.[129]

Maritime Boundaries and Maritime Zone Patrol

EEZ Patrol and Surveillance. Coastal states have sovereign rights over the living and non-living resources in their EEZ. Indian maritime security agencies, the Indian Navy and the Coast Guard, having supported Indian Ocean island nations—Maldives, Seychelles and Mauritius—in the surveillance and patrol of their respective EEZ.[130] These patrols, undertaken biannually since 2009, with 'sea-riders' from the host nations, contribute to mitigating capacity gaps, safety and security in respective maritime zones, and in building interoperability.[131] In 2020, the Indian Navy deployed a P-81 LRMP aircraft to the Reunion Islands for joint patrol with French Navy personnel thereby further expanding its engagement.[132] Further, in 2023, an Indian Naval ship, with three officers from the Mozambique Navy, undertook joint surveillance in Mozambiquan EEZ for the first time.[133] In addition to naval assets, a Coast Guard Advanced Light Helicopter (ALH) along with a Coast Guard contingent had also been stationed in Maldives.[134] These patrols, in addition to the operational effects, also reinforce the historic ties and the special relationship India shares with island nations.

CORPAT. India shares its maritime boundaries with seven countries. The Indian Navy undertakes Coordinated Patrol (CORPAT) with four of the seven neighbouring navies.[135] CORPATs not only entail coordinated patrols along the IMBL, but also port visits and exercises at sea with shore-based aircraft.[136] CORPATs are reflective of the shared concern amongst neighbouring countries in maintaining security of contiguous seas,[137] and contribute to building operational synergy, and standardising procedures to prevent and suppress transnational maritime crimes.[138] Details of CORPATs undertaken by the Indian Navy are tabulated below:

Table 4.1: Coordinated Patrol

Sl. No.	Navy	Year	Frequency
1.	Indonesia Navy	2002	Biannually
2.	Thailand Navy	2005	Biannually
3.	Myanmar Navy[139]	2013	Annual
4.	Bangladesh Navy	2018	Annual

If mission-based deployments in the wider IOR reflect the SAGAR vision, strengthening bilateral relations with countries with whom India shares maritime boundaries, by extension, also reflects the 'Neighbourhood First' policy. Strengthening the CORPAT mechanisms could possibly include, more frequent CORPATs, trilateral CORPATS for patrol of the areas adjoining three tri-junction points which India shares with Indonesia and Thailand, Maldives and Sri Lanka, and Myanmar and Thailand, integration with domestic coastal security exercises, and, as should be the case in every operational endeavour, progressive expansion of the scope of complexity of exercises. Deploying frontline ships and aircraft, in addition to patrol vessels, can also be a way to signal the importance India attaches to its maritime neighbours.

Benign Missions

HADR. The 2004 Tsunami that originated in the Indian Ocean majorly affected 11 littoral countries in South Asia and South East Asia. In addition to its domestic response, the Indian Navy launched HADR operations to assist Indonesia (Operation GAMBHIR), Maldives (Operation CASTOR), and Sri Lanka (Operation RAINBOW), in concert with other navies. It was perhaps the first time that the Indian Navy was simultaneously operating on a major scale both domestically in coastal states affected by the Tsunami viz. Andhra Pradesh, Kerala, Tamil Nadu, and Pondicherry, and overseas, stretching available resources to the maximum. Subsequently, the Indian Navy has also assisted Bangladesh (Cyclone Sidr, 2007; Cyclone Mora, 2017), Cambodia (flood relief, 2020), Madagascar (Cyclone Diane, 2020), Mauritius (Cyclone Berguitta, 2018; Cyclone Idai, 2019) and Myanmar (Cyclone Nargis, 2008). Increasing frequency and ferocity of extreme weather events driven by climate change will only exacerbate the present challenges, and despite improved preparedness, as Cyclones Ockhi (2017) and Tauktae (2021) have demonstrated, there will remain unforeseen challenges to risk mitigation and response.[140] Therefore, building national capabilities in maritime disaster management, and forging partnerships will facilitate the expeditious provisioning of succour nationally, and regionally.

Another facet of HADR relates to humanitarian assistance during pandemics. During the COVID-19 pandemic, between May 2020 and December 2021, the Indian Navy deployed warships to 15 countries as part of Mission SAGAR to assist the extended maritime neighbourhood.[141] These deployments spanning over 215 days at sea provided a cumulative assistance of more than 3,000 MT of food aid, over 300 MT Liquid Medical Oxygen (LMO), 900 Oxygen Concentrators, and 20 containers.[142] Mission SAGAR continued into 2022, albeit with an expanded mandate of transhipment of other material to FFCs on their request.[143] Towards developing regional cooperation in HADR, in August 2022, the leaders of the QUAD announced the establishment of the 'Quad Partnership on Humanitarian Assistance and Disaster Relief (HADR) in the Indo-Pacific' aimed at strengthening regional collaborative for effective response to disasters.[144] This, almost two decades after the 2004 Tsunami, is another approach by the erstwhile 'core group' to collectively approach regional issues.

NEO. Indian naval ships have been engaged in Non-Combatant Evacuation Operations (NEO) for evacuation of distressed Indian and foreign citizens. Some of the notable NEO operations have included evacuations from Lebanon (2006), Libya (2011), and Yemen (2015).[145] In 2023, three Indian Navy ships were deployed as part of Operation KAVERI undertook five 'sorties' to evacuate Indian nationals from Sudan.[146] Indian naval ships were also standing-by for evacuations from Yemen (1986) and Kuwait (2004). More recently, between May 2020 and July 2020 in the wake of the COVID-19 pandemic, the Indian Navy launched Operation SAMUDRA SETU to repatriate Indians from Iran, Maldives, and Sri Lanka.[147] In the operation, the Indian Navy evacuated 3,992 Indian nationals. In 2023, the Indian Navy ships deployed off the African coast also evacuated stranded Indian citizens in Sudan as part of Operation KAVERI.[148] In a globalised world with Indian diaspora spread across the world, and tensions simmering in various hot spots, the need for such evacuation is likely to remain; evacuations from Afghanistan (2021) and Ukraine (2022), despite being undertaken by air, only underscore the point.

SAR. From a maritime perspective, Search and Rescue (SAR) is intrinsic to the human security dimensions of maritime security. India has an international responsibility for maritime SAR in accordance with the International Convention on Maritime Search and Rescue, 1979. The International Civil Aviation Organisation (ICAO) and IMO, in consultation with member states, has designated SAR regions for coordination of international SAR.[149] The Indian SAR region—termed the Indian Search and Rescue Region (ISRR)—covers an area of 4.6 million square kilometres, more than double of the Indian EEZ and adjoins ten other SAR regions.[150] In 2019, the Coast Guard conducted over 300 SAR missions involving more than 1,000 lives, including 27 MEDVAC operations, and in 2022, the Coast Guard saved over 1,200 lives.[151] Overall, the Coast Guard has saved over 11,000 lives since its raising in 1977.

Progressively, the Coast Guard has also strengthened regional cooperation in SAR. In September 2020, India signed the 'MOU between IORA Member States for the Coordination and Cooperation of Search and Rescue Services in the Indian Ocean Region,'[152] The Coast Guard is the implementing agency of the MOU.[153] Subsequently in 2021, 'nodal agency' for SAR in the Indo-Pacific Region.'[154] In addition, since 2014, the Coast Guard is also the nodal agency for forwarding two nominations every year to the IMO award for exceptional bravery at sea.[155]

The Coast Guard regularly conducts SAR Communication Exercises (SARCOMEX) with Maritime Rescue Coordination Centres (MRCCs)/ Rescue Coordination Centres in the maritime neighbourhood, and beyond, for strengthening regional responses to SAR, developing interoperability, and capacity building.[156] In 2021, the Coast Guard engaged in 14 SARCOMEXs with 11 countries.[157] Furthermore, the tenth edition of the National Maritime Search and Rescue Exercise (SAREX -22), was attended by 24 foreign observers from 16 FFCs.[158] In addition to SARCOMEX, the Coast Guard also conducts a MRCC Operations and SAR Course for personnel from FFCs.[159]

Depending on the mission, SAR operations could require coordination amongst multiple international agencies, and Indian agencies too have to coordinate SAR efforts involving Indian ships/citizens outside the Indian SSRR. For example, the 2018 rescue of Indian yachtsperson Commander Abhilash Tomy in the South Indian Ocean (Australian SRR), coordinated by the Australian Rescue Coordination Centre, also involved surface and air assets of the Indian Navy, the Royal Australian Navy, and a French fisheries patrol boat.[160] The Indian Navy described the rescue as evidence of its reach, mobility, and versatility and as a testimony to the Indian Navy being a credible 'net security provider' in the region.[161] Likewise in May 2023, Indian Navy's P8I aircraft had located a Chinese Fishing Vessel with 39 crew which had capsized in the Southern Indian Ocean in a multinational operation.[162]

Earlier in 2014, ships and aircraft of the Indian Navy, the Indian Air Force, and the Coast Guard from multiple commands/equivalents were pressed into service in the Bay of Bengal, the Andaman Sea, and adjoining seas for the search of the missing Malaysian Airliner MH 370.[163] The Indian Navy and the Indian Air Force also deployed aircraft to Malaysia for the search.[164] While the Indian Navy was designated the lead service for the operation, the operation was coordinated by Headquarters, Integrated Defence Staff (HQIDS) with Commander-in-Chief Andaman and Nicobar Command (CINCAN) as the Overall Force Commander (OFC). Subsequently in July 2016, an Indian Air Force AN 32-transport aircraft went missing over the Bay of Bengal. In one of the largest operations of its kind, led by the Indian Navy, ships and aircraft of the Indian Navy, Indian Air Force, Coast Guard, Ministry of Earth Sciences (MoES) [Geological Survey of India (GSI) and National Institute of Ocean Technology (NIOT)], and surveillance satellites of Indian Space Research Organisation (ISRO) were pressed into service for the search.[165] Both the search for MH 370 and the AN 32 did not meet with success despite the unprecedented scale of the operations.

The above incidents are testimony to the fact that SAR operations, especially in extended ranges, and in situations where information is scant, may require massive deployment of assets with specialised equipment and also coordination. Response to complex SAR missions within the ISRR, and beyond, also requires coordination amongst multiple ministries, departments, and agencies, including SAR agencies, Indian defence forces, the Coast Guard, space and scientific organisations, etc.

Figure 4.2: Indian Search and Rescue Region

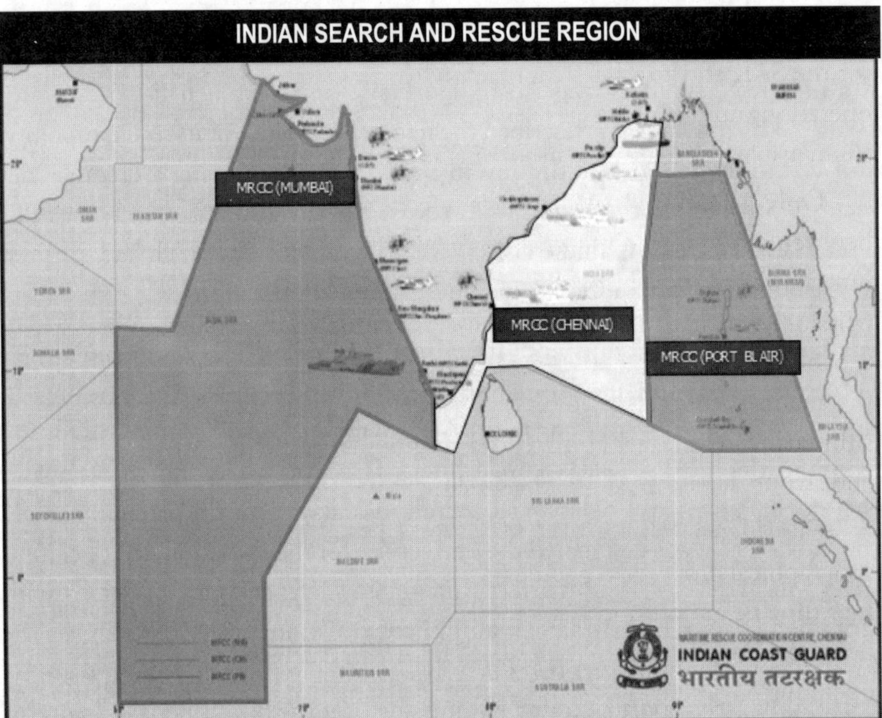

Another aspect of SAR pertains to rescue from underwater vessels and submarines. Rescue of personnel from distressed submarines requires specialised capabilities, and presently, only a few submarine-operating navies have requisite capabilities, with India being one of them.[166] In 2018—half-a-century after India acquired its first submarine—the Indian Navy acquired its first integral rapidly deployable Deep Sea Rescue Vehicle (DSRV). The DSRV, manned by a crew of three, is capable of rescuing submarine crew from a depth of 650 m and operating up to Sea State six conditions.[167] Like India, it is likely that other submarine-operating countries will initially prefer the route of assured rescue support, rather than develop integral capabilities for rescue. It is therefore only in the interest of submarine-operating navies that they establish formal mechanisms with agencies capable of providing submarine rescue. In April 2021, in a first, India deployed the DSRV to assist the Indonesian Navy in the SAR effort for the missing Indonesian Submarine KRI *Nanggala* off the coast of Bali.[168]

Notwithstanding the induction of the DSRV, India's overall capacities appear to be relatively limited. The Chinese, for example, deployed three ships for the SAR effort of KRI *Nanggala* with the capability to undertake salvage operations up to a depth of over 4,500 m (15,000 feet) along with a manned submersible reportedly capable of operations close to 10,000 m (32,000 feet).[169]

Only a few countries have manned submersibles capable of operating between 4,500 m (14,800 feet) to 7,500 m (23,000 feet) and beyond. This limitation is likely to be overcome to some extent with the MoES 'Deep Ocean Mission' which includes developing a manned submersible, *Samudrayan,* capable of operating at 6000 m (19,685 m).[170] The technology for developing the manned submersible could also have utility in developing indigenous submarine rescue capability, and augmenting military use of scientific endeavours in the underwater domain.

Considering the criticality of time in submarine rescue and India's geographical proximity to some submarine operating navies in the immediate maritime neighbourhood, such as Bangladesh and Myanmar, India is ideally positioned to be the 'first responder'. Formalised agreements with submarine-operating navies, such as with Singapore, will help in increasing familiarisation to operate together. Overall, future imperatives will include exercising submarine rescue drills with foreign navies, especially neighbouring submarine operating navies to streamline procedures for submarine crew rescue, including related logistics, and developing indigenous capabilities for underwater SAR and salvage. Exercises with offshore operators could also streamline processes for underwater SAR.[171]

Marine Environment Protection. The concept of maritime security is also linked to marine environment protection. Prime Minister Modi, speaking at the UN Security Council in August 2021, highlighted the need for cooperation for facing natural disasters, and that India has been a first responder to assist in maritime disasters, including maritime pollution. In India, the Coast Guard is the agency responsible for preservation and protection of the marine environment and control of marine pollution.[172]

Two incidents in 2020 involving to MV *Wakashio* (off Mauritius in July 2020) and MT *New Diamond* (off Sri Lanka in September 2020, code named Operation SAGAR ARAKSHA) and one incident in 2021 involving MV *X-Press Pearl* (off Sri Lanka in May 2021, code named SAGAR ARAKSHA II) underscored the importance of regional cooperation in response to incidents of marine environmental pollution, or incidents which could potentially lead to oil spillages. The efforts to douse the fire onboard the MT *New Diamond* and MV *X-Press Pearl*,[173] a collaborative effort amongst multiple agencies from Indian and Sri Lanka, also invoked the provisions of the SACEP/Coast Guard MOU. A short brief on India's contribution to regional efforts is enumerated below:

- In August 2020, to assist in pollution response activities associated with the grounding of MV *Wakashio*,[174] India deployed diving support ship, INS *Nireekshak,* and a ten-member response team from the Coast Guard with specialised equipment, was airlifted by the Indian Air Force to Mauritius, INS *Nireekshak* also provided assistance in locating a sunken tug *Gaetan* and to contain possible spillage.[175]
- In September 2020, navies and coast guards of India and Sri Lanka, along with other agencies of both countries were involved in efforts to douse the fire onboard the MT *New Diamond.*[176] On the request of the Sri Lanka Navy, INS *Sahyadri* assumed duties of On Scene Commander (OSC).[177] According to a press release by the Ministry of Defence, effective coordination amongst Indian and Sri Lankan agencies facilitated the prevention of a possible ecological disaster.[178]

- In May 2021, Coast Guard ships were also involved in fighting a fire onboard MV *X-Press Pearl* of the Colombo coast along with tugs deployed by Sri Lankan authorities, however, after relentless efforts the ship sank with a cargo of dangerous goods raising concerns of pollution.[179] Subsequent to the sinking, INS *Sarvekshak* surveyed the site of the ill-fated MV *X-Press Pearl* and handed over the survey data to Sri Lanka authorities.[180]

These incidents only call attention to the fact that capabilities in the region are limited, and that international cooperation is key to ensuring safe and secure seas, and that the capabilities required for safety and security are often interchangeably or complementarily employed. For example, during Cyclone *Tauktae* (2021) the mission to rescue offshore workers was beyond the operating profile of OPV class ships and had to be undertaken by larger destroyer class vessels available with only the Indian Navy. Regional agreements on oil spill contingencies are therefore likely to gain traction.

Enhancing regional cooperation for oil pollution response is, therefore, an agenda for the future, particularly in South Asia and the Bay of Bengal. Consequently, operationalisation of regional contingency plans, and conduct of regular exercises at the regional level are imperatives.

MDA AND INTERNATIONAL INFORMATION SHARING

MDA is a *sine qua non* for effective maritime security, and in the 21st century, driven by ICT, there has been a transformative shift in the ways and means to develop MDA and to exchange information. Today there is unprecedented awareness about the maritime domain. However, until the end of the 20th century, this was largely in the realm of fiction. Despite the unprecedented transparency of the maritime domain, there remain significant gaps in awareness that could be exploited by actors with malicious intent. In the past decade or so there have been increasing international collaborations for information sharing, and the proliferation of MDA and international information sharing hubs is ample proof of such collaborations. These centres not only collaborate with each other, but also disseminate their analysis and reports through the Internet for wider distribution to the maritime community. The presence of

International Liaison Officers (ILOs) in international information centres is considered as the bedrock of international information sharing and a manifestation of mutual trust and confidence.

There has been increasing recognition of the need for developing mechanisms for regional and sub-regional coordination to counter threats to maritime security. The outcome document of the maiden high-level open debate in the UN Security Council in August 2021 for enhancing maritime security cooperation recognised the importance of enhancing international and regional cooperation to counter threats to maritime security and safety.[181] The document also commended the efforts by individual countries, regional and sub-regional organisations, including through information sharing. Notably, the concept of MDA has wide utility not only as a tactical tool for security agencies, but also as an instrument in understanding the 'big picture' in multifarious strategic dimensions, such as for energy security and trade.

In addition to the increasing maritime security challenges, some of the main drivers for enhanced cooperation in MDA and information sharing are capacity constraints, jurisdictional limitations, and challenges associated the technical means for developing MDA. These very challenges and drivers provide avenues for furthering international cooperation to achieve common objectives in ways that are mutually beneficial. Individually, obtaining a comprehensive understanding of the wider oceanic spaces is difficult, if not impossible, but collectively through cooperative endeavours, a better understanding of the environment is surely possible. As countries and regional groupings develop their own strategies for enhancing cooperation, cooperation in MDA and information sharing has emerged as one of the most promising areas for enhanced cooperation amongst likeminded countries. There is therefore immense potential and opportunities for expanding these linkages and developing a regional framework for cooperative MDA. In 2021, issues related to developing regional MDA and information sharing were discussed at workshops and conferences steered by the EU CRIMARIO, the IFC-IOR and the NMF.[182] It emerged that despite the attractiveness of the concept, there remain inherent challenges both in developing MDA itself, and in facilitating regional cooperation.

White Shipping Information Exchange Agreement

In 2014, the GoI approved conclusion of agreements to exchange unclassified data on bilateral and multilateral basis with foreign agencies entrusted with maritime security for augmenting MDA capacity.[183] The Indian Navy is accordingly progressing conclusion of Technical Agreements/MOUs on Shipping Information—also termed the White Shipping Information Exchange Agreements (WSIE)—with 36 countries and three multilateral constructs.[184] Until December 2020, the Indian Navy had concluded WSIE with 22 countries and one multilateral construct.[185] Some of the countries with which India has negotiated WSIE include Australia, Brazil, France, Israel, Maldives, Mauritius, Myanmar, Oman, US, UK, and Vietnam.[186] In 2022, India has also concluded a WSIE with New Zealand.[187] India's agreement with Trans-Regional Maritime Network (T-RMN), steered by Italy, gives India access to a construct which has 30 other international members, exponentially increasing the availability of global shipping information.[188]

In effect these agreements give access to additional shipping information on a reciprocal basis—information that will not be normally available through organic sensor capabilities. In a globalised world, where trade and threats move seamlessly from one region to another, and the effect of activities in one impact another, there is a justifiable need for situational awareness in regions beyond a country's own maritime zones and sensor capabilities (which is normally limited to coastal/offshore areas). The principal limitation of WSIE, however, is that information flow is limited to unclassified information on shipping. Therefore, additional complementary ways and means need to be adopted for further increasing maritime transparency. While WSIE are a good start, it must not be seen as an end, but as a foundation for more robust information sharing in the classified domain, as is conceivably already happening with some partners.

The Information Fusion Centre–Indian Ocean Region

The Information Fusion Centre–Indian Ocean Region (IFC-IOR), located at Gurugram, was launched on 22 December 2018 by the then Raksha Mantri, Shrimati Nirmala Sitharaman with the aim of engaging partner nations and multinational maritime constructs to develop comprehensive MDA and for information sharing.[189] While initially information exchange was undertaken through 'virtual' means, progressively, as planned, information sharing has moved beyond virtual means. IFC-IOR has inducted ILOs from several countries, including from France, Japan, US, Seychelles, Maldives, and more ILOs are expected to join.[190] The IFC has also established linkages with over 50 partners across the world, including industry bodies and NGOs. As evinced from the monthly updates of the centre, the IFC-IOR monitors not only the IOR, but also East Africa and South East Asia. Considering India's widening interests across the globe, progressively, the centre could expand its linkages and coverage beyond its present areas of interest, to the Indo-Pacific, if not the world. As such, considering the areas of interest of the IFC-IOR, the suffix 'IOR' appears to be a misnomer, necessitating a future name change to more accurately reflect its wider area of interest. Likewise, there is also scope to expand the scope of engagement and portfolio of activities, such as through more robust engagements with the wider maritime security sector and through customised deliverables. Progressively, if the IFC-IOR is to establish itself as the leading player in the IOR (and beyond), there will be a need to develop infrastructure, augment capacity, and develop cutting-edge capabilities. This necessitates not only wider participation from Indian agencies, but also induction of more ILOs, and leveraging India's technology base.[191]

Indo-Pacific Partnership for MDA

Under the aegis of the QUAD framework, the Indo-Pacific Partnership for MDA (IPMDA) is a 2022 initiative focused on MDA capacity building in the Indo-Pacific.[192] Broadly, the IPMDA endeavours to build on existing MDA structures, by infusing emerging technologies for increased transparency of the maritime environment across the Indian Ocean, South East Asia, and the Pacific Islands.[193] While two operational areas of focus of the IPMDA include HADR and IUU fishing, increased transparency of the oceans by enhanced collaboration amongst regional countries, as well as regional MDA centres, will also facilitate rapid detection and response to a range of maritime security threats, as also humanitarian crises.[194] It is envisaged that the IPMDA will be a "cutting-edge partnership that promotes peace and stability throughout the region."[195] Considering India's own developed capabilities for national and regional capabilities for MDA viz. IMAC and the IFC-IOR, India can indeed play a vital role in the initiative, and in turn strengthen its own capabilities.[196]

However, there remain challenges to overcome such as those related to investments for persistent tracking, mobilisation of resources that may be necessary, as also the degree of participation by other regional countries/ international MDA centres, outside of the QUAD framework, etc.[197]

Other Linkages

The Indian Navy and the Coast Guard have positioned ILOs at a few information-sharing centres overseas. This includes Indian Navy ILOs at IFC Singapore and US Naval Forces Central Command (NAVCENT), and a Coast Guard ILO at ReCAAP ISC.[198] India is also a member of the Mercury network which is an informal collaborative information sharing tool for countering piracy in the Gulf of Aden developed by the EU Maritime Security Centre-Horn of Africa (MSC-HOA).[199] Progressively, personnel from Indian agencies may be positioned in additional centres, albeit based on a prioritised action plan.

CAPACITY BUILDING AND CAPACITY ENHANCEMENT

Training Cooperation

The Indian maritime security strategy focuses on training to "facilitate a shared understanding of maritime issues, strengthen relations, enhance interoperability, and enable broader cooperation."[200] The Indian Navy's Training Command, located at Kochi, is responsible for training in the Indian Navy, including 16 naval training establishments encompassing over 30 training centres.[201] As part of 'soft power' projection, the Indian Navy offers over 20 training courses for officers and over 90 courses for sailors for foreign trainees, and has trained over 15,000 personnel from 45 countries.[202] The Naval War College (NWC), Goa conducts an eight week Maritime Security Council (MSC), an international Professional Military Exchange (PME) programme, for officers from FFC.[203] Training is undertaken either under the MEA's Indian Technical and Economic Cooperation (ITEC) Programme for foreign beneficiaries or through self-financed schemes.[204] ITEC, instituted in 1964, is India's flagship programme for capacity building which although initially was conceived on a bilateral basis, has over the years been extended to multilateral groupings, such as ASEAN, BIMSTEC, IORA, etc.[205] The Indian Navy also deploys mobile training teams overseas and has also been involved in the 'operational sea training' of foreign warships.[206] In addition, practical training cooperation is also furthered during other opportune engagements with foreign agencies, such as during exercises. The Coast Guard also undertakes a course on 'Maritime Law and Operations' for foreign countries.[207] The Indian Navy has also taken steps to provide placement opportunities to veterans in capacity building of friendly countries, such as with the Qatar Navy under an MOU.[208] Ostensibly, these placements also relate to training of the Qatari Emiri Navy (QEN).

Conceivably, as India foreign policy assumes greater maritime dimensions in the 21st century, boosting training under the ITEC programme can contribute significantly to meeting the objectives of furthering Indian maritime policies such as SAGAR. A proposal for development for Centres of Excellence and collaborative training programmes under the aegis of the GMC potentially can give a fillip to regional cooperation in training.[209] Progressively, as the Coast Guard develops its proposed academy, the Coast Guard could also contribute to furthering international cooperation in specialised areas, such as those related to SAR and oil pollution response. However, despite a proven record of accomplishment, considering the shortage of personnel in the Indian Navy, expanding training linkages overseas, like other initiatives, can perhaps also lead to a stretch and have an adverse effect on internal training efforts. The increasing use of the virtual medium for training and education, driven by the COVID pandemic, despite its limitations, can, to some extent, facilitate such a balance. In other words, training efforts could adopt a mix of physical and virtual means to maximise training effort.

Indian security forces also avail training courses with foreign navies under similar arrangements, or on a reciprocal basis.[210] A specific problem with training of own personnel overseas is the possibility of indoctrination of future leaders. This may in the long term affect naval policy through unperceived biases. Consequently, to hedge against the possibility of indoctrination, a balanced approach to imbibe the best practices from different partners needs to be adopted, wherein the future leaders are exposed to alternative views and approaches, and not a set of views, which majorly hitherto have reflected western thinking.

Military-Technical Cooperation

The growth of the Indian Navy to be amongst the largest and most capable navies in the world in the 21st century has been supported by several countries, particularly the erstwhile Union of Soviet Socialist Republics (USSR), and subsequently Russia, as the successor of the USSR, in the latter half of the 20th century.[211] The USSR provided the Indian Navy with required military-technology (and assets) to operate in all the dimensions of naval warfare, as well as strategic assets, such as an aircraft carrier and nuclear submarines. Progressively, the relationship has grown beyond a buyer-seller relationship, to joint Research and Development (R&D) and production of state-of-the-art military platforms, such as frigates, and weapon systems, such as the BrahMos missile.[212] While over the years India's dependence on Russian technology has reduced, even as late as 2020, Russia still accounted for almost half of India's defence imports.[213] India's preponderant dependence on Russia for defence technology is one of the pillars of the Indo-Russian relationship. While the Indian Navy took the lead in domestic warship-building at about the same time as it went about acquiring Russian technology, its rapid growth could not have been possible without foreign military-technical cooperation, not only with Russia, but also with several other countries, including France, Israel, Germany, and more lately, the US. However, Indian maritime security forces are increasingly striving to be self-reliant (*Atmanirbhar*).

Between 2016-17 and 2021-22, Indian defence exports more than tripled, and touched a record Rs 13,000 crore with exports to over 75 countries.[214] Progressively, as India's own Defence Industrial Base (DIB) has grown, India has also began providing technical assistance to several FFC. Broadly, military technical cooperation includes repairs and refits, maintenance support for assets delivered by India, development of maintenance support facilities, specialised technical assistance, and gifting of assets, or transfer/lease of assets of the Indian Navy and the Coast Guard.

Over the years, Interceptor Boats (IB), Fast Interceptor Craft (FIC), Fast Patrol Craft (FPC), Fast Attack Craft (FAC), and Offshore Patrol Vessel (OPV) class of ships of the Indian Navy and Coast Guard have been provided for capacity building of maritime security agencies in Seychelles, Maldives, Mauritius, Mozambique, and Vietnam. In July 2023, India handed over an indigenously built operational missile vessel corvette, INS *Kirpan*, to

Vietnam.[215] Reportedly, this was the first time that an operational corvette has been handed over to any country.[216] India has also handed over submarines, and aircraft to FFCs, such as a submarine to Myanmar in 2020, and a Dornier Maritime Reconnaissance (MR) aircraft to Sri Lanka in 2022.[217] Overall, India's efforts at capacity building of FFCs has significantly expanded over the years.

In addition, personnel from Indian maritime security agencies have been deployed for operations and maintenance of assets overseas, such as in Mauritius and Mozambique.[218] Military-technical cooperation not only strengthens capacities of regional maritime forces, but also fosters operational interoperability. As India expands its own domestic shipbuilding infrastructure, India could expand its technical cooperation with a larger number of countries than hitherto on a larger number of areas for cooperation.

Hydrographic Cooperation

Over the years, hydrographic cooperation has emerged as one of the pillars of the India Navy's international cooperative efforts, and was extensively discussed at the GMC-21. The Indian Naval Hydrographic Department (INHD), one of the leading hydrographic agencies in the IOR, actively supports coastal states in the IOR in hydrographic surveys, capacity building, and nautical charting.[219] India, which joined the International Hydrographic Organization (IHO) in 1955, is a member of the 30-member IHO Council and is actively engaged in its activities. The INHD is also a member in regional bodies and other international groupings, such as the North Indian Ocean Hydrographic Commission (NIOHC), the Southern African and Islands Hydrographic Commission (SAIHC), and the International Cartographic Association.

The international responsibilities of the INHD in the IOR, which extend well beyond Indian maritime zones, include being the regional coordinator for International (INT) charts for Region "J" and the coordinator for NAVAREA VIII for Maritime Safety Information Services (MSIS). The National Institute of Hydrography (NIH) at Goa, an IHO recognised regional training centre for countries in the IOR, has trained personnel from over 39 countries. Besides this, bilaterally, India has cooperative mechanisms with several countries, such as Mauritius, Seychelles, Tanzania, Maldives, Mozambique, Vietnam, Myanmar, Kenya, and Sri Lanka, for the conduct of joint surveys and production of charts and Electronic Nautical Charts (ENC).

In Mauritius, the INHD along with local surveyors has also set up a joint training team.

In addition to its primary role in the promotion of maritime safety, the National Hydrographic Office (NHO), located at Dehradun, has prepared an 'Indian Maritime Safety and Security Chart' in 2019, a pioneering effort to support maritime safety and security. The chart provides comprehensive safety and security-related information not only in the Indian maritime zones, but also in the wider IOR.[220] With the increasing challenges to safety and security of mariners, the NHO can play a significant role in the promotion of safety and security through cartographic products and the dissemination of safety and security information in partnership with regional and sub-regional organisations and other countries of Region "J"/NAVAREA VIII.

Infrastructure Development

India has installed an indigenously developed coastal radar system for maritime surveillance of the coastal areas in Sri Lanka, Mauritius, and Seychelles.[221] Installation of such systems is also planned in Maldives, Myanmar, and Bangladesh. Reportedly 12 other countries have also expressed an interest in the system.[222] The Coastal Radar System (CRS) contributes to developing domain awareness in coastal areas with radar as the primary sensor. A coastal radar system is an integral part of the surveillance matrix for any coastal state, and the integration of radar information from multiple CRS systems can potentially contribute to enhancing regional MDA. As India, particularly M/s Bharat Electronics Limited (BEL), has gained significant experience, in developing naval systems for MDA, through the domestic Coastal Surveillance Network (CSN), National Command Control Communication and Intelligence (NC3I) network, and in installing CRS in several countries, India can leverage this expertise to offer cost-effective solutions not only to IOR littorals, but also beyond.

Operational Support Agreements

India signed its first logistic support agreement with the US, the Logistics Exchange Memorandum of Agreement [LEMOA] in 2016. The agreement facilitates replenishment of military assets from each other's bases, as also logistic and maintenance support at respective bases on reimbursement basis.[223]

Subsequently, India has inked similar agreements with several countries as tabulated below:

Table 4.2: Logistic Agreements

Sl. No.	Country	Agreement	Year
1.	US	Logistics Exchange Memorandum of Agreement [LEMOA] between the Ministry of Defence and the Department of Defence[224]	2016
2.	Singapore	Indian Navy and Republic of Singapore Navy agreement for mutual coordination, logistics and services support for naval ships', submarines, and naval aircraft (including Ship borne Aviation Assets) visits[225]	2018
3.	France	Agreement regarding the Provision of Reciprocal Logistics Support[226]	2018
4.	South Korea	Military Logistic Agreement[227]	2019
5.	Australia	Mutual Logistics Support Agreement (MLSA)[228]	2020
6.	Japan	Reciprocal Provisions for Support and Services (RPSS) Agreement[229]	2020
7.	Vietnam	MOU on Mutual Logistic Support	2023

In addition to the above, India also has also inked several important agreements with the US as tabulated below:[230]

Table 4.3: India-US Agreements

Sl. No.	Agreement	Year
1.	General Security of Military Information Agreement (GSOMIA)	2002
2.	Helicopter Operations from Ships other than Aircraft Carriers (HOSTAC)	2017
3.	Communications Compatibility and Security Agreement (COMCASA)	2018
4.	Basic Exchange and Cooperation Agreement for Geo-spatial Cooperation (BECA)	2020
5.	Maritime Information Sharing Technical Agreement (MISTA)[231]	2020

Collectively, BECA, COMCASA, LEMOA, and, along with GSOMIA, are considered 'foundational' security agreements with the US for facilitating interoperability, and for sale of high-end technology, such as encrypted communication equipment, for optimal exploitation of assets procured from the US.[232] A short overview of the foundational agreement is provided below:

- BECA facilitates access to US geospatial intelligence and contributes to improved terrain awareness and targeting by weapon systems, and can also contribute to benign operations such as HA/DR operations.[233]
- COMCASA, an India-specific version of the Communication and

Information on Security Memorandum of Agreement (CISMOA), facilitates transfer of specialised equipment for encrypted communications on US-built platforms in the Indian inventory, and supports classified information sharing, such as those related to terrorist threats.[234] The agreement importantly incorporates specific provisions for safeguarding Indian security interests, including clauses related to non-disclosure of information to third-parties without India's consent.[235] Under the agreement, a secure communication link, facilitating real-time information sharing, has been established between IHQ MoD(N) and the US Central and Indo-Pacific Commands.[236]
- The GSOMIA, one of the earliest agreements with the US, as the name indicates, provides for security of classified military information.[237]

In addition to the foundational agreements, HOSTAC facilities safe cross-deck helicopter operations between naval and coast ships, and MISTA lays down protocols for real-time intelligence exchange between the two countries. Unlike WSIE, which focuses on merchant shipping, MISTA focuses on warship-related information exchange.[238] For strengthening intelligence sharing, a US Congressional committee expressed its desire to strengthen the Anglophone 'Five Eyes' intelligence alliance comprising Australia, Canada, New Zealand, UK, and the US by collaborating with India, Japan, South Korea.[239] While strengthening intelligence sharing can be mutually beneficially, India has been traditionally averse to alliances, and whether India chooses to go for such arrangements will need much debate and consultation.

The US Navy has also concluded a Master Ship Repair Agreement (MSRA) with M/s Larsen and Toubro (L&T) Shipbuilding Ltd in India.[240] Agreements such as the MSRA support naval operations between multiple theatres of naval operations.[241] Between August 2022 and June 2023 three US naval ships had undergone repairs at L&T's Katupalli shipyard.[242] Similar agreements are also planned with other shipyards in India.[243]

While the increasing cooperation with the US through formal agreements is encouraging and speaks volumes about the growing partnership between the two countries, when interests collide, every nation places its own interests above others. Sceptics also question the talk about 'convergences,' the US, for example, is a global player with global interests, which India is not. In the past, the US has been called out for being an undependable ally, such as in the context of withdrawal from Afghanistan in August 2021.[244] The operational assertion by USS *John Paul Jones* in the Indian EEZ in April 2021, as well its public release by the US Navy, is an example of the US placing its own fundamental interests ahead of its partners. India's own interests can at times be in variance with its strategic partner (US), such as on the UN vote on condemning the Russian invasion of Ukraine in February 2022, or on issues of climate change. The AUKUS deal in September 2021 is another example of realism when Australia presumably back-tracked on its conventional submarine deal with France, to acquire nuclear submarines with help from the US and the UK. India has over the years chosen to develop strategic partnerships with several countries, including in military cooperation; a diversified approach, especially in view of its defence dependency on Russia, perhaps is still the best hedging strategy for India.

This chapter focused on the operational aspects of maritime security cooperation, including constructs, various forms of engagements amongst maritime security agencies, operational engagements, such as through exercises, operational deployments, specific maritime safety and security missions, such as anti-piracy and drug trafficking, cooperative mechanisms for developing MDA and information sharing, and finally capacity building and capability enhancement initiatives. The next chapter focuses on some of the key issues related to maritime security cooperation.

NOTES

1 Jaishankar, *The India Way: Strategies for an Uncertain World*, 198.

2 Stable Seas, *Challenges and Solutions for Maritime Security in the Indian Ocean*, 8.

3 Indian Ocean Naval Symposium, *Charter of Business* (2016), 2. http://www.ions.global/sites/default/files/IONS-Charter-Version-2.0.pdf, accessed on 15 January 2021.

4 Indian Ocean Naval Symposium, *Charter of Business* (2016), 3.

5 Ministry of Defence, "Indian Ocean Naval Symposium (IONS) Working Group Meeting on Humanitarian Assistance And Disaster Relief," Press Information Bureau, 16 December 2020, https://pib.gov.in/Pressreleaseshare.aspx?PRID=1681319, accessed on 14 January 2021.

6 "IONS Working Groups," Indian Ocean Naval Symposium, http://www.ions.global/ions-working-groups, accessed on 15 January 2021.

7 Indian Ocean Naval Symposium, *Charter of Business* (2016), 6.

8 "10th Anniversary of Indian Ocean Naval Symposium to be hosted on 13-14 November 2018," Indian Navy, https://www.indiannavy.nic.in/content/10th-anniversary-indian-

ocean-naval-symposium-be-hosted-13-14-november-2018, accessed on 15 January 2021.

9 https://www.indiannavy.nic.in/content/ions-maritime-exercise-2022-imex-22

10 Sawan, "Problems and prospects of maritime security cooperation in the Indian Ocean Region."

11 "COVID-19," Indian Ocean Naval Symposium, http://www.ions.global/covid-19, accessed on 15 January 2021.

12 Interaction between NMF and visiting foreign delegation at NMF on 12 November 2021.

13 Sawan, "Problems and prospects of maritime security cooperation in the Indian Ocean Region."

14 Sawan, "Problems and prospects of maritime security cooperation in the Indian Ocean Region."

15 Sawan, "Problems and prospects of maritime security cooperation in the Indian Ocean Region."

16 Sawan, "Problems and prospects of maritime security cooperation in the Indian Ocean Region."

17 Upadhyaya, "Maritime Security Cooperation in the Indian Ocean Region." 253.

18 Sawan, "Problems and prospects of maritime security cooperation in the Indian Ocean Region."

19 Sawan, "Problems and prospects of maritime security cooperation in the Indian Ocean Region." 29.

20 Ministry of Defence, "Joint Maritime Exercise." Press Information Bureau, 03 February 2021, https://pib.gov.in/Pressreleaseshare.aspx?PRID=1694881

21 "Heads of Asian Coast Guard Agencies Meeting (HACGAM)," Turkish Coast Guard Command, https://en.sg.gov.tr/hacgam, accessed on 13 January 2021.

22 Ministry of Defence, "India Stands for Open & Rule-Based Maritime Borders in Indo-Pacific: Raksha Mantri during 18th Heads of Asian Coast Guard Agencies Meeting in New Delhi," Press Information Bureau, 15 October 2022, https://pib.gov.in/PressReleasePage.aspx?PRID=1868008, accessed on 20 August 2023.

23 Ministry of Defence, "India Stands for Open & Rule-Based Maritime Borders."

24 "Objective," Heads of Asian Coast Guard Agencies Meeting, https://hacgam.org/about, accessed on 13 March 2022.

25 "Objective," Heads of Asian Coast Guard Agencies Meeting.

26 Ministry of Defence. "India Stands for Open & Rule-Based Maritime Borders in Indo-Pacific"

27 Gulbin Sultana, "Inauguration of NSA Trilateral Secretariat: A step forward for maritime security cooperation with Sri Lanka, and the Maldives," *Financial Express*, 04 March 2021, https://www.financialexpress.com/defence/inauguration-of-nsa-trilateral-secretariat-a-step-forward-for-maritime-security-cooperation-with-sri-lanka-and-the-maldives/2206173/, accessed on 03 January 2022.

28 Sultana, "Inauguration of NSA Trilateral Secretariat"

29 Ministry of Defence, "Tri Nation Table Top Naval Exercise 'SHIELD' Held at WNC, Mumbai," Press Information Bureau, 15 July 2021. https://pib.gov.in/PressReleasePage.aspx?PRID=1736197, accessed on 03 January 2022.

30 Ministry of Defence, "Colombo Security Conclave Focused Operation between India,

Maldives and Sri Lanka," Press Information Bureau, 28 November 2021, https://pib.gov.in/PressReleaseIframePage.aspx?PRID=1775797, accessed on 03 January 2022.

31 Integrated Headquarters of Ministry of Defence (Navy), *Ensuring Secure Seas,* 90.

32 Ministry of Defence, "4th Indian Navy (IN) - Russian Federation Navy (RuFN) Staff Talks," Press Information Bureau, November 01, 2019, https://pib.gov.in/Pressreleaseshare.aspx?PRID=1589955, accessed on 14 January 2021; various tweets from Spokesperson Indian Navy.

33 Integrated Headquarters of Ministry of Defence (Navy), *Ensuring Secure Seas,* 85.

34 Collated from multiple sources by the author.

35 Ministry of Defence, "Admiral Sunil Lanba chairman COSC and Chief of the Naval Staff visits UK from 12-15 March 2019," Press Information Bureau, 11 March 2019, https://pib.gov.in/Pressreleaseshare.aspx?PRID=1568527, accessed on 16 January 2021.

36 Ministry of Defence, "Admiral Sunil Lanba chairman COSC and Chief of the Naval Staff visits UK"

37 US Joint Forces, Joint Publication 3-13 *Information Operations,* II-13, https://www.jcs.mil/Portals/36/Documents/Doctrine/pubs/jp3_13.pdf, accessed on 16 January 2021.

38 "Memorandum of Understanding," Indian Coast Guard.

39 Discussions at the National Maritime Foundation.

40 Ministry of Defence, "For our collective aspirations to bear fruition and their impact to be sustainable, having a peaceful, stable and secure maritime environment in the region is a pre-requisite" - Smt Nirmala Sitharaman, Raksha Mantri," Press Information Bureau, November 01, 2017, https://pib.gov.in/PressReleasePage.aspx?PRID=1507800, accessed on 02 January 2022.

41 Ministry of Defence, "Curtain Raiser Goa Maritime Conclave – 2021," Press Information Bureau, November 05, 2021, https://pib.gov.in/PressReleaseIframePage.aspx?PRID=1769505, accessed on 02 January 2022.

42 Ministry of Defence, "For our collective aspirations"

43 Ministry of Defence, "Goa Maritime Symposium (GMS) – 2021," Press Information Bureau, May 13, 2021, https://pib.gov.in/PressReleasePage.aspx?PRID=1718329, accessed on 02 January 2022.

44 Integrated Headquarters of Ministry of Defence (Navy), *Ensuring Secure Seas*, 90; "Sri Lanka, India navies hold 26th IMBL meeting aboard Sri Lankan naval ship," *Daily FT*, 30 April 2016, http://www.ft.lk/article/539196/Sri-Lanka—India-navies-hold-26th-IMBL-meeting-aboard-Sri-Lankan-naval-ship, accessed on 14 January 2021.

45 "30th IMBL meeting held onboard SLNS Sayurala," Sri Lanka Navy, https://news.navy.lk/eventnews/2019/05/25/201905251620/, accessed on 14 January 2021.

46 Scroll Staff, "India, Sri Lanka to set up coast guard hotline to deal with fishermen crossing territorial waters," Scroll.in, November 06, 2016, https://scroll.in/latest/820864/india-sri-lanka-to-set-up-coast-guard-hotline-to-deal-with-fishermen-crossing-territorial-waters, accessed on 27 February 2022.

47 Sidhant Sibal,"Pakistan pulls out of annual maritime dialogue with India," *Daily News and Analyses*, 21 March 2019, https://www.dnaindia.com/india/report-pakistan-pulls-out-of-annual-maritime-dialogue-with-india-2731514, accessed on 14 January 2021; "Extension of MOU between Indian Coast Guard and Pakistan Maritime Security Agency," Ministry of External Affairs, 26 February 2016. https://mea.gov.in/press-

releases.htm?dtl/26426/Extension+of+MOU+between+Indian+Coast+Guard+and+Pakistan+Maritime+Security+Agency, accessed on 14 January 2021.

48 "Extension of MOU," Ministry of External Affairs,

49 "Statement on Fifth meeting between Indian Coast Guard [ICG] and Pakistan Maritime Security Agency [PMSA]," Ministry of External Affairs, https://mea.gov.in/press-releases.htm?dtl/27027/Statement+on+Fifth+meeting+between+Indian+Coast+Guard+ICG+and +Pakistan+Maritime+Security+Agency+PMSA, accessed on 14 January 2021.

50 Chief of the Naval Stsff, Admiral Karambir Singh, "Where does the Indian Navy Stand today?" Press Conference on A Decade of Transformation: The Indian Navy, 2011-21, 03 December 2019, https://www.youtube.com/watch?v=aZmVdpb87E8, accessed on 20 August 2023.

51 Integrated Headquarters of Ministry of Defence (Navy), *Indian Maritime Doctrine*, 114.

52 Integrated Headquarters of Ministry of Defence (Navy), *Ensuring Secure Seas,* 86.

53 Ministry of Defence, "Eastern Fleet Ships on Overseas Operational Deployment," Press Information Bureau, 02 August 2021, https://pib.gov.in/PressReleasePage.aspx?PRID=1741640, accessed on 24 August 2021.

54 Ministry of Defence. "Ministry of Defence – Year End Review 2022."

55 Ministry of Defence. "Ministry of Defence – Year End Review 2022."

56 Integrated Headquarters of Ministry of Defence (Navy), *Ensuring Secure Seas,* 86.

57 Ministry of Defence, "Integrated bilateral exercise of Indian Navy and Indian Air Force with US Navy concludes in Indian Ocean Region," Press Information Bureau, 25 June 2021, https://pib.gov.in/PressReleasePage.aspx?PRID=1730308, accessed on 05 September 2021.

58 Spokesperson Navy(@indiannavy), Twitter, 26 August 2021, https://twitter.com/indiannavy/status/1430761200720105472, accessed on 03 September 2021.

59 Australian Government: Defence. "Australia to Host Exercise MALABAR for the First Time," 11 August 2023. https://www.minister.defence.gov.au/media-releases/2023-08-11/australia-host-exercise-malabar-first-time, accessed on 20 August 2023.

60 Ministry of Defence, "28th Edition of Singapore-India Maritime Bilateral Exercise 'SIMBEX'," Press Information Bureau, 04 September 2021, https://pib.gov.in/PressReleasePage.aspx?PRID=1751973, accessed on 05 September 2021.

61 Ministry of Defence, "28th Edition of Singapore-India Maritime Bilateral Exercise 'SIMBEX'."

62 "Transforming The Indian Navy to be a Key Maritime Force in the Indo-Pacific," Address by Admiral Karambir Singh, Chief of the Naval Staff, at United Services Institute, New Delhi, Youtube, 27 August 2021, https://www.youtube.com/watch?v=JliLaXx46AI, accessed on 30 August 2021.

63 "Memorandum of Understanding," Indian Coast Guard.

64 "Trilateral Joint Coast Guard Exercises – DOSTI XI" Ministry of External Affairs, 24 April 2012. https://mea.gov.in/press-releases.htm?dtl/19436/Trilateral+Joint+Coast+Guard+Exercises++DOSTI+XI, accessed on 13 January 2021.

65 Ministry of Defence, "Colombo Security Conclave Focused Operation between India, Maldives And Sri Lanka," Press Information Bureau, 28 November 2021, https://pib.gov.in/PressReleasePage.aspx?PRID=1775797, accessed on 03 March 2022.

66 Ministry of Defence, *Annual Report 2018-19*, 52.

67 Ministry of Defence, "IN Ships to participate in International Fleet Review at Qingdao, China," Press Information Bureau, 19 April 2019, https://pib.gov.in/Pressrelease share.aspx?PRID=1570906, accessed on 12 January 2022.

68 Ministry of Defence, "IN Ships to participate in International Fleet Review at Qingdao, China."

69 J.G. Nadkarni, "Spectacular Fleet Review Salutes Navy's Grand Tradition,' Rediff.com, 07 February 2001. https://www.rediff.com/news/2001/feb/17nad.htm, accessed on 27 February 2022; Ministry of Defence, "IN Ships to participate in International Fleet Review at Qingdao, China."

70 Integrated Headquarters of Ministry of Defence (Navy), *Ensuring Secure Seas*, 87; Ministry of Defence, "Indian Navy's Multi-National Exercise MILAN-2022 to commence 25 February 2022." Press Information Bureau, 23 February 2022, https://pib.gov.in/PressReleaseIframePage.aspx?PRID=1800604, accessed on 27 February 2022.

71 "MILAN 2018," Indian Navy, https://www.indiannavy.nic.in/content/milan-2018, accessed on 14 January 2021; Ministry of Defence, "Indian Navy's Multi-National Exercise MILAN-2022 to commence 25 February 2022." Participation in the exercise could be either through sending assets, such as ships and aircraft, or through delegations, or both.

72 Round-table discussion at the NMF under Chatham House Rules.

73 Ministry of Defence, "Indian Navy's Multi-National Exercise MILAN-2022 to commence 25 February."

74 "MILAN 2018," Indian Navy.

75 "MILAN 2018," Indian Navy.

76 "MILAN 2018," Indian Navy.

77 Upadhyaya, "Maritime Security Cooperation in the Indian Ocean Region," 247.

78 Ministry of Defence, "Indian Navy's Multi-National Exercise MILAN-2022 to commence 25 February."

79 Ministry of Defence, "Navy Day Press Conference at New Delhi: Opening Address by Admiral Sunil Lanba Chief of The Naval Staff," Press Information Bureau, 01 December 2017, https://pib.gov.in/PressReleasePage.aspx?PRID=1511487, accessed on 07 September 2021.

80 Ministry of Defence, "Raksha Mantri Shri Rajnath Singh asks Naval Commanders to deliberate on key focus areas," Press Information Bureau, 19 August 2020, https://pib.gov.in/PressReleasePage.aspx?PRID=1646978, accessed on 07 September 2021.

81 Ministry of Defence, "Year End Review – 2021 of Ministry of Defence," Press Information Bureau, 31 December 2021, https://pib.gov.in/PressReleasePage.aspx?PRID=1786640, accessed on 01 March 2022.

82 "Coordinated Maritime Presences," European Union External Action Service, https://eeas.europa.eu/headquarters/headquarters-homepage/91927/factsheet-coordinated-maritime-presences_en, accessed on 09 March 2022.

83 "Coordinated Maritime Presences: Council extends implementation in the Gulf of Guinea for two years and establishes a new Maritime Area of Interest in the North-Western Indian Ocean," European Council,

84 Sujan Dutta, "Indian Navy informs government about the fleet's reoriented mission pattern," *The New Indian Express*, 01 April 2018, https://www.newindianexpress.com/nation/2018/apr/01/indian-navy-informs-government-about-the-fleets-reoriented-

mission-pattern-1795404.html, accessed on 07 September 2021.

85 Ministry of Defence, "Year End Review – 2021 of Ministry of Defence."

86 Ministry of Defence, "Year End Review – 2021 of Ministry of Defence."

87 Ministry of Defence, "Ministry of Defence - Year End Review 2022."

88 Ministry of Defence, "Ministry of Defence - Year End Review 2022."

89 Ministry of Defence, "Press Brief on Operation Sankalp," Press Information Bureau, January 08, 2021, https://pib.gov.in/PressReleasePage.aspx?PRID=1598858, accessed on 07 September 2021.

90 Dutta, "Indian Navy informs government about the fleet's reoriented mission pattern."

91 Abhijit Singh, "India's 'Mission Ready' naval posture must extend beyond the Indian Ocean," Observer Research Foundation, November 01, 2017. https://www.orfonline.org/research/indias-mission-ready-naval-posture-must-extend-beyond-the-indian-ocean/, accessed on 07 September 2021.

92 "Overseas Deployments," Indian Coast Guard, https://www.indiancoastguard.gov.in/content/1730_3_OverseasDeployment.aspx, accessed on 13 January 2021; Ministry of Defence, *Annual Report 2018-19*, 54; Ministry of Defence,"Year End Review – 2019 Ministry of Defence," Press Information Bureau, 27 December 2020, https://pib.gov.in/PressReleasePage.aspx?PRID=1597842, accessed on 13 January 2021.

93 Ministry of Defence, "Year End Review – 2021 of Ministry of Defence,"

94 Ministry of Defence. "Ministry of Defence – Year End Review 2022,"

95 *US DOD Dictionary of Military and Associated Terms* (November 2021, online), s.v. "maritime security cooperation," https://www.jcs.mil/Portals/36/Documents/Doctrine/pubs/dictionary.pdf, accessed on 01 March 2022.

96 "Media Briefing on the Occasion of India Assuming UNSC Presidency for August 2021," Permanent Mission of Indian to the UN, 02 August 2021, https://pminewyork.gov.in/IndiaatUNSC?id=NDMxNw, accessed on 16 August 2021.

97 "Remarks by External Affairs Minister at the UN Security Council Open Debate on Technology & Peacekeeping," Ministry of External Affairs, 18 August 2021, https://www.mea.gov.in/Speeches-Statements.htm?dtl/34192/Remarks, accessed on 22 August 2021.

98 "Media Briefing on the Occasion of India Assuming UNSC Presidency for August 2021."

99 "Remarks by External Affairs Minister" Ministry of External Affairs.

100 "Remarks by External Affairs," Ministry of External Affairs; C4ISR: Command, Control, Communications, Computers, Intelligence, Surveillance, and Reconnaissance.

101 Doraibabu and Godbole, *A Decade of Transformation: The Indian Navy, 2011-21*, 256.

102 Spokesperson Navy (@indiannavy), Twitter, 20 July 2021, https://twitter.com/indiannavy/status/1417511429691772934, accessed on 17 August 2021.

103 Spokesperson Navy (@indiannavy), 20 July 2021, https://twitter.com/indiannavy/status/1417511429691772934, accessed on 12 January 2022.

104 "International Response: Contact Group," US Department of State.

105 Ministry of Defence, "Piracy in Indian Ocean," Press Information Bureau, 22 April 2013, https://pib.gov.in/newsite/PrintRelease.aspx?relid=94883, accessed on 12 January 2022.

106 Ministry of Shipping, "India becomes co-chair of Working Group on Maritime Situational Awareness under Contact Group on Piracy off the Coast of Somalia," Press Information

Bureau, June 04, 2016, https://pib.gov.in/newsite/PrintRelease.aspx?relid=145976, accessed on 12 January 2022.

107 The piracy HRA had been extended to the west coast of India,

108 Ministry of Shipping, "India becomes co-chair of Working Group on Maritime Situational Awareness under Contact Group on Piracy off the Coast of Somalia."

109 Baltic and International Maritime Council (BIMCO), "Indian Ocean High Risk Area for Piracy to Be Removed on 1 January," 16 December 2022. https://www.bimco.org/insights-and-information/safety-security-environment/20221216-hra-indian-ocean, accessed on 20 August 2023.

110 Ministry of Defence,"Piracy in Indian Ocean."

111 P.K. Ghosh, "Shared Awareness and Deconfliction: Can the success story be applied to Southeast Asia?," Indo-Pacific Defence Forum, 23 February 2016. https://ipdefenseforum.com/2016/02/shared-awareness-and-deconfliction-initiative/, accessed on 12 January 2022.

112 Ghosh, "Shared Awareness and Deconfliction: Can the success story be applied to Southeast Asia?."

113 "India joins the Djibouti Code of Conduct as Observer," Ministry of External Affairs, 16 September 2020, https://www.mea.gov.in/press-releases.htm?dtl/32977/India+joins+the+Djibouti+Code+of+Conduct+as+Observer, accessed on 12 January 2022.

114 "G7++ Friends of the Gulf of Guinea Plenary Meeting Agenda and Information," US Department of State, December 2020. https://www.state.gov/wp-content/uploads/2020/12/Fogg-Plenary-Agenda-With-Day-2-Updates.pdf, accessed on 12 January 2022.

115 Ministry of Defence, "Ministry of Defence – Year End Review 2022."

116 Ministry of Defence, "Press Statement by Raksha Mantri Shri Rajnath Singh after India-US 2+2 Ministerial Dialogue," Press Information Bureau, 12 April 2022. https://pib.gov.in/PressReleasePage.aspx?PRID=1815838, accessed on 20 August 2023.

117 U.S. Naval Forces Central Command, "Combined Maritime Forces." https://www.cusnc.navy.mil/Combined-Maritime-Forces/, accessed on 20 August 2023; Combined Maritime Forces, "Combined Maritime Forces," https://combinedmaritimeforces.com/, accessed on 20 August 2023.

118 UNODC, *World Drug Report 2020* (Vienna: UN Publication, 2020), 20, https://wdr.unodc.org/wdr2020/field/WDR20_BOOKLET_1.pdf, accessed on 14 March 2022.

119 Himadri Das, "Drug Trafficking in India: Maritime Dimensions," National Maritime Foundation, 31 December 2021, https://maritimeindia.org/drug-trafficking-in-india-maritime-dimensions/#_ftn83, accessed on 14 March 2022.

120 Department of Revenue Intelligence, *Smuggling in India Report 2020-21,* 20, https://www.dri.nic.in/dri_report/ebook/, accessed on 14 March 2022.

121 Asian News International, "Alerted by Indian agencies, Sri Lankan coast guard intercepts boats carrying drugs from Karachi," *Business Standard*, 11 July 2019, https://www.business-standard.com/article/news-ani/alerted-by-indian-agencies-sri-lankan-coast-guard-intercepts-boats-carrying-drugs-from-karachi-119071100161_1.html, accessed on 28 May 2023.

122 Ministry of Home Affairs, "Unstarred Question 459: Drug Trafficking," Lok Sabha, 20 July 2021, https://www.mha.gov.in/MHA1/Par2017/pdfs/par2021-pdfs/LS-20072021/459.pdf, accessed on 14 December 2021.

123 These include the South Asian Association for Regional Cooperation (SAARC) Drug Offences Monitoring Desk (SDOMD); Brazil, Russia, India, China, and South Africa (BRICS); Colombo Plan; Association of Southeast Asian Nations (ASEAN); ASEAN Senior Officials on Drug Matters (ASOD); Bay of Bengal Initiative for Multi-Sectoral Technical and Economic Cooperation (BIMSTEC); UNODC; and the International Drug Control Bureau.

124 Ministry of Home Affairs, "Shri Hansraj Gangaram Ahir participated in the High Level Meeting of Interior Ministers of the Indian Ocean Region to Counter Drug Trafficking in Colombo, Sri Lanka," Press Information Bureau, 10 November 2016, https://pib.gov.in/newsite/PrintRelease.aspx?relid=153498., accessed on 12 January 2022.

125 Das, "Drug Trafficking in India: Maritime Dimensions."

126 Das, "Drug Trafficking in India: Maritime Dimensions."

127 Das, "Drug Trafficking in India: Maritime Dimensions."

128 Press Information Bureau, "Seizure of Approximately 2500kg High Purity Methamphetamine Sourced from Death Crescent Valued around Rs. 15,000 Cr in the Indian Waters." May 13, 2023. https://pib.gov.in/PressReleaseIframePage.aspx?PRID = 1923937, accessed on 20 August 2023.

129 Press Information Bureau, "Seizure of Approximately 2500kg High Purity Methamphetamine."

130 Integrated Headquarters of Ministry of Defence (Navy), *Ensuring Secure Seas,* 96; "Joint Exclusive Economic Zone Surveillance of Maldives," Indian Navy, https://www.indiannavy.nic.in/content/joint-exclusive-economic-zone-surveillance-maldives-0, accessed on 14 January 2021; Dinakar Peri, "In a first, India, France conduct joint patrols from Reunion Island," *The Hindu,* 21 March 2020, https://www.thehindu.com/news/international/in-a-first-india-france-conduct-joint-patrols-from-reunion-island/article31129323.ece, accessed on 14 January 2021.

131 Ministry of Defence, "INS Shardul on Joint Exclusive Economic Zone (EEZ) Surveillance in South India Ocean," Press Information Bureau, 05 April 2017, https://pib.gov.in/newsite/PrintRelease.aspx?relid=160497, accessed on 14 January 2021.

132 Peri, "In a first, India, France conduct joint patrols from Reunion Island."

133 "Joint EEZ Surveillance off Mozambique Coast," INS Shivaji International Alumni Portal, 21 March 2023, https://alumni.indiannavy.gov.in/public/index.php/shivaji/news-details/3lZ36E, accessed on 20 August 2023.

134 Ministry of Defence, "Year End Review – 2019 Ministry of Defence."

135 "Indo-Thai Coordinated Patrol (CORPAT)," Indian Navy, https://www.indiannavy.nic.in/content/indo-thai-coordinated-patrol-corpat-2, accessed on 14 January 2021.

136 "8th Indo-Myanmar Coordinated Patrol Commences at Andaman and Nicobar Command," Indian Navy, https://www.indiannavy.nic.in/node/22802, accessed on 14 January 2021.

137 "27th India - Indonesia Coordinated Patrol (CORPAT)," Indian Navy, https://www.indiannavy.nic.in/content/27th-india-indonesia-coordinated-patrol-corpat, accessed on 14 January 2021.

138 "Indo-Thai Coordinated Patrol (CORPAT)," Indian Navy.

139 Indo-Myanmar Coordinated Patrol Exercise is termed IMCOR.

140 Cyclone *Ockhi* witnessed rapid intensification of the cyclone and Cyclone *Tauktae* caused unprecedented damage in the offshore areas.

141 Collated from multiple sources, including the Indian Navy website.

142 Ministry of Defence, "Mission Sagar," Press Information Bureau, 26 December 2021, https://pib.gov.in/PressReleaseIframePage.aspx?PRID=1785282, accessed on 12 January 2022.

143 Ministry of Defence, "Ministry Of Defence - Year End Review 2022."

144 Prime Minister's Office, "Quad Joint Leaders' Statement," Press Information Bureau, 24 May 2022, https://pib.gov.in/PressReleseDetail.aspx?PRID=1827892, accessed on 20 August 2023.

145 Indian Navy, *Ensuring Security Seas*, 99.

146 Press Trust of India, "17 IAF Flights, Five Sorties of Navy Ships Rescue 3,862 Indians from Sudan." *The Times of India,* May 05, 2023. https://timesofindia.indiatimes.com/india/17-iaf-flights-five-sorties-of-navy-ships-rescue-3862-indians-from-sudan/articleshow/100021613.cms?from=mdr, accessed on 20 August 2023.

147 Ministry of Defence, "Year End Review – 2020 Ministry of Defence," accessed on 08 January 2022.

148 "Operation KAVERI," Indiannavy.nic.in. Accessed on 28 May 2023. https://indiannavy.nic.in/content/operation-kaveri.

149 "International search and rescue conventions," Australian Maritime Safety Authority, https://www.amsa.gov.au/safety-navigation/search-and-rescue/international-search-and-rescue-conventions, accessed on 14 January 2021.

150 Ministry of Defence, "Indian Coast Guard holds 18th National Maritime Search and Rescue Board meeting," Press Information Bureau, 18 December 2019, https://pib.gov.in/Pressreleaseshare.aspx?PRID=1596845, accessed on 14 January 2021; "Coordinating Agencies," Indian Coast Guard, https://www.indiancoastguard.gov.in/content/1676_3_CoordinatingAgencies.aspx, accessed on 14 January 2021.

151 Ministry of Defence, "Indian Coast Guard holds 18th National Maritime Search and Rescue Board meeting."; Coast Guard, "COAST GUARD DAY – 01 FEB 2022." Press Release. https://indiancoastguard.gov.in/WriteReadData/Tender/202202040843072326468CGDAY.pdf, accessed on 20 August 2023.

152 "Specialised Agencies and MOU's," Indian Ocean Regional Association, https://www.iora.int/en/structures-mechanisms/specialised-agencies-and-mous/specialised-agencies-and-mous, accessed on 13 January 2021.

153 Ministry of Defence, "Year End Review – 2020 Ministry of Defence."

154 Ministry of Defence, "Year End Review – 2021 of Ministry of Defence."

155 Ministry of Defence, "Year End Review – 2021 of Ministry of Defence."

156 Coast Guard, "Maritime SAR Events," *Safe Waters* XVIII, no. 1 (July 2018), https://www.indiancoastguard.gov.in/WriteReadData/bookpdf/201810240259321153666SafeWatersJul18.pdf, accessed on January 14, 2021.

157 Ministry of Defence, "Year End Review – 2021 of Ministry of Defence."

158 Asia News International, "Indian Coast Guard conducts Exercise SAREX 22 in Chennai." *The Statesman*, 28 August 2022. https://www.thestatesman.com/india/indian-coast-guard-conducts-1503105086.html, accessed on 20 August 2023.

159 Coast Guard, "MRCC OPS & SAR COURSE; FRIENDLY FOREIGN COUNTRIES

(FFCs)" Press Release, https://indiancoastguard.gov.in/WriteReadData/Tender/202301230915274857265pressrelease.pdf, accessed on 20 August 2023.

160 Ministry of Defence, "Cdr Abhilash Tomy, KC reaches Visakhapatnam safely," Press Information Bureau, 06 October 2018, https://pib.gov.in/PressReleaseIframePage.aspx?PRID=1548810, accessed on 19 August 2021; other media reports.

161 Ministry of Defence, "Cdr Abhilash Tomy, KC reaches Visakhapatnam safely."

162 Reuters, "Indian Navy Locates Capsized Chinese Fishing Vessel, Life Raft." Reuters, 19 May 2023, https://www.reuters.com/world/india/indian-navy-locates-capsized-chinese-fishing-vessel-2023-05-19/, accessed on 28 May 2023.

163 Ministry of Defence, "Indian Navy, Air Force and Coast Guard Pressed into Service for the Search of the Missing Malaysian Airline Aircraft," Press Information Bureau, 13 March 2014, https://pib.gov.in/newsite/PrintRelease.aspx?relid=104596, accessed on 19 August 2021.

164 "Lost Malaysian Aircraft - Indian Navy Joins search operations," Indian Navy, https://www.indiannavy.nic.in/content/lost-malaysian-aircraft-indian-navy-joins-search-operations, accessed on 19 August 2021.

165 Indo-Asian News Service, "All 29 people on board missing AN-32 plane presumed dead, says Indian Air Force," Firstpost, 15 September 2016, https://www.firstpost.com/india/all-29-people-on-board-missing-an-32-plane-presumed-dead-says-indian-air-force-3006142.html, accessed on 31 August 2021; Press Trust of India, "No concrete evidence emerged with respect to IAF AN-32 that went missing in 2016: Government," *Economic Times*, 28 November 2019, https://economictimes.indiatimes.com/news/defence/no-concrete-evidence-emerged-with-respect-to-iaf-an-32-that-went-missing-in-2016-government/articleshow/72271433.cms?utm_source=contentofinterest&utm_medium=text&utm_campaign=cppst, accessed on 31 August 2021.

166 Abhishek Bhalla, "Indian Navy to rush in assets to help Singapore in case of submarine disasters," *India Today*, January 21, 2021, https://www.indiatoday.in/india/story/indian-navy-to-rush-in-assets-to-help-singapore-in-case-of-submarine-disasters-1761169-2021-01-21, accessed on 01 February 2021.

167 Ministry of Defence, "Deep Sea Submarine Rescue System Inducted into the Indian Navy at Mumbai," Press Information Bureau, 12 December 2018, https://pib.gov.in/PressReleasePage.aspx?PRID=1555672, accessed on 14 January 2021. The rescue is limited to 14 crew at a time.

168 Ministry of Defence, "Indian Navy dispatches its Deep Submergence Rescue Vessel to support Search and Rescue of Missing Indonesian Submarine," Press Information Bureau, 22 April 2021, https://pib.gov.in/PressReleasePage.aspx?PRID=1713390, accessed on 19 August 2021.

169 Dzirhan Mahadzir, "Chinese Navy to Help with Recovery of Indonesian Sub Wreck," United States Naval Institute News, May 4, 2021, https://news.usni.org/2021/05/04/chinese-navy-to-help-with-recovery-of-indonesian-sub-wreck, accessed on 19 August 2021.

170 Cabinet Committee on Economic Affairs, "Cabinet approves Deep Ocean Mission," Press Information Bureau, June 16, 2021, https://pib.gov.in/PressReleasePage.aspx?PRID=1727525, accessed on 19 August 2021; G.A. Ramdass, "Eminent Person's Lecture (EPL)," National Maritime Foundation Eminent Person Lecture Series, May 11, 2021, https://

maritimeindia.org/events/eminent-persons-lecture-dr-g-a-ramadass/?occurrence=2021-05-11, accessed on 20 August 2023.

171 T. Rajkumar, "Challenges of Salvage Operations in the IOR and Beyond." Presentation at Webinar on "Anti-Submarine Warfare & Underwater Search & Recovery: A New Perspective based on the Underwater Domain Awareness (UDA) Framework," Maritime Research Centre, 26 June 2021.

172 "Marine Environment Protection," Indian Coast Guard, https://indiancoastguard.gov.in/content/246_3_MarineEnvironmentProtection.aspx, accessed on 28 May 2023.

173 "Dornier aircraft launched from Chennai for firefighting aboard MT New Diamond off Sri Lanka coast," Asian News International, 08 September 2020, https://www.aninews.in/news/national/general-news/dornier-aircraft-launched-from-chennai-for-fire-fighting-aboard-mt-new-diamond-off-sri-lanka-coast20200908093501/, accessed on 13 January 2021.

174 Embassy of India, Mauritius(@HCI_PortLouis), Twitter post, 16 August 2020, https://twitter.com/hci_portlouis/status/1294959722290753538?lang=en [Not available subsequently], accessed on 13 January 2021.

175 Ministry of Defence, "Year End Review – 2020 Ministry of Defence."

176 Ministry of Defence, "Year End Review – 2020 Ministry of Defence." *Sagar Araksha* means Sea Protection.

177 Ministry of Defence, "Year End Review – 2020 Ministry of Defence."

178 Ministry of Defence, "Indian Coast Guard will celebrate 45th Raising Day," Press Information Bureau, January 31, 2021, https://pib.gov.in/Pressreleaseshare.aspx?PRID=1693670, accessed on 28 May 2023.

179 Ministry of Defence, "Assistance to Sri Lanka – Operation SAGAR AARAKSHA II," Press Information Bureau, 03 June 2021, https://pib.gov.in/PressReleseDetailm.aspx?PRID=1724313, accessed on 18 August 2021.

180 Ministry of Defence, "Indian Naval Ship (INS) Sarvekshak Departs Colombo on completion of survey assistance," Press Information Bureau, 02 July 2021, https://pib.gov.in/PressReleaseIframePage.aspx?PRID=1732390 , accessed on 18 August 2021.

181 UN Security Council, "Presidential Statement."

182 In 2021, in India, three major events discussed issues related to regional MDA and information sharing. The first event was jointly organised by the NMF along with the CRIMARIO Project and the IFC-IOR (June 2021), the second was the Indo-Pacific Regional Dialogue (October 2021), and finally was a regional workshop organised by the IFC-IOR and CRIMARIO (December 2021). Taken together, these events provided a multiregional perspective on MDA and information sharing. The author was speaker in one of the events and the rapporteur for the other two. The points expressed in this section draw extensively from the deliberations at the three events.

183 "Agreements for Exchange of White Shipping Information," *Business Standard*, 25 November 2016, https://www.business-standard.com/article/government-press-release/agreements-for-exchange-of-white-shipping-information-116112400631_1.html, accessed on 17 January 2021.

184 Dinakar Peri, "India looks at integrating more countries into coastal radar network," *The Hindu*, 20 December 2020, https://www.thehindu.com/news/national/india-looks-at-integrating-more-countries-into-coastal-radar-network/article33379243.ece, accessed on

17 January 2021.

185 Dinakar Peri, "India looks at integrating more countries into coastal radar network."

186 Rajat Pandit, "India strengthens its eagle-eye over Indian Ocean with pacts," *The Times of India,* 13 December 2018, https://timesofindia.indiatimes.com/india/india-strengthens-its-eagle-eye-over-indian-ocean-with-pacts-with-different-countries/articleshow/67081923.cms, accessed on 17 January 2021; various.

187 Ministry of Defence, "Visit of Adm R Hari Kumar, CNS to New Zealand," Press Information Bureau, 02 October 2022, https://pib.gov.in/PressReleasePage.aspx?PRID=1864538, accessed on 20 August 2023.

188 Press Trust of India, "India signs ascension pact to the 30-member Trans Regional Maritime," 11 December 2018, https://economictimes.indiatimes.com/news/defence/india-signs-ascension-pact-to-the-30-member-trans-regional-maritime-network/articleshow/67037915.cms?from=mdr, accessed on 17 January 2021.

189 Ministry of Defence, "Raksha Mantri Inaugurates Information Fusion Centre – Indian Ocean Region (IFC-IOR)," Press Information Bureau, 22 December 2018, https://pib.gov.in/Pressreleaseshare.aspx?PRID=1557074, accessed on 03 January 2022.

190 "About IFC," Information Fusion Centre, Singapore, https://www.ifc.org.sg/ifc2web/app_pages/User/common/aboutus.cshtml, accessed on 17 January 20211; Dinakar Peri, "India looks at integrating more countries into coastal radar network."

191 Himadri Das, "Maritime Domain Awareness in India: Shifting Paradigms," National Maritime Foundation, 30 September 2021. https://maritimeindia.org/maritime-domain-awareness-in-india-shifting-paradigms/, accessed on 03 January 2022.

192 Prime Minister's Office, "Quad Joint Leaders' Statement,"

193 Press Release, "FACT SHEET: Quad Leaders' Tokyo Summit 2022." The White House, May 23, 2022. https://www.whitehouse.gov/briefing-room/statements-releases/2022/05/23/fact-sheet-quad-leaders-tokyo-summit-2022/, accessed on 20 August 2023; Australian Government: Department of the Prime Minister and Cabinet, "Indo-Pacific Partnership for Maritime Domain Awareness," https://www.pmc.gov.au/resources/quad-leaders-summit-2023/indo-pacific-partnership-maritime-domain-awareness, accessed on 20 August 2023.

194 Australian Government, "Indo-Pacific Partnership for Maritime Domain Awareness." https://www.pmc.gov.au/resources/quad-leaders-summit-2023/indo-pacific-partnership-maritime-domain-awareness, accessed on 20 August 2023.

195 The White House, "FACT SHEET: Quad Leaders' Tokyo Summit 2022." May 23, 2022, https://www.whitehouse.gov/briefing-room/statements-releases/2022/05/23/fact-sheet-quad-leaders-tokyo-summit-2022/, accessed on 20 August 2023.

196 C. Raja Mohan, "India, the Quad and Indo-Pacific Maritime Security." Institute of South Asian Studies, national University of Singapore, June 03, 2022, https://www.isas.nus.edu.sg/papers/india-the-quad-and-indo-pacific-maritime-security/, accessed on 20 August 2023.

197 Shruti Pandalai and Abhay Kumar Singh, "Quad's Maritime Domain Awareness Initiative Needs Time to Deliver," Manohar Parrikar Institute for Defence Studies and Analyses, 24 June 2022, https://idsa.in/idsacomments/Quads-Maritime-Domain-240622, accessed on 20 August 2023.

198 Ministry of Defence, "Press Statement by Raksha Mantri Shri Raj Nath Singh following

India- USA"

199 "MSCHOA and Maritime Domain Awareness. How?," Maritime Security Centre-Horn of Africa, https://on-shore.mschoa.org/mschoa-and-maritime-domain-awareness-how/#Mercury, accessed on 03 January 2022.

200 Integrated Headquarters of Ministry of Defence (Navy), *Ensuring Secure Seas,* 93.

201 "The Training Command," Indian Navy, https://www.indiannavy.nic.in/sites/default/themes/indiannavy/images/pdf/the-training-command.pdf, accessed on 12 January 2022.

202 "Home," Indian Navy International Alumni Portal, https://www.alumni.indiannavy.gov.in/index, accessed on 12 January 2022; Ministry of Defence, "Year End Review – 2021 of Ministry of Defence."

203 Indian Navy, "6th Maritime Security Course Concludes at Naval War College Goa." https://www.indiannavy.nic.in/content/6th-maritime-security-course-concludes-naval-war-college-goa, accessed on 20 August 2023.

204 "Administrative Instructions," Indian Navy, https://www.indiannavy.nic.in/sites/default/themes/indiannavy/images/pdf/administrative-instructions.pdf, accessed on 28 February 2022.

205 "Indian Technical And Economic Cooperation (ITEC) Programme," ITEC Programme, MEA, https://www.itecgoi.in/about, accessed on 28 February 2022.

206 Integrated Headquarters of Ministry of Defence (Navy), *Ensuring Secure Seas*, 93-94.

207 Ministry of Defence, *Annual Report 2018-19*, 52.

208 Press Trust of India, "Indian Navy seeks placement opportunities for veteran sailors in Qatar Navy," India TV, 10 November 2019, accessed on 28 February 2022.

209 The author attended the GMS 2022 as a moderator on a session for training cooperation.

210 Integrated Headquarters of Ministry of Defence (Navy), *Ensuring Secure Seas*, 94.

211 "Military and military-technical cooperation," Embassy of the Russian Federation in the Republic of India, https://india.mid.ru/en/countries/bilateral-relations/military_and_military_technical_cooperation/, accessed on 28 February 2022.

212 "India-Russia Defence Cooperation," Embassy of India, Moscow, https://indianembassy-moscow.gov.in/india-russia-defence-cooperation.php, accessed on 28 February 2022.

213 Press Trust of India, "Indian military cannot operate effectively without Russian supplied equipment: CRS report," *The Economic Times*, 27 October 2021, https://economictimes.indiatimes.com/news/defence/indian-military-cannot-operate-effectively-without-russian-supplied-equipment-crs-report/articleshow/87293784.cms?from=mdr, accessed on 28 February 2022.

214 Ministry of Defence, "Ministry of Defence - Year End Review2022."

215 Kamal Joshi, "Boosting Presence in China's Backyard, India Gifts Missile Corvette INS Kirpan to Vietnam," Republic World, 22 July 2023.https://www.republicworld.com/india-news/general-news/boosting-presence-in-chinas-backyard-india-gifts-missile-corvette-ins-kirpan-to-vietnam-articleshow.html, accessed on 20 August 2023.

216 Joshi, "Boosting Presence in China's Backyard, India Gifts Missile Corvette INS Kirpan."

217 Anirban Bhaumik, "Myanmar commissions submarine gifted by India," *The Deccan Herald*, 26 December 2020, https://www.deccanherald.com/international/myanmar-commissions-submarine-gifted-by-india-931931.html, accessed on 28 February 2022.

218 Ministry of Defence, "Year End Review – 2019 Ministry of Defence."

219 "Foreign Cooperation," National Hydrographic Office, https://hydrobharat.gov.in/

international-co-op/introduction/, accessed on 12 January 2022.

220 "Chart 5020: Indian Maritime Safety and Security Chart," https://hydrobharat.gov.in/wp-content/uploads/2019/07/5010.pdf, accessed on 08 January 2022.

221 Abhishek Bhalla, "Eye on China, India Sets up Coastal Radars in neighbourhood," *India Today, 27* November 2020, https://www.indiatoday.in/india/story/india-sets-up-coastal-radars-in-neighbourhood-to-keep-eye-on-china-1744751-2020-11-27, accessed on 16 January 2021.

222 Bhalla, "Eye on China, India Sets up Coastal Radars in Neighbourhood."

223 Shubhajit Roy, "Explained: BECA, and the importance of 3 foundational pacts of India-US Defence cooperation," *The New Indian Express*, November 03, 2020, https://indianexpress.com/article/explained/beca-india-us-trade-agreements-rajnath-singh-mike-pompeo-6906637/, accessed on 17 January 2021.

224 Ministry of Defence, "Signing of Agreements with other Countries," Press Information Bureau, 05 February 2018, https://pib.gov.in/PressReleaseIframePage.aspx?PRID=1519147, accessed on 17 January 2021.

225 Ministry of Defence, "List of MoUs signed between India and Singapore during visit of Prime Minister to Singapore," Press Information Bureau, June 01, 2018, https://pib.gov.in/Pressreleaseshare.aspx?PRID=1541259, accessed on 17 January 2021.

226 "India-France Joint Statement on Visit of Prime Minister to France (22-23 August 2019)," Ministry of External Affairs, 22 August 2021, https://www.mea.gov.in/bilateral-documents.htm?dtl/31755/IndiaFrance+Joint+Statement+on+Visit+of+Prime+Minister+to+ France+2223+August+2019, accessed on 12 January 2022.

227 Ministry of Defence, "Raksha Mantri Shri Rajnath Singh holds talks with Minister of National Defence of Republic of Korea, Mr. Jeong Kyeongdoo in Seoul," Press Information Bureau, 06 September 2020, https://pib.gov.in/PressReleaseIframePage.aspx?PRID=1584291, accessed on 17 January 2021.

228 Ministry of Defence, "Year End Review – 2020 Ministry of Defence."

229 Ministry of Defence, "Year End Review – 2020 Ministry of Defence."

230 Ministry of Defence, "Full text of Raksha Mantri's press statement after India-US 2+2 dialogue," Press Information Bureau, 06 September 2018, https://pib.gov.in/PressReleaseIframePage.aspx?PRID=1545151, accessed on 17 January 2021; Dinakar Peri, "What is COMCASA?," *The Hindu,* 06 September 2018, https://www.thehindu.com/news/national/what-is-comcasa/article24881039.ece, accessed on 17 January 2021; Ministry of Defence, " Press Statement by Raksha Mantri Shri Raj Nath Singh following India- USA 2+2 Meeting in New Delhi on 27 October 2020," Press Information Bureau, 27 October 2020, https://pib.gov.in/PressReleseDetailm.aspx?PRID=1667841, accessed on 17 January 2021.

231 Rajat Pandit, "India-US gear up to share maritime military intel," *Times of India,* 07 December 2020.

232 Peri, "What is COMCASA?"

233 Roy, "Explained: BECA, and the importance of 3 foundational pacts of India-US defence cooperation."

234 Peri, "What is COMCASA?"

235 Peri, "What is COMCASA?"

236 Pranab Dhal Samanta, "First Secure Link Between India, US Navies Set Up ," *The*

Economic Times, 02 April 2019, https://economictimes.indiatimes.com/news/defence/first-secure-link-between-india-us-navies-set-up/articleshow/68681214.cms, accessed on 17 January 2021.

237 Press Trust of India, "India, U.S. Ink Strategic Defence Pact," *The Hindu*, 27 October 2022, https://www.thehindu.com/news/national/india-us-ink-strategic-defence-pact/article32953275.ece, accessed on 28 February 2022.

238 Pandit, "India-US gear up to share maritime military intel."

239 Press Trust of India, "Congressional Committee Wants India, Japan and S Korea at Par with Five Eyes on Intelligence Sharing," *The Economic Times*, 14 December 2019, https://economictimes.indiatimes.com/news/defence/congressional-committee-wants-india-japan-and-s-korea-at-par-with-five-eyes-on-intelligence-sharing/articleshow/72587975.cms?from=mdr, accessed on 29 May 2023.

240 Dalip Singh, "US Navy Inks Agreement with L&T, to Also Tie up with Mazagon Dock and Goa Shipyard," *BusinessLine*, 23 June 2023. https://www.thehindubusinessline.com/news/national/us-navy-inks-agreement-with-lt-to-also-tie-up-with-mazagon-dock-and-goa-shipyard/article67000603.ece

241 Singh, "US Navy Inks Agreement with L&T."

242 Singh, "US Navy Inks Agreement with L&T."

243 Singh, "US Navy Inks Agreement with L&T."

244 Swaminathan Anklesaria Aiyar, "Lessons for India from Af retreat: US is an undependable ally." *Economic Times*, 29 August 2021, http://timesofindia.indiatimes.com/articleshow/85717863.cms?utm_source=contentofinterest&utm_medium=text&utm_campaign=cppst_prime, accessed on 03 September 2021.

5

Key Issues

> *...navies and foreign ministries need to develop a strategic approach to naval diplomacy, designed to integrate it effectively with all other relevant aspects of a country's security policy.... For their part, navies need to develop a rigorous way of thinking about naval diplomacy (perhaps even a doctrine?) and reflect the importance of the mission in their budgetary and force structure decisions.*
>
> —Geoffery Till[1]

The need for international cooperation is integral to the concept of maritime security, and its governance. However, notwithstanding the overall progress in strengthening cooperation for maritime security, as India strives for a greater role in the global order there is indeed room for furthering maritime security cooperative endeavours. Having explored the Indian approach to maritime security cooperation, and its various dimensions, this chapter endeavours to dwell upon some of the key issues that have a bearing on India's cooperative efforts for maritime security.

Jo Inge Bekkevold and Geoffrey Till identified six main and interlinked issues which will influence the future of the international order at sea. These issues largely focus on the need for balance, including between the maritime and continental domains; great power rivalry and cooperation; access and denial; warfighting and constabulary roles; safeguarding national interests and contributing to collective efforts, and the management of non-traditional threats.[2] The striking feature of the future of the international order, as described by Bekkevold and Till, is the need to balance between competing imperatives. The need for striking balance has important implications for maritime security cooperation and some of these, along with some others, are discussed in succeeding paragraphs.

Competing Interests: The Need for Balance

Despite the significance and increasing priority given by the Indian Government to the maritime domain, including by the political leadership, territorial challenges, such as India's territorial disputes with China and Pakistan, continue to occupy centre-stage in the security discourse in India; even more so lately in view of the ongoing standoff with China in border areas since 2020. Unlike land borders, maritime border delimitation with maritime neighbours, barring the dispute with Pakistan on the Sir Creek, have been peacefully negotiated through agreements and in one case with Bangladesh through arbitration. Consequently, the continental preoccupation of the security establishment, will continue to divert attention away from the national maritime space. However, with India's relative dominance in the Indian Ocean, along with Chinese dependence on the Indian Ocean, gives India an impactful lever, which can be further strengthened by partnerships with the QUAD and other countries. It is therefore imperative for the maritime security agencies, and the wider maritime community, to ensure that the national security establishment retains its focus on the maritime dimensions of security. It is only then that all the dimensions of maritime security, including maritime security cooperation, can be taken forward to the next level. The appointment of the National Maritime Security Coordinator (NMSC) in 2022 is a positive step for stewardship of maritime security at the national level.

India has attempted to leverage security cooperation in the maritime domain to deal with the full spectrum of security threats, both traditional and non-traditional; while the threats may appear distinct there are interlinkages, and security cooperation in one dimension can also influence security cooperation in another. In fact, it has been argued that strategic goals can also achieved through sub-strategic means such as through cooperation in countering non-traditional threats.[3] To hedge against China's growing presence in the Indian Ocean, India has strengthened cooperation with all major naval powers, including acquisition/lease of force multipliers, transfer of defence technology, developing interoperability and information sharing, logistic support, etc. To shape the environment, to develop and retain influence, to promote maritime security, and to counter an increasingly influential China, India has also significantly enhanced maritime security cooperation across the multilateral and the bilateral spectrum with a host of partners, especially in areas of non-traditional and non-military security.

India has amongst the largest and most capable maritime security forces in the world, and without doubt possesses the most powerful navy and the largest coast guard in the IOR; this provides India with adequate flexibility to further maritime security cooperative efforts in the IOR like no other country. Furthermore, the overall mechanisms for maritime security in India have also matured, especially after the '26/11' incident. Risk assessments, funding, and political will, underlined by a long-term vision, are some of the major factors in determining capacity building to counter potential long-term threats. Competing demands and limited funding are particularly major challenges for almost every country. Overall, the need is for harmonising of capacities and capabilities with political will and funding, for without funding, capacity and capabilities cannot be generated, and without political will, capacities and capabilities may remain underutilised.

Within the realm of cooperation, the question that emerges is which should be the most appropriate approach: multilateral, plurilateral (minilateral), or bilateral. While some authors see a movement away from multilateralism, some even calling it dead, others advocate a movement away from bilateralism towards multilateralism.[4] Increasingly, there is a growing proclivity in international relations, and in maritime security cooperation, to gravitate towards plurilateral/sub-regional mechanisms, which bridge the shortcomings of both multilateralism and bilateralism, and are primarily driven by like-mindedness, the convergence of interests, shared values, and common security concerns. Such groupings also reflect collective capacities to deter possible threats across the threat spectrum. However, despite the promise and preference for smaller plurilateral arrangements, large multilateral arrangements, such as IORA and IONS, in which India has invested significantly, are likely to remain relevant. The fact that India is a co-chair or a member of each of the Working Groups and continues to participate actively in affairs of IONS is testimony to this fact. Likewise, bilateralism is to continue to be a bedrock of international nations. The steadfast support of the erstwhile USSR (and now Russia) in the UN Security Council, by exercising its veto power, including in the 1971 India-Pakistan war, and India's abstinence from voting against Russia in UN bodies during its invasion of Ukraine, five decades later in 2022, reflect the enduring value of special strategic partnerships in international relations.

While the underlying rationale for strengthening international cooperation in maritime security is a compelling one, including the fact that robust linkages and cooperative mechanisms have indeed contributed significantly to the growth of the Indian Navy and its capabilities, there is also a need to balance between competing domestic, regional, and international imperatives. Despite India's political vision of a wider role in the IOR and in the Indo-Pacific, in May 2020, General Bipin Rawat, the Chief of Defence Staff (CDS) said that "We are not expeditionary forces that have to deploy around the globe. We have to guard and fight only along our borders and, of course the Indian Ocean Region."[5] The CDS clearly articulated that the principal security priority was to protect the sovereignty of the country from external aggression, and also underscored the limitations of the Indian defence forces. Conversely, engagements other than those for the protection of external aggression can be viewed as unnecessary. This view, however, contradicts the larger Indian vision of maritime security cooperation not only in the IOR, but also in the Indo-Pacific.

In several instances, the US, has had to abort its efforts at extending its influence in distant lands, and so there are historical lessons about the limits of such influence, even by superpowers. Even in the US there are voices that urge for a reorientation of the foreign policy to a neighbourhood first policy, rather than that of intervention in conflicts elsewhere.[6] India is not yet a superpower, and while the desire to play a greater security role in the Indo-Pacific is desirable, and perhaps even necessary, and in line with its standing as a major regional player, it surely needs to be balanced against its own security requirements, including the possibility of dilution of the principal military role of maritime security agencies, in favour of the more 'glamourous' diplomatic role. As an analogy, during the COVID-19 pandemic the government faced criticism for its vaccine diplomacy when there were domestic shortages.[7] The EAM, underscoring the need for international cooperation to fight common challenges, rightly clarified that India could not expect assistance from others if it itself was not forthcoming to assist others. He also stated that such criticism was 'irresponsible' and 'short-sighted.'[8] Naval and maritime security diplomacy perhaps needs to learn a few things from vaccine diplomacy about balancing domestic requirements with international obligations.

There can be little doubt that for a developing power like India with several security challenges, internal and external, the prime responsibility for the defence services will be the defence of the nation from external aggression. As a developing power, and a major player in the region that has enunciated its wider regional maritime policy at the highest political levels, it also needs to act in accordance with its own vision. Indian defence services have gained, and continue to gain, from defence and security cooperation with major countries and therefore the benefits of international maritime security cooperation are hardly questionable in India. Likewise, a host of countries have also benefited from their security cooperation with India. It is perhaps India's turn now to contribute in larger measure, but surely without prejudice to domestic imperatives. The national security complex and the HDO will have to balance a host of competing (and conflicting) imperatives, lest maritime security cooperation face the same criticism as vaccine diplomacy did for neglecting domestic priorities in favour of diplomatic priorities.

Walking the Talk

India has made a strident pitch for international security cooperation in maritime security and India's foreign policy is driven by the interplay of regional and thematic cooperation for maritime security; SAGAR for the IOR, and IPOI for the Indo-Pacific, are the most notable examples.[9] Bilaterally, India's preferred partnerships are categorised as strategic partnerships, and even such strategic partners have been further categorised. As a majority of India's strategic partners are maritime nations, partnerships in the maritime domain, including in maritime security, are a potential area of strengthening strategic cooperation. Roadmaps for pursuing India-France cooperation in ocean governance and blue economy, and India-EU roadmap to 2025 are good examples of taking forward strategic partnerships in the maritime domain in a structured way.[10]

The *Indian Maritime Security Strategy* of the Indian Navy lists primary and secondary areas of interests, which reflect naval prioritisation. As India embraces a multi-polar approach to international relations, pushes for greater plurilateralism, and sees itself as a force for global good, its engagements with countries, regions and regional bodies for security cooperation, particularly maritime security cooperation, are only expanding.[11] As such, being a larger country with greater resources than all of its regional partners, it is expected that India, in accordance with its own vision of being a security provider in the region, does some of the 'heavy-lifting' in the IOR, if not the entire Indo-Pacific. India's multi-dimensional maritime security cooperation initiatives therefore need to embrace different pulls and pushes emerging from its strategic partnerships, foreign policy vision, and defence diplomacy/maritime security imperatives. This is unlike earlier times when its engagements were largely restricted, based on its policy of non-alignment and of strategic autonomy.

In a democratic set up, there are mechanisms between the agencies and ministries concerned and the MEA, the nodal ministry, which ensure coordination of international cooperation efforts, including for maritime security. However, in the absence of coherent overarching strategy, it is likely that there are gaps in cooperative endeavours at one end, and possible overreach at the other. According to a research article of 2009, in the absence of an overarching guidance, the approach to defence diplomacy is 'bottom-up' with the services drawing out plans which are then approved by the Government after consultations.[12] However, it would be naive to assume that 'top-down' approaches driven by strategic concerns are absent. The contours of planning of international cooperative efforts are unlikely to have the granularity of the defence acquisition process, which includes 15 year, five year, and annual plans.[13]

While counting quantitative criterion to measure the success of maritime security cooperation has its own merit, ever increasing cooperative efforts, galvanised by emerging threats, could come at a cost. Overall, with limited budgets and resources, and a threat environment that is volatile, maritime security cooperation initiatives need to be balanced, prioritised, and driven by purposeful ends. Consequently, the need is for the development of a jointly formulated comprehensive long term plan amongst the MEA, MoD, HQIDS, services HQs, which cater for the multiple factors that influence the dynamics of international cooperation, including for maritime security, by incorporating both a 'bottom-up' approach as well as a 'top-down' approach.[14] A prioritised work plan in different time frames (from short-term to long-term), while catering for multiple requirements, would facilitate inter-ministerial alignment and mutual commitment while catering for limited resources and finances, and diverse requirements. Acquisitions/processes too would need to cater for facilitating long term international security cooperation requirements. Such a plan may also need alignment of the Coast Guard's international cooperation efforts with the overall national efforts, and particularly that of the Indian Navy. Further from the strategy/plan, at an operational level, developing an engagement matrix also needs to be developed for maritime security cooperation so that there is clarity on what needs to be achieved in every partnership, like the India-EU Roadmap for the period 2020-25. Furthermore, a dedicated maritime security cooperation plan would need to also consider bodies outside the MoD such as cooperation efforts in customs control, counter drug trafficking, etc. The NMSC could play an important role in this regard.

Impact of Foreign Cooperation on Primary Responsibilities

The primary role of Indian maritime security agencies is to ensure the defence of India, and the security in India's maritime zones. As India envisions a wider role for itself in the IOR and the Indo-Pacific, India has proactively responded to crises in the region especially in the past two decades, including natural disasters and the COVID-19 pandemic, and its foreign cooperation efforts which have been increasing rapidly and have been widely appreciated. The rise of China, and the increasing presence of the PLA(N) and other Chinese vessels in the IOR, has been worrisome for the Indian security establishment and consequently, there has also been a rise of partnership amongst likeminded nations, such as the QUAD, which aim to uphold rules and values which are increasingly under threat in the emerging world order. While the need to enhance India's international efforts in maritime security and to develop partnerships is understandable and needed, an increase in foreign cooperation initiatives could lead to dilution of focus from the primary roles of maritime security agencies. There is therefore a need to guard against hidden costs which come with such engagements and the possible unintended consequences of such engagements. There is also a need to guard against the possibility of unwittingly getting entrenched in situations which may not be a primary interest for India.

While making an objective analysis of the gains may be a challenging exercise, there may be a need for a periodic subjective cost-benefit analysis of continually increasing foreign cooperation efforts vis-à-vis the primary roles that maritime security agencies need to perform; the defence of India in the case of the Indian Navy and in the case of the Indian Coast Guard the security of the maritime zones. Such an analysis may also need to be undertaken objectively, purely from a financial perspective, for optimal utilisation of budgetary allocation. At the bare minimum, an 'annual report' has been recommended which would "assist in creation of desired institutional memory and maintenance of requisite focus on quality vis-à-vis the quantity of events."[15]

Need for Holistic Approach to Cooperation

Another facet of having greater say in regional and international maritime security affairs is through engagements with international and regional bodies dealing with maritime issues in leadership roles. China, for example, has worked at securing more clout in the UN for over a decade and as of 2020 Chinese representatives were holding leadership positions in four of the 15 specialised agencies and groups of the UN.[16] The ability to participate in international and multilateral administrative bodies, both maritime and non-maritime, and the ability to deploy knowledgeable diplomatic personnel in support of maritime-related interagency activities are two of the capabilities required under the 'diplomatic and foreign affairs support' sub-function for maritime security governance.[17]

India has slowly and steadily enhanced its representation in top positions in international organisations/bodies. In recent years, three significant elections won by India include that of Dr Neeru Chadha as judge of the International Tribunal for the Law of the Sea (ITLOS) in 2017), membership of the Council of the IMO under Category 'B' in 2017, and election of Mr K Natrajan as the Executive Director of the ReCAAP ISC in 2021.[18] Dr Chadha is the first Indian woman to be elected as judge of the ITLOS and reportedly only the second Indian woman to occupy a top position in the UN system after Ms Vijay Lakshmi Pandit who was the 8th President of the UN General Assembly between 1953-54. Considering the plethora of international and regional organisations dealing with maritime (and maritime security) issues, enhancing representation at multiple levels in international/regional bodies would not only be reflective of India's willingness to shoulder wider international responsibilities, but would also contribute to its own long term capacity building. Veterans and retired personnel could also be employed in such efforts. In addition to representations, there is also a need to build capacity by the education and training of Indians in international maritime institutions, such as the World Maritime University (WMU), Malmo; International Maritime Law Institute (IMLI), Malta; the International Institute of Humanitarian Law (IIHL), San Remo, etc.

At a more fundamental level, there is a need for greater cross-pollination amongst Indian agencies for maritime security cooperation. While the NWC does conduct the GMC and Maritime Security Course, there is no Indian equivalent course for Indian agencies on areas of maritime security cooperation. The Sushma Swaraj Institute of Foreign Service (SSIFS) has included maritime issues and maritime security in some of its programmes, and considering the impetus to maritime security from the foreign ministry, there is perhaps scope for further enhancement of training efforts on issues related to maritime security for both Indian and foreign diplomats, and for setting up/strengthening linkages with the NWC and the NMF.

Human Resource Development: Specialised Cadre

As per the Lowy Institute Global Diplomacy Index (2019), India, with close to 190 diplomatic missions, including 123 embassies/high commissions, 54 consulates/consulates-general, five permanent missions, and four other representations is ranked 12th in world and 3rd in Asia.(after China and Japan).[19] India's maritime security cooperation efforts need to be pursued by Indian embassies/high commissions/consulates and the Defence/Naval Advisors/ Attaches (DAs/NAs) are the nodal points for pursuing such efforts. In 2018, India had resident DAs in 44 countries, who were accredited to 95 countries.[20] In 2020, the Raksha Mantri stated that towards strengthening defence diplomacy 10 more DAs could be appointed.[21] In contrast, the US Defence Attaché System is represented in over 140 countries.[22]

The generic role of a DA/NA include pursuance and advocacy of national military and security interests; representing national military authorities/ security agencies in the host nation; liaising with host country agencies; acting as military advisor to the ambassador/high commissioner; make assessments of events with a bearing on the host country; overseeing and managing military outreach and other cooperative efforts bilaterally, multilaterally or regionally; promotion of defence industry; coordinating crisis response, etc.[23] Oftentimes a naval officer may be the only maritime or marine specialist in an embassy or High Commission further expanding the role of the DA/NA. In 2018, the first annual conference of Indian DAs with the objective of enhancing the role of the DAs "towards implementation of India's defence cooperation and engagement with foreign countries."[24] Such efforts also include encouragement of participation in events like the DEFEXPO [Defence Exposition].[25] The annual conference typically includes sessions with the MoD, including the Department of Defence Production, Service HQs, DRDO, Defence PSUs and industry representatives.[26] Towards achieving the objectives of the Draft Defence Production Policy (2018) which sets an export target of Rs 35,000 crore, in May 2019, a scheme for export promotion by the DAs was approved.[27] The introduction of these measures point to the increasing importance being accorded to the DA community.

Increasingly, the role of the DA/NA is no longer restricted to 'defence' cooperation, but also security cooperation, including maritime security cooperation.[28] The role of a DA being a specialised role, different from the 'normal' role of defence officers, countries approached the position of DA differently in terms of qualifying requirements, selection processes, training, tenure, reporting lines, and the nature of employment.[29] Typically, in the US, training for the post of a DA includes language training, specialised training, as well as cultural training.[30] While little material is available on the DA system in India, anecdotally it is apparent that the DA system typically is tenure appointment, and that there is no dedicated training facility for DAs akin to that in the US.

From a maritime security cooperation perspective, the range of areas for cooperation in the past decade have grown exponentially placing added demands on the DA community, and with the continuing focus on enhancing international maritime security cooperation, including at the UN. There is a need for reforming the DA system to progress defence and maritime security cooperation to ensure that expertise developed is not lost and ploughed back into the system. As DAs/NAs are the focal points for maritime security cooperation, a dedicated core cadre of foreign cooperation personnel, and formalised training mechanisms are some of the measures that merit attention, including for the staff.[31] Notably, in a generic context in relation to the 'diplomatic and foreign affairs support' sub-function for maritime security, the need for recruitment and maintenance of professional staff with requisite expertise has been included as a specific capability requirement.[32] Since maritime security itself encompasses multiple dimensions, the structures within stakeholder ministries/department/agencies, which also contribute to specific dimensions of maritime security, must also foster foreign cooperation and necessary linkages must be established between the agency and the DA/NA who may be the only maritime security specialist in the concerned Indian embassy.

MDA and Information Sharing Imperatives[33]

Technological Imperatives. Technology has been one of the most important drivers for the paradigm shift in domain awareness; for example, the increasing availability of the internet, for information sharing has been a facilitator for information sharing. Notwithstanding, it is a fact that limitations in material wherewithal are constraining the ability of countries to both, share information, and to respond to security threats. It is also a fact that niche technologies are finding increasing utility in both the development of MDA and in information sharing, such as the use of satellite technologies for IR detection and Synthetic Aperture Radar (SAR) imaging, as well as for monitoring of vessel-borne electronic emissions. Progressively, there would be a need for international collaborations in the development and adoption of niche technologies, and for sharing such technologies with nations that may not have the resources for doing so. Another area that requires niche technologies is that of Underwater Domain Awareness (UDA), an emerging area of interest in some Indo-Pacific countries. Partnering in developing UDA, in particular, may need 'tighter' partnerships.[34] A growing need has also been felt for a common platform that can facilitate the interfacing of information systems that are operated in a standalone mode by individual IFCs, such as the Indian Ocean Regional Information Sharing and Incident Management Network (IORIS) developed by EU CRIMARIO, IFC Real-time Info-sharing System (IRIS), Merchant Shipping Information System (MSIS) systems developed and used by the EU, Singapore, and India respectively.[35] The Share.IT platform, developed by EU CRIMARIO, can facilitate interoperability between information systems.[36]

Therefore, MDA and information sharing systems also need to conform with global standards that promote interoperability. The overbearing quantum of data and limited human capacity to process the data makes the use advanced algorithms, Artificial Intelligence/Machine Learning (AI/ML), and Big Data Analytics (BDA) an imperative to uncover patterns and trends, and possibly also provide predictive features. Considering the growing threats in cyberspace, MDA systems and information sharing systems also must be protected from threats in cyberspace and must develop resilience. Finally, MDA-related technologies must be made cost-effective, and if India is to be an exporter of such systems, also cost-competitive. While technology must indeed be leveraged to facilitate seamless sharing of information and develop interoperability amongst partners, there is a need to underscore the fact that despite the overwhelming focus on technology, information sharing in any form has value, and is not always technology-dependent.

Human Resources Development. Related to capacity building is also the need for human resource development. Any system is only as good as the people who operate the system. Collaborative efforts in training, co-development of solutions, conduct of workshops, 'train-the-trainer' programmes, and positioning of ILOs in information centres from the widest array of maritime sectors are possible ways for development of human resources to facilitate international information sharing.

Regional Cooperation. Presently, there is no overarching regional cooperative framework for MDA and information sharing in the IOR, and consequently, a recommendation for a pan-IOR information grid has been proposed linking all stakeholders in the region.[37] While sub-regional architectures have been operationalised in some regions, such as under the aegis of the IMO and the Indian Ocean Commission (IOC) in the western IOR, similar architectures could be developed in other regions as well. The Information Sharing and Interoperability IONS Working Group (IS & IIWG) has been deliberating on the modalities for developing an information sharing mechanism amongst IONS members. This initiative needs to be given due impetus to achieve the overall objectives of regional MDA. Initiatives under the IORA and BIMSTEC construct also have the potential to support regional coordination. There are inherent challenges to facilitate information sharing amongst large constructs, and considering capacity constraints there is possibly a need to harmonise overall efforts, perhaps through interfacing of smaller groupings/centres. India, with extensive linkages across the IOR, and active participation in regional forums, can play a lead role in developing a regional architecture. Even then, developing a pan-IOR information grid soon appears difficult as countries can often face challenges even in developing a national information sharing grid. Likewise, there is a case for harmonising and integrating with regional initiatives led by international organisations such as INTERPOL and UNODC.

In any regional framework, there is likely to be in inherent disparity in the exchange of information, driven by multiple factors such as geography, available technology, national capabilities, etc. It is natural that some members would have the capacity and the capability to share larger amounts of information than others. However, aggregated information from multiple sources has the potential to significantly enrich regional MDA, and despite the disparity, relevant actionable information can provide asymmetric gains. In any collective framework, every bit and byte of information exchanged, therefore, counts. In short, the possibility of information disparity by itself should not be a barrier for information sharing.

Strengthening Existing Linkages. As confidence grows, existing linkages can be further expanded to include the exchanging of more granular data, and also go beyond sharing of white shipping information. Likewise, there is the scope of expanding the basket of information sharing engagements (agreements and partnerships) with more partners; and also leveraging other existing mechanisms for maritime security cooperation, such as Coast Guard MOUs, to strengthen information sharing.

Legal Imperatives. Another issue that merits attention is the legal framework for information sharing. Domestic legal processes to facilitate international engagement in information sharing has been identified as a major challenge; while legal processes are inherently complex in any democratic country, bureaucratic procedures, too can also be protracted and long-winding. Notwithstanding formal agreements, such as the WSIE, information is also shared through informal non-binding arrangements on 'good faith' considerations. While informal arrangements are a good start and have utility (the Mercury net is a good example), in the long term informal arrangements cannot be a substitute for formal partnerships which ensure relatively greater reliability. Moving forward, as the MDA concept strives for greater integration there may also be issues of private, privileged, and proprietary information of private players, the sharing of which could have legal ramifications. Therefore, information sharing agreements need to also cater to related provisions.

Trust Building. Whereas the discourse of MDA and information sharing is largely focused on technology, cooperative endeavours need to be based on mutual and collective trust. While technology is the facilitator, maritime cooperation for MDA can only succeed if it is based on trust. Trust cannot be surged, and is patiently developed over time; trust can also potentially be irretrievably lost, if compromised. Countries engage with multiple partners simultaneously, including those with adversarial relationships; however, such partnerships, are, by themselves, not prejudicial to the interest of parties, unless undermined. While the exchange of liaison officers has been recognised as one of the ways for trust-building for information sharing, trust can also be developed through other means, such as exercises and virtual engagements. With multiple sources of information and inter-linkages, trust can also be eroded, when it becomes clear that information is being withheld, or misused. Therefore, trust will remain at the core of any cooperative information sharing endeavour.

Domestic Imperatives. A robust domestic framework in the form of capabilities and capacities, developed organically, as has been largely done in India, or through international partnerships, as in several littoral countries of the IOR, or a hybrid approach, involving organic development and foreign assistance, is a facilitator, but by no means the only prerequisite for international information sharing. However, domestic institutional mechanisms need to be strengthened, and domestic initiatives streamlined and synergised. The National Maritime Domain Awareness (NMDA) project in India is a case-in-point. Capacity building efforts to address the constraints (domestically or for partners), also need to be taken at multiple levels of domestic governance, viz by states and by the Centre. Further, since MDA is not an end by itself, there is also a need for complementary approaches to HOA capacity building, especially in operational units such as ships, craft, and aircraft, for transforming

MDA into effective operational response at sea. Academia can also play an important part in developing awareness, including amongst the political leadership. Likewise, international partners need to develop a clear understanding of the domestic structures of proposed partners to develop partnerships; Track 1.5 and Track 2 organisations can provide a platform to facilitate better understanding of MDA government structures.

In brief, strengthening regional cooperation in MDA and information sharing needs a multi-dimensional approach and different tools in the toolkit; the requirement is for customised approaches to address information sharing needs: there is no 'one-size-fits-all' solution. Second, there is a need for sustained and honest conversations, dialogues, and engagements to develop trust and understanding, a prerequisite for furthering information sharing; despite the preponderance of technology, human factors, such as trust, will continue to shape the dimensions of future engagements. Finally, the need is to 'walk-the-talk' on regional cooperation in MDA and information sharing.

Having examined India's approach to maritime security cooperation in previous chapters this chapter focused on some of the key issues associated with furthering maritime security cooperation. The need to balance between competing requirements emerges as one of the key issues in progressing maritime security cooperation. In the last thirty years, there has been significant progress in furthering maritime security cooperation, however, it does appear that there is scope for refining processes. Amongst others, budgets, plans, and capacity, are key requirements for an effective maritime security cooperation. The NMSC will have an important role to play in developing a coherent and integrated approach, and in coordinating maritime security cooperation efforts in consultation with maritime stakeholders and the MEA.

NOTES

1 Geoffrey Till, *Seapower: A Guide for the 21st Century*, (Oxford, Routledge, 2013)), 285
2 Bekkevold and Till, eds., *International Order at Sea: How it·is challenged; How it is maintained*, 308.
3 Frédéric Grare and Mélissa Levaillant, "Getting Real about the Indo-Pacific Redefining European Approach to Maritime Security," The Hague Centre for Strategic Studies, March 2022, https://hcss.nl/wp-content/uploads/2022/03/GTC4-Levaillant-Grare-HCSS-2022.pdf, accessed on 14 March 2022.
4 Sawan, "Problems and prospects of maritime security"; Upadhyaya, "Maritime Security

Cooperation," 298.

5 Rajat Pandit, "Forces must shun imports, go for 'Make in India', says Gen Bipan Rawat," *The Times of India*, 10 May 2020, http://timesofindia.indiatimes.com/articleshow/75652962.cms?from=mdr&utm_source=contentofinterest&utm_medium=text&utm_campaign=cppst, accessed on 03 September 2021.

6 "Is Captain America Ready to Reboot? US Should Give Up On Its National Myth" *The Times of India*, 27 August 2021, https://timesofindia.indiatimes.com/blogs/toi-edit-page/is-captain-america-ready-to-reboot-us-should-give-up-on-its-national-myth/, accessed on 20 August 2023.

7 Suhasini Haider, "What went wrong with India's vaccine diplomacy?" *The Hindu*, 23 April 2021, https://www.thehindu.com/news/national/worldview-with-suhasini-haidar-what-went-wrong-with-indias-vaccine-diplomacy/article34394622.ece, accessed on 03 September 2021.

8 Nayanima Basu, "Those questioning Covid vaccine exports are short-sighted, 'really irresponsible': Jaishankar," *The Print*, 19 April 2021, https://theprint.in/india/those-questioning-covid-vaccine-exports-are-short-sighted-really-irresponsible-jaishankar/642462/, accessed on 14 March 2022.

9 Ministry of External Affairs "Foreign Secretary's Vimarsh Talk on "Global Rebalancing and India's Foreign Policy", Vivekananda International Foundation, June 30, 2021, https://www.mea.gov.in/Speeches-Statements.htm?dtl/33965/Foreign_Secretarys_Vimarsh_Talk_on_Global_Rebalancing_and_ Indias_Foreign_Policy_Vivekananda_ International_ Foundation_June_30_2021, accessed on 11 October 2021.

10 "India-France Roadmap on The Blue Economy And Ocean Governance," Ministry of External Affairs, 20 February 2022, https://www.mea.gov.in/bilateral-documents.htm?dtl/34882/INDIAFRANCE+ROADMAP+ON+THE+BLUE+ ECONOMY+AND+OCEAN +GOVERNANCE, accessed on 17 March 2022.

11 Ministry of External Affairs, Speech by Foreign Secretary on on "Global Rebalancing and India's Foreign Policy", Vivekananda International Foundation, June 30, 2021, https://www.mea.gov.in/Speeches-Statements.htm?dtl/33965/Foreign_Se, accessed on 10 October 2021.

12 Arvind Dutta, "Role of India's Defence Cooperation Initiatives in Meeting the Foreign Policy Goals," *Journal of Defence Studies* 3, no. 3 (July 2009): 33, https://www.idsa.in/system/files/jds_3_3_adutta.pdf, accessed on 20 August 2023.

13 "Defence Acquisition," Integrated Defence Staff, https://www.ids.nic.in/defence-acquisition.php, accessed on 11 October 2021; Defence acquisitions and capability development are undertaken through a 15 year 'Technology Perspective and Capability Roadmap' (TPCR), services Long Term Perspective Plan (LTPP) and the 15-year Long Term Integrated Perspective Plan (LTIPP), which is further divided into five-year Service Capital Acquisition Plans (SCAP) and two year roll-on Annual Acquisition Plans (AAP)

14 Dutta, "Role of India's Defence Cooperation Initiatives in Meeting the Foreign Policy Goals,".33

15 Dutta, "Role of India's Defence Cooperation Initiatives in Meeting the Foreign Policy Goals," 43.

16 Yaroslav Trofimov, Drew Hinshaw and Kate O'Keeffe, "How China is Taking Over

International Organizations, One Vote at a Time," *Wall Street Journal,* 29 September 2020, https://www.wsj.com/articles/how-china-is-taking-over-international-organizations-one-vote-at-a-time-11601397208, accessed on 11 October 2021.

17 U.S. Government, *Maritime Security Sector Reform,* 22.

18 "Dr Neeru Chadha bags top United Nations post, becomes second Indian woman to make this achievement after Lakshmi Pandit," *Financial Express*, June 15, 2017, https://www.financialexpress.com/india-news/neeru-chadha-becomes-first-indian-woman-as-member-of-international-tribunal-for-the-law-of-the-sea/719258/, accessed on 11 October 2021; Press Trust of India, "India re-elected to International Maritime Organisation Council," *Hindustan Times*, 02 December 2017, https://www.hindustantimes.com/india-news/india-re-elected-to-international-maritime-organisation-council/story-3xhvfWLMcS2kMqTZ1cPPTO.html, accessed on 11 October 2021; "Election of Mr. K. Natarajan as next Executive Director of ReCAAP," Ministry of External Affairs, 05 August 2021, https://www.mea.gov.in/press-releases.htm?dtl/34138/Election+of+Mr+K+Natarajan+as+next+Executive+Director+of+ReCAAP, accessed on 11 October 2021.

19 "Lowy Institute Global Diplomacy Index: 2019," Lowy Institute, https://globaldiplomacyindex.lowyinstitute.org/, accessed on 13 March 2022.

20 "Defence Attaches Conclave," Sainik Samachar, http://www.sainiksamachar.nic.in/englisharchives/2018/apr16-18/h12.htm, accessed on 10 October 2021.

21 Ministry of Defence, "Raksha Mantri Shri Rajnath Singh says terror poses a serious challenge but India has displayed that it can disrupt & deter terrorist groups and their patrons," Press Information Bureau, 03 February 2020, https://www.pib.gov.in/PressReleseDetailm.aspx?PRID=1601766, accessed on 10 October 2021.

22 US Defence Intelligence Agency, *Joint Military Attaché School*, 1, https://www.dia.mil/Portals/27/Documents/About/JMAS/JMAS_Brochure_JUL_2020.pdf, accessed on 10 October 2021.

23 Geneva Centre for Democratic Control of Armed Forces, *Defence Attaches*, July 2007, 2-3, https://www.files.ethz.ch/isn/38583/dcaf-backgrounder-defence-attaches.pdf, accessed on 20 August 2023.

24 "Defence Attaches Conclave," Sainik Samachar.

25 Ministry of Defence, "Raksha Mantri Shri Rajnath Singh says terror poses a serious challenge."

26 "Defence Attaches Conclave," Sainik Samachar.

27 Ministry of Defence, "Funding to Defence Attaches for Export Promotion," https://defenceexim.gov.in/showfile.php?fname=attache-scheme, accessed on 10 October 2021.

28 Geneva Centre for Democratic Control of Armed Forces, *Defence Attaches*, July 2007, 6.

29 Geneva Centre for Democratic Control of Armed Forces, *Defence Attaches*, July 2007, 3.

30 Geneva Centre for Democratic Control of Armed Forces, *Defence Attaches,* July 2007, 3-4.

31 Dutta, "Role of India's Defence Cooperation Initiatives in Meeting the Foreign Policy Goals," 43.

32 US Government, *Maritime Security Sector Reform,* 22.

33 This section is based on the author's participation in a number of events in the period

2020-2022 at the NMF, and the views of a number of panelists during the events.

34 Inputs by a visiting dignitary to the National Maritime Foundation in a closed-door meeting.

35 IORIS: Indo-Pacific Regional Information Sharing; IRIS: IFC Real-time Information-sharing System; MSIS: Merchant Shipping Information System.

36 CRIMARIO II, "SHARE.IT" https://www.crimario.eu/share-it/, accessed on 20 August 2023.

37 Upadhyaya, "Maritime Security Cooperation in the Indian Ocean Region." v.

6

Conclusion

The need for international cooperation is integral to the concept of maritime security, and its governance. This chapter endeavoured to examine the mechanisms for maritime security cooperation that are being pursued by India from a holistic maritime perspective, rather than a purely naval or regional perspective as is normally the case. The nature of the maritime domain which is seamless and interconnected requires cooperation amongst States, and international laws therefore provide for international and regional maritime cooperation; further, national interests also drive the need for maritime security cooperation. The security environment characterised by day-to-day strategic competition has resulted in even greater need for multidimensional cooperation amongst partners. Notwithstanding the need for cooperation, cooperation is often driven by underlying national interest, rather than altruism. The progressive rise of threats to international peace and security, such as terrorists and pirates, in the early part of the 21st century led to a greater focus on flexible cooperative partnerships to deal with such threats. The rise of China as a major maritime player, and its unilateral actions in the South China Sea, and elsewhere, which are threatening the international order, including along the Indian land borders, has also galvanised *ad hoc* 'coalitions' amongst like-minded nations. Unlike alliances in the 20th century, 21st century security cooperation is characterised by partnerships which are diffused, informal, inclusive, and bereft of formal structures. The entire range of cooperative endeavours encompasses a range of objectives and different partners need to be synchronised through effective governance to optimise such efforts.

Maritime security cooperation, despite its apparent attractiveness, is not without challenges. Some of the broad challenges include: mistrust and suspicion about underlying motives; cultural and social differences; wide disparities in capabilities; limited budgets, and consequently, resources; differing priorities; and policies and governance structures which may not engender cooperation. Pursuing cooperation, therefore, needs to address some of these generic challenges and more specific ones relating to the proposed areas of cooperation.

The development of international partnerships is not new to Indian statecraft. India's ancient wisdom is encapsulated in the phrase 'the world is one family,' and the framers of the Indian Constitution also recognised India's role in international peace and security. India's foreign policy, despite its changing outlook, continues to be driven by the enduring principles of *Panchsheel*, non-alignment, and strategic autonomy, despite increasing questions about their relevance. In the 21st century, India has chosen to expand its role in the global order, and the maritime domain is one of the chosen areas. India's political leadership has progressively articulated India's maritime security vision over the past decade: net security provider (2011), SAGAR (2015), free and open Indo-Pacific and five 'S' vision (2018), IPOI (2019), and most recently the five principles for maritime security cooperation at the UN Security Council (2021). The articulation of India's maritime vision by the Prime Minister himself, and the expanding remit of these articulations, underscores the importance that India attaches to maritime security in the 21st century, not only in the immediate region, but also on a regional and global basis. In addition, foreign policy articulations such as 'Act East' and 'Neighbourhood First,' and a host of ever growing strategic partnerships provide requisite policy focus to maritime security partnerships. Maritime security cooperation, from a foreign policy perspective, is driven by interplay of both 'thematic' cooperation, as well as bilateral, regional, and international cooperation. In other, words there is no single overarching policy, or a national plan to give effect to policies, but a collection of political articulations—this approach may provide flexibility, but not the requisite 'ways' to achieve the ends. Development of thematic or regional strategies, as has been done by several countries and regional blocks, therefore, is one imperative.

In the 21st century, the failure of multilateral and regional organisations to deliver, has marked a movement towards smaller multilateral formats ('plurilaterals'/'minilaterals'); the QUAD and the CSC are examples of promising arrangements focusing on the wider Indo-Pacific on one hand and the proximate neighbourhood on the other. It is for regional organisations to reinvent themselves if they are to remain relevant and fulfil the initial promise. With proliferating groupings, one way to do that is to leverage existing mechanisms to pursue regional goals, for example IORA could leverage the IONS, the MILAN platform (and similar engagements elsewhere) to also pursue IONS objectives. India has close bilateral relationships with most countries in the IOR (including some strategic partnerships), and the relationships are only growing, perhaps catalysed by the growing influence of the Chinese which is eroding traditional Indian influence. One view has been that investments in bilateral relations to counter China may be wasteful effort, but not everybody would subscribe to that view. India also has close relationships with several extra-regional powers on bilateral and plurilateral formats, including strategic partnerships, and its relationship with the US is a particularly close one, despite some differences. The India-Russian bilateral relationship is a particularly enduring relationship in which both countries have stood by each other in difficult times. Despite the promise of plurilateral engagements, multilateral and bilateral engagements continue to be relevant, and cannot be disregarded. In a dynamic world order, where India (and others) engage in multiple formats, it is only prudent to engage in all formats, while prioritising one over another on the basis on national interests. However, national interests themselves may change and come into conflict with other partners; the AUKUS deal of 2021 is one example of national interests trumping partnerships. Therefore, it is also important to hedge against possibilities such as these through diversified approaches. Maritime security cooperation, fundamentally built on trust, has many dimensions, and each relationship must be customised; it may involve engaging with adversaries when and where necessary, providing reassurance to those who may be developing misgivings, and aid to those who may need it.[1]

The diplomatic role is one of the enduring roles of navies, and perhaps one of the more rewarding ones, especially in times of peace. Commencing in the early 1990s, when the Indian Navy initiated bilateral/regional cooperative efforts with IOR and South East Asian littoral, the efforts were progressively consolidated over the years, followed by an exponential growth in the mid-2010s. In line with political vision and foreign policy, in the past decade, the Indian Navy has developed its own strategy for shaping the environment (2015) and defined its own role as a 'preferred security partner' with the aims of developing 'collective maritime competence' (2019). Despite the right sentiments, it is another matter that such lofty goals are challenging to achieve, even domestically. More lately, in 2021, the CNS has also articulated the India Navy's approach to cooperation publicly on different occasions and the lines of effort are focused on leveraging key naval capabilities and existing regional mechanisms, especially those in which India is active. As its own resources are limited, the Indian Navy's approach is focused on developing partnerships, building capabilities, and sustaining dialogue, and it would do well to leverage its strengths. In addition to traditional areas of focus, such as training and hydrographic cooperation, MDA and information sharing, cooperation in submarine rescue, and conclusion of operational support agreements, are areas of emerging focus. Looking ahead, with growing focus on *Atmanirbharta* and 'Make in India,' India could strengthen its focus on capacity-building through defence exports, such as ships, craft, aircraft, radars, etc. Becoming a 'preferred' or 'dependable' partner comes from day-to-day dealings, and not only from one-off engagements, however important they may be, or from grand pronouncements. Therefore, the need to have plans in place that balance the numerous ways and limited means to assure dependability. The Coast Guard too has deepened its international cooperation efforts, primarily on areas related to its charter, such as oil pollution response and SAR, and must be integrated into the overall national plans for most effectively leveraging limited national resources for pursuing maritime security cooperation across its multiple dimensions, especially in the immediate neighbourhood and within its areas of international responsibilities, such as MSRR. While the enormous progress in naval diplomacy is proof of the convergence of diplomacy with the security establishment, developing human resources in the form specialised and dedicated personnel within the defence forces is an imperative if such efforts need to be taken to the next level.

Operations are the practical manifestations of noble intent, and perhaps should be one of the major criteria to measure effectiveness of security cooperation. At the operational level, at one end, the international anti-piracy patrols in the GoA under a UN Security Council mandate, coordinated by an informal mechanism such as SHADE has exemplified the effectiveness of informality in real situations vis-à-vis the inability of large formal organisations, like IONS, to work together on professed areas of cooperation. On the other hand, QUAD a politically-led grouping has gained significant traction in the Indo-Pacific, not specifically as an alliance against a rampaging China, but as partnership for public good, which through the MALABAR series of exercises also projects its collective power and a message of deterrence. In the immediate neighbourhood, the CSC, a smaller high-level grouping, after a slow start, has been able to 'operationalise' itself in a short while after its rejuvenation. Political will and political leadership are the key differentiators for the success or failure of cooperative efforts; it is political will that can bring capacity and capabilities to deliver on intent. While Indian maritime security agencies are operationally engaged with several countries, which could be further expanded and consolidated, India should be willing to take a wider part in naval peacekeeping under the UN umbrella, especially as it is unlikely to be part of any alliance. This will give the Indian Navy valuable experience in participation and leadership of multinational forces, something which it has not been able to gain despite being deployed in the Gulf of Aden for over a decade. Likewise, India should be willing to go beyond participation, and shoulder lead responsibilities in operational constructs, such as SHADE.

While maritime security cooperation is often visualised in terms of naval engagements, which has indeed been the overwhelming case thus far, 21st century imperatives demand that maritime security cooperation be viewed holistically encompassing not only regional perspectives, but also specific themes, such as maritime crime and marine environment pollution, and maritime sectors, such as shipping, fisheries, biodiversity, etc. Therefore, the national approach to maritime security cooperation must incorporate and integrate the multiple elements of maritime security and move from its predominant naval diplomacy approach to a maritime diplomacy approach. In addition to themes and sectors, academia, particularly think tanks, can contribute to multi-track engagements across the official, quasi-official, and informal formats. India must strive to embody its representatives in international and regional bodies and to hold leadership positions in such bodies; to do so, a fundamental requirement is the development of capable human resources to take on global leadership roles. This will require strengthening maritime education in India, and till that happens, it has no recourse but to educate potential candidates in the best academic institutions in the world.

In line with the India's vision of being a major regional player and of a wider role in the world order, and considering the importance of the seas for meeting India's overall national interests, a wider role for India in regional maritime security is an inescapable one. While the exponential increase in engagements is indeed laudable, the increase is unlikely to be without impact on the other primary roles for maritime security agencies, and this needs to be guarded against. A detailed examination of this emerges as an area for future study, and examination by government bodies. For the present, a fine balance needs to be maintained, including between the necessary competing needs for cooperation itself; for the future, it would serve India well to develop the requisite capabilities which cater for its wider role in regional and international security, much like the US, which after aiming for '1000-ship navy' by combining international efforts, is now aiming for a 500-ship US Navy to fulfil its global ambitions on its own. Finally, the NMSC will have a key role in prioritising, synchronising, and balancing the growing cooperation agenda in maritime security cooperation. Maritime security cooperation cannot be pursued without a robust mechanism for governance and that maritime security cooperation needs a Whole-of-Government approach. India has truly covered a huge distance in this century, and looking at its avowed commitment, hopefully, the future will see an even greater role for India in international security cooperation; however, there are challenges to be overcome.

NOTE

1. Inputs from a closed-door meeting at the National Maritime Foundation.

ANNEXURE A

SELECT INSTRUMENTS: MARITIME SECURITY COOPERATION [1]

International Instruments

1. Charter of the United Nations, 1945.
2. International Convention for the Prevention of Pollution from Ships, 73/78
3. International Convention for the Safety of Life at Sea, 1974
4. International Convention on Maritime Search and Rescue, 1979
5. Convention for the Suppression of Unlawful Acts against the Safety of Maritime Navigation, 1988/2005, and Protocol for the Suppression of Unlawful Acts Against the Safety of Fixed Platforms Located on the Continental Shelf
6. Regional Cooperation Agreement on Combating Piracy and Armed Robbery against Ships in Asia, 2004.
7. BIMSTEC Convention on Cooperation in Combating International Terrorism, Transnational Organized Crime and Illicit Drug Trafficking, 2009

Other Instruments

8. Code of Conduct concerning the Repression of Piracy, Armed Robbery against Ships, and Illicit Maritime Activity in West and Central Africa, 2013
9. The Jeddah Amendment to the Djibouti Code of Conduct, 2017
10. Indian Ocean Naval Symposium, Charter of Business, 2016.
11. Code of Unalerted Encounters Sea, 2014

Bilateral Agreements

12. India-US General Security of Military Information Agreement, 2002.
13. Agreement on development of facilities on Assumption Island, 2015 [Seychelles].
14. India-US Logistics Exchange Memorandum of Agreement [LEMOA] between the Ministry of Defence and the Department of Defence, 2016
15. India-US Helicopter Operations from Ships Other Than Aircraft Carriers, 2017.
16. India-US Communications Compatibility and Security Agreement, 2018.
17. Indian Navy and Republic of Singapore Navy agreement for mutual coordination, logistics and services support for naval ships', submarines, and naval aircraft (including Ship borne Aviation Assets) visits, 2018
18. India-France Agreement regarding the Provision of Reciprocal Logistics Support, 2018
19. India-South Korea Military Logistic Agreement, 2019
20. Australia-India Mutual Logistics Support Agreement, 2020
21. India-Japan Reciprocal Provisions for Support and Services Agreement, 2020.
22. India-US Basic Exchange and Cooperation Agreement for Geo-spatial Cooperation, 2020.
23. India-US Maritime Information Sharing Technical Agreement, 2020.
24. White Shipping Information Exchange Agreement [with multiple countries]

Memorandum of Understanding

25. MOU between the Coast Guards for Establishment of Collaborative Relationship to Combat Transnational Illegal activities at sea and Develop Regional Cooperation, 2015 [Australia].
26. MOU between the Coast Guards for establishment of Collaborative Relationship to Combat Transnational Illegal activities at sea and Develop Regional Cooperation, 2015 [Bangladesh].
27. MOU for the improvement in Sea and Air Transportation Facilities at Agalega Island of Mauritius, 2015.

28. MOU between Indian Coast Guard in the Republic of India and Vietnam Coast Guard in the Socialist Republic of Vietnam for Establishment of Collaborative Relationship to Combat Transnational Crime and Develop Mutual Cooperation, 2015
29. MOU between the navies of Chile and India Establishing a Frame work for Cooperation and Confidentiality in Navy Issues. 2016.
30. MOU between the Coast Guards in the field of Marine Crime Prevention at Sea, 2016 [Oman].
31. MOU to Cooperate on Maritime Issues, 2016 [Oman].
32. MOU for Establishment of a Communication Link between Indian Coast Guard and Pakistan Maritime Security Agency Extended, 2016 [Pakistan].
33. MOU on Maritime Security Cooperation, 2017 [Myanmar].
34. Bilateral Agreement for Navy Cooperation, 2017 [Singapore].
35. MOU on Co-operation on the Response to Oil Spill and Chemical Pollution in the South Asia Seas Region, 2018 [with SACEP]
36. MOU on Mutual Logistic Support, 2023 [with Vietnam].

Other Agreements

37. Master Ship Repair Agreement, 2022 [US and M/s L&T]

NOTES

1 Ministry of Defence, "Signing of Agreements with Other Countries," Press Information Bureau, 05 February 2018 https://pib.gov.in/Pressreleaseshare.aspx?PRID=1519147, accessed on 23 August 2023; Ministry of Defence, "Military Ties with Foreign Countries," 08 August 2017, https://pib.gov.in/newsite/PrintRelease.aspx?relid=169712 , accessed on 23 August 2023.

ANNEXURE B

BILATERAL MARITIME SECURITY COOPERATION

The table below provides an overview of the *highest-level* of bilateral cooperative endeavours which has been achieved by India with specific countries. The table is based on the earlier work of Shishir Updadhya, as updated, with a focus on the 'military' and 'constabulary' engagements.

Towards a more comprehensive understanding of maritime security cooperation, the table also includes:

(1) Strategic partnerships with the country, indicated in **bold**;
(2) Presence of defence/naval attaché/advisor in the country, indicated with an 'asterisk.'
(3) The assessed export potential for Indian defence products, indicated by its categorisation by the MoD with 'A' as the highest potential and 'C' as the lowest potential (also refer footnote below for the additional information on this table).[1]

Table B.1: Bilateral Cooperation

Sl. No.	Country/Export Potential	Level 1	Level 2	Level 3[2]
		South Asia[3]		
1.	*Bangladesh** A	*C1: CG MOU*[4]	M2: Defence export C2: CORPAT	-
2.	Maldives* A	-	*C2: EEZ patrols/ WSIE*	M3: Basing of aircraft/ infrastructure development *M2: Transfer of non-strategic platform*[5]
3.	Pakistan*	*C1: CG MOU* M1: CBM	-	-
4.	Sri Lanka* A	-	*C2: WSIE/CRS*	*M3: Transfer/Sale of platforms*

Sl. No.	Country/Export Potential	Level 1	Level 2	Level 3[2]
		West Asia[6]		
5.	Bahrain* A	M1: Defence Co-operation Agreement	-	-
6.	**Iran*** C	-	M2: Defence exports	-
7.	Iraq/ -	-	D2: Training	-
8.	**Israel*** C	-	*C2: WSIE*	M3: Joint development of military technology
9.	Kuwait* C	-	M2: Defence export	-
10.	**Oman*** A	*C1: CG MOU*	M2: OTR support	D3: Basing of Indian Navy training team
11.	Qatar* B	-	M2: Defence export	D3: Basing of Indian Navy training team
12.	Saudi Arabia* A	M1: Defence Co-operation Agreement	-	-
13.	**UAE*** A	-	M2: Defence export	-
14.	Yemen/ -	D1: Ship visits	-	-
		East Africa and Indian Ocean Island States[7]		
15.	Comoros -	D1: Ship visits	-	-
16.	Djibouti C	D1: Ship visits	-	-
17.	*Egypt** A	-	M2: Defence export/ Joint Defence R&D	*M3: Joint Defence R/D*
18.	*Madagascar*		*D2: Training*	*M3: transfer of platforms*
19.	Kenya* B	-	*C2: WSIE* M2: Defence export	-
20.	**Mauritius/** -	-	C2: EEZ patrols/ *WSIE/CRS*	M3: Embedded Indian Navy personnel *M3: Transfer/Sale of platforms*
21.	Mozambique C	-	*C2: EEZ patrols* M2: Defence export	*M3: Gifting of boats/craft*
22.	**Seychelles** A	-	*C2: EEZ patrols/WSIE* M2: Defence export	M3: Embedded Indian Navy personnel; gifting of assets, etc.
23.	Somalia	-	*C2: Anti-piracy cooperation*	-

Sl. No.	Country/Export Potential	Level 1	Level 2	Level 3[2]
24.	South Africa* A	-	-	M3: Defence export/Joint Defence R&D
25.	Sudan C	D1: Visits by officials	-	-
26.	Tanzania B	-	D2: Training/ hydrographic assistance M2: Defence exports	-
		Southeast Asian and Australia[8]		
27.	**Australia*** B	-	C2: WSIE M2: Advanced exercises; joint SOP/doctrine	-
28.	Cambodia A	D1: Visits by officials	-	-
29.	**Indonesia*** B	*C1: CG MOU*	C2: CORPAT	M3: Defence technology transfer
30	**Malaysia** A	-	*M2: Defence exports*	-
31	Myanmar* B	-	C2: CORPAT	*M3: Transfer of strategic platform*
32	Singapore * B	-	C2: WSIE	M3: Joint defence R&D
33.	Thailand* A	-	C2: CORPAT M2: Defence export	-
34.	Timor Leste	D1: Foreign Aid		
35.	*Vietnam* *A*	*C1: CG MOU*	*C2: WSIE*	*M3: Transfer of naval platform*

NOTES

1 Ministry of Defence Note No. 20/2018/Export Promotion/EPC Cell dated 20 May 2019, https://www.defenceexim.gov.in/showfile.php?fname=attache-scheme, accessed on 05 January 2022.
2 Annotation: D (Diplomatic); C (Constabulary); M (Military); The designation is based on meeting any one of the criteria as originally elucidated by Shishir Upadhyaya: Defence/ Naval Attaché/Advisor.
3 Upadhyaya, "Maritime Security Cooperation in the Indian Ocean Region."
4 CG: Coast Guard.
5 Italics indicate variation from original articulation based on author's view and/or updates, including additions.
6 Upadhyaya, "Maritime Security Cooperation in the Indian Ocean Region," 115.
7 Upadhyaya, "Maritime Security Cooperation in the Indian Ocean Region," 168-69.
8 Upadhyaya, "Maritime Security Cooperation in the Indian Ocean Region," 183.

Annexure C

List of Exercises

Institutionalised Bilateral Exercises: Chronologically

Table C.1: Indian Navy Bilateral Exercises: Chronologically

S.No.	Country	Exercise	Year	Remarks
		1990-2000		
1	US	MALABAR	1992	Expanded to multilateral exercise in 2007
2	Oman	NASEEM-AL-BAHAR	1993	Earlier THAMMAR-AL-TAYYIB
3	Singapore	SIMBEX	1994	Earlier SEA LION
		2001-10		
4	France	VARUNA	2001	
5	Russia	INDRA NAVY	2003	
6	UK	KONKAN	2004	
7	Sri Lanka	SLINEX	2005	
		2011-20		
8	Japan	JIMEX	2012	
9	Australia	AUSINDEX	2015	
10	Indonesia	SAMUDRA SHAKTHI	2015	
11	Maldives	EKATHA	-	Special Operation Exercise
12	Myanmar	INMEX	2018[1]	
13	UAE	GULF STAR	2018	
14	Vietnam[2]	IN-VPN BILAT	2018	
15	Bangladesh	BONGO SAGAR	2019[3]	
16	Malaysia	SAMUDRA LAXMANA	2019	
17	Qatar	ZAIRE AL BADR	2019[4]	
		2021 onwards		
18	EU	-	2021	
19	Saudi Arabia	AL-MOHED AL-HINDI[5]	2021	

Source: Various.[6]

Institutionalised Bilateral Exercises: Country-wise

Table C.2: Indian Navy Bilateral Exercises: Country-wise

S.No.	Country	Navy	Year	Remarks
1	Australia	AUSINDEX	2015	Biennial
2	Bangladesh	BONGO SAGAR[7]	2019[8]	Annual
3	EU	-	2021	-
4	France	VARUNA	2001	Annual
5	Indonesia	SAMUDRA SHAKTHI	2015	Annual
6	Japan	JIMEX	2012	Biennial
7	Malaysia	SAMUDRA LAXMANA	2019	Biennial
8	Maldives	EKATHA	-	Annual/SF exercise
9	Myanmar[9]	INMEX	2018	Annual
10	Oman	NASEEM-AL-BAHAR[10]	1993	Biennial
11	Qatar	ZAIRE AL BADR	2019[11]	Biennial
12	Russia	INDRA NAVY	2003	Biennial
13	Saudi Arabia	AL-MOHED AL-HINDI	2021	Annual
14	Singapore	SIMBEX[12]	1994	Annual
15	Sri Lanka	SLINEX[13]	2005	Annual
16	UAE	GULF STAR/ZAYED TALWAR	2018	Biennial
17	UK	KONKAN	2004	Annual
18	US	MALABAR[14]	1992	Annual
19	Vietnam	IN-VPN BILAT	2018	Annual

Source: Various [15]

Multilateral Exercises[16]

Table C.3: Indian Navy—Multilateral Exercises

S.No.	Host Country/Organisation	Exercise/Periodicity[17]	Year[18]
1	Australia	KAKADU/Biennial[19]	2018
2		BLACK CARILLION/Annual[20]	2018
3	ASEAN	ARF DiREx/Biennial	2011
4		AIME[21]	2023
5	France	LA PEROUSE/Annual	2021
6	Australia, India, Japan, US	MALABAR/Annual	2007
7	India, Brazil, South Africa	IBSAMAR/Biennial	2008
8	India, Tanzania, Mozambique[22]	IMT TRILAT	2022
9	India	MILAN/Biennial	1995

S.No.	Host Country/Organisation	Exercise/Periodicity	Year
10	Indonesia	KOMODO (HADR exercise)/Biennial	2016
11	IONS	IMMSAREX[23]	2017
12	IONS[24]	IMEX	2022
13	Israel	MIGHTY SHIELD	-
14	Japan	EOD J2A (Ordnance disposal)/Annual	2019
15	Singapore	SITMEX (with Thailand)/Annual	2019
16		MARISX/Biennial [25]	-
17	US	SANGAM[26]	1994
18		SALVEX[27]	2005
19		SPITTING COBRA[28]	-
20		RIMPAC/Biennial	2014[29]
21		IMX/CUTLASS EXPRESS/[30] Annual	2019/2023[31]
22		SEACAT[32]/Annual	2021
23		SOUTHERN READINESS[33]	2022
24		SEA DRAGON/Annual	2022
25	WPNS	WPNS Exercise/Annual	2018

Source: Various.[34]

Tri-Service Exercises

Table C.4: Indian Navy in Tri-Service Exercises

S.No.	Country	Exercise	Periodicity
1.	ADMM Plus countries	ADMM Plus	As Scheduled
2.	Russia	INDRA (Tri Service)	Biennial
3.	Russia	VOSTOK	Annual
4.	Thailand	Ex Cobra Gold	Annual
5.	USA	Ex Tiger Triumph	Annual
6.	UK	Konkan Shakti	

Source: Ministry of Defence.[35]

NOTES

1 "Indian, Myanmar Navies Commences Maiden Bilateral Exercise, INMEX-18," *Defpost,* https://defpost.com/indian-myanmar-navies-commences-maiden-bilateral-exercise-inmex-18/, accessed on 14 January 2021.

2 Ministry of Defence, "Second Edition of Indian Navy-Vietnam Peoples' Navy Bilateral Exercise (IN – VPN BILAT EX) Concludes," Press Information Bureau, 17 April 2019, https://pib.gov.in/newsite/PrintRelease.aspx?relid=189794, accessed on 20 August 2023.

3 Ministry of Defence, "Indian Navy (IN) - Bangladesh Navy (BN) Bilateral Exercise

Bongosagar and IN-BN CORPAT," Press Information Bureau, 02 October 2020, https://pib.gov.in/PressReleseDetailm.aspx?PRID=1661064, accessed on 15 January 2021.

4 Ministry of Defence, "Joint Exercise between the Qatari Emiri Navy and the Indian Navy Forces (the Roar of the Sea)," Press Information Bureau, 18 November 2019, https://pib.gov.in/PressReleasePage.aspx?PRID=1591973, accessed on 14 January 2021.

5 Ministry of Defence, "Maiden *Al-Mohed Al-Hindi* Exercise set to begin Between Indian Navy and Saudi Arabia Navy," Press Information Bureau, 12 August 2021, https://www.pib.gov.in/PressReleasePage.aspx?PRID=1745103, accessed on 05 September 2021.

6 While the table has been sourced from multiple sources, the basic structure was sourced from Roby Thomas, "Leveraging India's Maritime Diplomacy," *Journal of Defence Studies* 14, no. 3 (July-September 2020): 1-27, accessed on 11 January 2021, https://idsa.in/jds/14-3-2020-leveraging-indias-maritime-diplomacy; Ministry of Defence, "Joint Maritime Exercise." Press Information Bureau, 03 February 2021, https://pib.gov.in/Pressreleaseshare.aspx?PRID=1694881, accessed on 20 August 2023; Ministry of Defence, "Maritime Cooperation With Regional Partners," Press Information Bureau, 21 March 2022, https://pib.gov.in/PressReleasePage.aspx?PRID=1807607, accessed on 20 August 2023; Integrated Headquarters of Ministry of Defence (Navy), *Ensuring Secure Seas,* 87.

7 Also, an annual Special Forces (SF) exercise.

8 Ministry of Defence, "Indian Navy (IN) - Bangladesh Navy (BN) Bilateral Exercise Bongosagar."

9 "Indian, Myanmar Navies Commences Maiden Bilateral Exercise, INMEX-18," Defpost,

10 Earlier Exercise THAMMAR-AL-TAYYIB

11 Ministry of Defence, "Joint Exercise between the Qatari Emiri Navy and the Indian Navy Forces (the Roar of the Sea)."

12 Earlier Exercise SEA LION

13 Also, SF exercise.

14 Also, SALVEX and SF exercise SANGAM.

15 While the table has been sourced from multiple sources, the basic structure was sourced from Roby Thomas, "Leveraging India's Maritime Diplomacy," *Journal of Defence Studies*; Ministry of Defence, "Joint Maritime Exercise."; Ministry of Defence, "Maritime Cooperation with Regional Partners," Integrated Headquarters of Ministry of Defence (Navy), *Ensuring Secure Seas*, 87.

16 Where the year could not be ascertained, the column has been left blank

17 Where data could not be confirmed, the periodicity has not been indicated.

18 Where data could not be confirmed, the year has not been indicated.

19 India participated in 2010 as an observer; Premesha, Saha and Angad Singh. "Securing two oceans: bolstering India-Australia defence cooperation in the Indo-Pacific." *Observer Research Foundation Occasional Paper* 346 (January 2022): 10, https://www.orfonline.org/wp-content/uploads/2022/01/ORF_OccasionalPaper_346_India-Australia.pdf, accessed on 20 August 2023.

20 Submarine Rescue Exercise; Saha and Singh, "Securing two oceans."

21 Ministry of Defence, "Sea Phase of ASEAN-India Maritime Exercise – 2023," Press Information Bureau, May 09, 2023, https://pib.gov.in/PressReleaseIframePage.aspx?PRID=1922815, accessed on 29 May 2023; AIME: ASEAN-India Maritime Exercise.

22 Ministry of Defence, "Indian Navy Participates in Maiden Trilateral Exercise with

Mozambique and Tanzania," Press Information Bureau, 29 October 2022, https://pib.gov.in/PressReleasePage.aspx?PRID=1871827, accessed on 20 August 2023.

23 Conducted by IONS Working Group (IWG) Chair.

24 Ministry of Defence, "Ministry of Defence - Year End Review 2022."

25 Information Sharing Exercise

26 Ministry of Defence, "IN MARCOs – USN Seals Joint Special Forces Exercise Commences at Goa." Press Information Bureau, 04 December 2022, https://pib.gov.in/PressReleaseIframePage.aspx?PRID=1880810, accessed on 20 August 2023.

27 Ministry of Defence, "IN-USN SALVAGE AND EXPLOSIVE ORDNANCE DISPOSAL EXERCISE – SALVEX." Press Information Bureau, 06 July 2023, https://pib.gov.in/PressReleaseIframePage.aspx?PRID=1937685, accessed on 20 August 2023.

28 Ordnance Disposal Exercise.

29 Dorai Babu and Gokhale, *A Decade of Transformation: The Indian Navy, 2011-21*, 75; Observers in 2006, 2008, and 2012.

30 Ministry of Defence, Government of India, "INS Trikand participates in exercise Cutlass Express 2019." Press Information Bureau, 08 February 2019. https://pib.gov.in/Pressreleaseshare.aspx?PRID=1563560

31 Ministry of Defence. "INS Trikand participates in International Maritime Exercise/Cutlass Express 23 (IMX/CE-23)." Press Information Bureau, 05 March 2023. https://www.pib.gov.in/PressReleasePage.aspx?PRID=1904376, accessed on 20 August 2023.

32 Piracy Exercise in Southeast Asia.

33 Ministry of Defence, "INS Sunayna in Seychelles: Indian Navy's Maiden Participation in Combined Maritime Forces Exercise." Press Information Bureau, 28 September 2022. https://pib.gov.in/PressReleasePage.aspx?PRID=1862198, accessed on 20 August 2023.

34 While the table has been sourced from multiple sources, the basic structure was sourced from Roby Thomas, "Leveraging India's Maritime Diplomacy;"; Ministry of Defence, "Joint Military Exercises," Press Information Bureau, 18 July 2018, https://pib.gov.in/Pressreleaseshare.aspx?PRID=1539020, accessed on 14 January 2021; Ministry of Defence, "Joint Military Exercises."; Ministry of Defence, "Maritime Cooperation with Regional Partners."

35 Ministry of Defence, "Maritime Cooperation with Regional Partners."

Select Bibliography

"India-France Roadmap on the Blue Economy and Ocean Governance." Ministry of External Affairs, 20 February 2022. https://www.mea.gov.in/bilateral-documents.htm?dtl/34882/INDIAFRANCE+ROADMAP+ON+THE+BLUE+ECONOMY+AND+OCEAN+GOVERNANCE.

"Remarks by External Affairs Minister at the UN Security Council Open Debate on Technology & Peacekeeping." Ministry of External Affairs, 18 August 2021. https://www.mea.gov.in/Speeches-Statements.htm?dtl/34192/Remarks_.

"Address by the President of India, Shri Ram Nath Kovind on the Occasion of Presentation of the President's Standard to 22nd Missile Vessel Squadron," 08 December 2021. https://presidentofindia.nic.in/speeches-detail.htm?887

"Memorandum of Understanding between the Coast Guard of the Republic Of India and the Coast Guard of the Democratic Socialist Republic of Sri Lanka for the establishment of a Collaborative Relationship to Combat Transnational Illegal Activities at Sea and develop Regional Co-Operation Between The Indian Coast Guard And The Sri Lanka Coast Guard" https://www.mea.gov.in/Portal/LegalTreatiesDoc/LK18B3322.pdf

"PM's speech at the foundation stone laying ceremony for the Indian National Defence University at Gurgaon," Former Prime Ministers of India. https://archivepmo.nic.in/drmanmohansingh/speech-details.php?nodeid=1316.

"Second ARF Workshop on Enhancing Regional Maritime Law Enforcement Cooperation." ASEAN Regional Forum. https://aseanregionalforum.asean. org/wp-content/uploads/2019/01/ANNEX-24-10th-ISM-on-MS.pdf.

"Transforming The Indian Navy to be a Key Maritime Force in the Indo-Pacific." Address by Admiral Karambir Singh, the Chief of the Naval Staff, at the United Services Institute, New Delhi, 27 August 2021.

"Transforming the Indian Navy to be a key Maritime Force in the Indo-Pacific."

Talk by the Chief of the Naval Staff, Admiral Karambir Singh at the United Services Institute, New Delhi, 27 August 2021.

Basu, Pratnashree. "Maritime India: The Quest for a Steadfast Identity." *ORF Occasional Paper* 339, November 2021. Observer Research Foundation. https://www.orfonline.org/research/maritime-india-the-quest-for-a-steadfast-identity/

Bekkevold, Jo Inge and Geoffrey Till, eds. *International Order at Sea: How it is challenged; How it is maintained.* London: Palgrave Macmillan, 2016.

Bharathiamma, Meenakumari. *Report of the Expert Committee constituted for Comprehensive Review of the Deep Sea fishing Policy and Guidelines.* https://www.researchgate.net/publication/322821544_Report_of_the_Expert_Committee_constituted_for_Comprehensive_Review_of_the_Deep_Sea_fishing_Policy_ and_ Guidelines/citation/download.

Bhattacharya, Debasis. "India's focus on enhancing maritime security as the UNSC president: Leadership envisioning a global roadmap." Observer Research Foundation, 26 August 2021. https://www.orfonline.org/expert-speak/indias-focus-on-enhancing-maritime-security-as-the-unsc-president/.

Borton, James. "UNCLOS Remains the Gold Standard in Maritime Security Cooperation." *Geopolitical Monitor*, 13 August 2021. https://www.geopoliticalmonitor.com/unclos-remains-the-gold-standard-in-maritime-security-cooperation/.

Bueger, Christian. "What is maritime security?" *Marine Policy* 53, (2015): 159-164. https://www.sciencedirect.com/science/article/pii/S0308597X14003 327.

Charter of the United Nations, Article 1(1).

Coast Guard. "Maritime SAR Events." *Safe Waters* 18, no. 1 (July 2018). https://www.indiancoastguard.gov.in/WriteReadData/bookpdf/20181024025932115 3666SafeWatersJul18.pdf.

Constitution of India.

Das, Himadri. "Drug Trafficking in India: Maritime Dimensions." National Maritime Foundation, 31 December 2021. https://maritimeindia.org/drug-trafficking-in-india-maritime-dimensions/#_ftn83.

Das, Himadri. "India @75: Reflections on the Homeland Dimensions of Maritime Security in India." National Maritime Foundation, 08 August 2022. https://maritimeindia.org/15395-2/

Das, Himadri. "Maritime Domain Awareness in India: Shifting Paradigms." National Maritime Foundation, 30 September 2021. https://maritimeindia.org/maritime-domain-awareness-in-india-shifting-paradigms/

Dedeoglu, C. "The Ontology of Security and its Implications for Maritime Security,"

Güvenlik Stratejileri Dergisi 15 (2019): 631-654. DOI: 10.17752/guvenlikstrtj.668182

Department of Animal Husbandry, Dairying and Fisheries. *Annual Report 2018-1919*. https://dahd.nic.in/sites/default/filess/Annual%20Report_0.pdf.

Department of Revenue Intelligence, *Smuggling in India Report 2020-21*. https://www.dri.nic.in/dri_report/ebook/.

Directorate General of Shipping. *Annual Report on Port State Control (PSC) And Flag State Implementation (FSI)*, 2017. https://www.dgshipping.gov.in/WriteReadData/userfiles/file/Annual%20Report%202017.pdf [Site has moved]

Doraibabu, M. and Amrut Dilip Godbole. *A Decade of Transformation: The Indian Navy, 2011-21*. Gurugram: Harper Collins, 2023.

Dutta, Arvind. "Role of India's Defence Cooperation Initiatives in Meeting the Foreign Policy Goals." *Journal of Defence Studies* 3, no. 3 (July 2009): 33. https://www.idsa.in/system/files/jds_3_3_adutta.pdf.

FISH-i Africa and West Africa Task Force. *Regional Cooperation to Stop Illegal Fishing: A Tale of Two Task Forces*. Botswana: 2021. https://1ae03060-3f06-4a5c-9ac6-b5c1b4a62664.usrfiles.com/ugd/1ae030_adff42091e77403d b1f894ff1d 17f986.pdf.

Geneva Centre for Democratic Control of Armed Forces. "Defence Attaches." In *Defence Backgrounder* July 2007, 2-3. https://www.files.ethz.ch/isn/38583/dcaf-backgrounder-defence-attaches.pdf.

Ghosh, P.K. "Shared Awareness and Deconfliction: Can the success story be applied to Southeast Asia?" Indo-Pacific Defence Forum, 23 February 2016. https://ipdefenseforum.com/2016/02/shared-awareness-and-deconfliction-initiative/.

Government of UK. *National Strategy for Maritime Security*. August 2022. https://assets.publishing.service.gov.uk/government/uploads/system/uploads/attachment_data/file/1100525/national-strategy-for-maritime-security-web-version.pdf.

Grare, Frédéric and Mélissa Levaillant. "Getting Real about the Indo-Pacific Redefining European Approach to Maritime Security." The Hague Centre for Strategic Studies, March 2022. https://hcss.nl/wp-content/uploads/2022/03/GTC4-Levaillant-Grare-HCSS-2022.pdf.

Hall, Ian. "Multialignment and Indian Foreign Policy under Narendra Modi." *The Round Table* 105, no. 3 (May 2016). https://doi.org/10.1080/00358533.2016.1180760.

Hazarika, Aneedrisha. "Fleshing out The Maritime Security Pillar of The India's Indo-Pacific Oceans' Initiative." *DEFSTRAT* 14, no. 5 (Nov-Dec 2020): 27.

https://www.defstrat.com/magazine_articles/fleshing-out-the-maritime-security-pillar-of-the-indias-indo-pacific-oceans-initiative/.

Hiranandani, Gulab Mohanlal. *Transition to Eminence: The Indian Navy 1976-1990*. Lancer, 2005. https://www.indiannavy.nic.in/sites/default/files/Transition-to-Eminence-07Apr16.pdf.

Integrated Headquarters of Ministry of Defence (Navy), *Ensuring Secure Seas: India's Maritime Security Strategy.*

Integrated Headquarters of Ministry of Defence (Navy). *Indian Maritime Doctrine*. New Delhi: 2004.

Jaishankar, S. *The India Way: Strategies for an Uncertain World.* New York: HarperCollins, 2021.

Jayatilake, S. M. D. P. Anura. "South Asian Seas Programme." Presentation at the Technical Workshop on Selecting Indicators for the State of Regional Seas. South Asia Co-operative Environment Programme, 2014. https://wedocs. unep.org/bitstream/handle/20.500.11822/11088/south_asian_seas _programme-a._jayatilake_-sacep.pdf?sequence=1&isAllowed=y

Jeyabaskaran, R. "Fisheries Management – An Indian Perspective." Presentation at an Online Workshop on Fisheries Issue, 07 November 2021.

Jeyabaskaran, R. "Fisheries Management as a Geostrategic Issue in the Indian Ocean." Presentation at an Online Workshop on Fisheries Issue, 01 November 2021.

Kautilya. *The Arthashastra.* Translated and Edited by L. N. Rangarajan. Penguin.

Khurana, Gurpreet. "BIMSTEC and Maritime Security; Issues, Imperatives, and Way Ahead." National Maritime Foundation, 16 November 2018. https://maritimeindia.org/bimstec-and-maritime-security-issues-imperatives-and-way-ahead/.

Khurana, Gurpreet. "Thousand-Ship Navy: A Reincarnation of the Controversial P.S.I.?" Institute of Defence Studies and Analyses, 28 December 2006. https://www.idsa.in/idsastrategiccomments/AReincarnationofthe Controversial PSI_GSKhurana_281206.

LaGrone, Sam and Mallory Shelbourne. "CNO Gilday: 'We Need a Naval Force of Over 500 Ships'." *US Naval Institute News*, 08 February 2022. https://news.usni.org/2022/02/18/cno-gilday-we-need-a-naval-force-of-over-500-ships.

Louys, Johnny. "Sustainable Fisheries Development and IUU Fishing." Presentation at IORA Capacity Building Workshop, Indian Council of World Affairs, 29 January 2021.

Malhotra, Achal. "India's Foreign Policy: Current priorities and relevance of SAARC."

Ministry of External Affairs, 08 October 2018. https://mea.gov.in/distinguished-lectures-detail.htm?766.

McDonagh, Naoise. "Is plurilateralism making the WTO an institutional zombie?" Institute for International Trade (University of Adelaide). https://iit.adelaide.edu.au/news/list/2021/02/23/is-plurilateralism-making-the-wto-an-institutional-zombie.

Ministry of Agriculture and Farmers Welfare. *National Policy on Marine Fisheries, 2017*. https://dahd.nic.in/news/notification-national-policy-marine-fisheries-2017.

Ministry of Defence, *Annual Report 2018-19*. https://www.mod.gov.in/dod/sites/default/files/MoDAR2018.pdf.

Ministry of Defence. "Aero India 2021: IOR Seminar Building Collective Maritime Competence Towards Security and Growth for All In The Region (SAGAR)," 04 February 2021. https://www.indiannavy.nic.in/content/aero-india-2021-ior-seminar-building-collective-maritime-competence-towards-security-and-0.

Ministry of Defence. *Year End Review – 2019*.

Ministry of Defence. *Year End Review – 2020*.

Ministry of External Affairs, *Annual Report 2020-21*. http://www.mea.gov.in/Uploads/PublicationDocs/33569_MEA_annual_Report.pdf.

Ministry of External Affairs. "BIMSTEC Convention on Cooperation in Combating International Terrorism, Transnational Organised Crime And Illicit Drug Trafficking," 11 December 2009. https://mea.gov.in/bilateral-documents.htm?dtl/5070/BIMSTEC+Convention+on+Cooperation+in+ Combating+ International+ Terrorism+Transnational+Organised+Crime+ And+ Illicit + Drug+Trafficking.

Ministry of External Affairs. "English translation of Prime Minister's remarks at the UNSC High-Level Open Debate on 'Enhancing Maritime Security: A Case For International Cooperation' (09 August 2021)." 10 August 2021. https://www.mea.gov.in/Speeches-Statements.htm?dtl/34151/English_tra.

Ministry of External Affairs. "External Affairs Minister participates in a panel discussion at the Raisina Dialogue 2021- 'Crimson Tide, Blue Geometries: New Partnerships for the Indo-Pacific'." https://www.mea.gov.in/interviews.htm?dtl/33806.

Ministry of External Affairs. "Foreign Secretary's Vimarsh Talk on 'Global Rebalancing and India's Foreign Policy'." Vivekananda International Foundation, 30 June 2021. https://www.mea.gov.in/Speeches-Statements.htm?dtl/33965/Foreign_Secretarys_Vimarsh_Talk_on_Global_ Rebalancing_ and_

Indias_Foreign_Policy_Vivekananda_International_ Foundation_ June_30_ 2021.

Ministry of External Affairs. "Foreign Secretary's Remarks on 'Quad and Future of the Indo-Pacific' at the 5th India-US Forum," 02 December 2021. https://www.mea.gov.in/Speeches-Statements.htm?dtl/34571/Foreign_Secretarys_Remarks _ on_Quad_and_Future_of_the_IndoPacific_at_the_5th_IndiaUS_Forum.

Ministry of External Affairs. "India-ASEAN Relations," August 2018. https://mea.gov.in/aseanindia/20-years.htm.

Ministry of External Affairs. "India-France-Australia Joint Statement on the occasion of the Trilateral Ministerial Dialogue (04 May 2021)." https://mea.gov.in/bilateral-documents.htm?dtl/33845/IndiaFranceAustralia+ Joint+ Statement + on+the+occasion+of+the+Trilateral+Ministerial+Dialogue+May+04+ 2021.

Ministry of External Affairs. "Keynote address by Secretary (East) at the BIMSTEC Coastal Security Workshop (20 November 2019)." https://www.mea.gov.in/Speeches-Statements.htm?dtl/32068/Keynote_address_by_Secretary_.

Ministry of External Affairs. "NSA level meeting on trilateral Maritime Security Cooperation between India, Sri Lanka, and Maldives." https://www.mea.gov.in/in-focus-article.htm?23037/NSA+level+meeting+on+ trilateral+ Maritime+ Security+ Cooperation+ between+ India+ Sri+ Lanka+ and+Maldives. [This web page is no longer available]

Ministry of External Affairs. "Prime Minister's Virtual Address at Eastern Economic Forum 2021," 03 September 2021. https://mea.gov.in/Speeches-Statements.htm?dtl/34216/prime+ministers+ virtualaddress+ at+ eastern+ economic+forum+2021.

Ministry of External Affairs. "External Affairs Minister's speech at the 4th Ramnath Goenka Lecture, 2019." 14 November 2019. https://www.mea.gov.in/Speeches-Statements.htm?dtl/32038.

Panda, Ankit. "Why Does India Have So Many 'Strategic Partners' and No Allies?" *The Diplomat*, 23 November 2013. https://thediplomat.com/2013/11/why-does-india-have-so-many-strategic-partners-and-no-allies/.

Panda, Jagganath. "The Australia-India-Indonesia Trilateral: Fostering Maritime Cooperation between Middle Powers." National Bureau of Asian Research, 23 April 2021. https://idsa.in/system/files/news/all-map-nbr-analysis-min.pdf.

Pandalai, Shruti and Abhay Kumar Singh. "Quad's Maritime Domain Awareness Initiative Needs Time to Deliver." Manohar Parrikar Institute for Defence Studies and Analyses, 24 June 2022. https://idsa.in/idsacomments/Quads-Maritime-Domain-240622.

Pant, Harsh V. "Lessons in new ways to lead." Observer Research Foundation, 16 August 2021. https://www.orfonline.org/research/lessons-in-new-ways-to-lead/

Raja Mohan, C. "India, the Quad and Indo-Pacific Maritime Security." Institute of South Asian Studies, national University of Singapore, 03 June 2022. https://www.isas.nus.edu.sg/papers/india-the-quad-and-indo-pacific-maritime-security/

Rajkumar, T. "Challenges of Salvage Operations in the IOR and Beyond." Presentation at Webinar on Anti-Submarine Warfare & Underwater Search & Recovery: A New Perspective Based on the Underwater Domain Awareness (UDA) Framework at the Maritime Research Centre, 26 June 2021.

Ramdass, G. A. "Eminent Person's Lecture (EPL)" National Maritime Foundation Eminent Person Lecture Series, 11 May 2021. https://maritimeindia.org/events/eminent-persons-lecture-dr-g-a-ramadass/?occurrence=2021-05-11.

Rothwell, Donald R. "Issues in Maritime Cooperation in the Region." Presentation at the 3rd ASEAN Regional Forum Workshop on UNLCOS, 01 June 2021.

Roy-Chaudhury, Rahul. "Modi spells out free, open, inclusive Indo-Pacific policy." International Institute of Strategic Studies, 17 August 2018. https://www.iiss.org/blogs/analysis/2018/08/modi-free-open-inclusive.

Roy-Chaudhury, Rahul. "Strengthening maritime cooperation and security in the Indian Ocean." International Institute of Security Studies, 06 September 2018. https://www.iiss.org/blogs/analysis/2018/09/maritime-cooperation-indian-ocean.

Sachdev, Mahesh Kumar. "Indian Diplomacy through Ages." Ministry of External Affairs, Government of India, Distinguished Lectures Details, 12 November 2014. https://mea.gov.in/distinguished-lectures-detail.htm?174

Sawan, Ranendra S. "Problems and prospects of maritime security cooperation in the Indian Ocean Region: a case study of the Indian Ocean Naval Symposium (IONS)," *Sea Power Soundings* 15, (2020). https://www.navy.gov.au/sites/default/files/documents/Soundings_Number_15.pdf.

Sawan, Ranendra S. "Problems and prospects of maritime security cooperation in the Indian Ocean Region: a case study of the Indian Ocean Naval Symposium (IONS)." National Maritime Foundation, 23 June 2022. https://maritimeindia.org/problems-and-prospects-of-maritime-security-cooperation-in-the-indian-ocean-region-a-case-study-of-the-indian-ocean-naval-symposium-ions-part-i/

Sharma, Bipandeep. "De-Securitising the Arctic': An Indian Perspective," *India Quarterly* 77, no. 4 (2021): 622–641. https://journals.sagepub.com/doi/abs/10.1177/09749284211047721.

Singh, Abhijit. "India's 'Mission Ready' Naval Posture Must Extend Beyond the Indian Ocean," Observer Research Foundation, 01 November 2017. https://www.orfonline.org/research/indias-mission-ready-naval-posture-must-extend-beyond-the-indian-ocean/.

Singh, Anup. *Blue Waters Ahoy!: The Indian Navy 2001–2010,* 2018.

Singh, Karambir. "Dynamics of Security in the Indo-Pacific." *Indian Naval Despatch* 1, no. 1 (Winter 2020): 4-5.

Singh, Karambir. "Transforming The Indian Navy to be a Key Maritime Force in the Indo-Pacific." Address by Chief of the Naval Staff at United Services Institute, New Delhi, 27 August 2021.

Sood, Rakesh. "Why France is a reliable strategic partner for India." Observer Research Foundation, 20 January 2020. https://www.orfonline.org/research/why-france-is-a-reliable-strategic-partner-for-india-60480/.

South Asia Co-operative Environment Programme. "South Asian Seas Programme - Action Plan." http://www.sacep.org/programmes/south-asian-seas/action-plan

South Asian Association for Regional Cooperation. "SAARC Ministerial Declaration on Cooperation in Combating Terrorism (2009)." 28 February 2009. https://www.iri.edu.ar/publicaciones_iri/anuario/cd%20Anuario% 202010/Asia/SAARC/SAARC%20Declaration%20Cooperation %20in%20Combating%20Terrorism.pdf.

Staats, Jennifer. "A Primer on Multi-track Diplomacy: How Does it Work?" United States Institute of Peace, 31 July 2019. https://www.usip.org/publications/2019/07/primer-multi-track-diplomacy-how-does-it-work.

Stable Seas. "Challenges and Solutions for Maritime Security in the Indian Ocean." One Earth Future, 05 March 2021. https://www.stableseas.org/post/challenges-and-solutions-for-maritime-security-in-the-indian-ocean.

Thai, Tran Viet. "Strategic partnership: a framework of foreign relations in the age of globalization." *Vietnam Law and Legal Forum*, 01 October 2013. https://vietnamlawmagazine.vn/strategic-partnership-a-framework-of-foreign-relations-in-the-age-of-globalization-3437.html.

The White House. *Indo-Pacific Strategy of the United States*, 2020. https://www.whitehouse.gov/wp-content/uploads/2022/02/U.S.-Indo-Pacific-Strategy.pdf.

Thomas, Roby. "Leveraging India's Maritime Diplomacy." *Journal of Defence Studies* 14, no. 3 (July-September 2020): 1-27. https://idsa.in/jds/14-3-2020-leveraging-indias-maritime-diplomacy.

Till, Geoffrey. *Seapower: A Guide for the Twenty-First Century.* Oxford: Routledge, 2004. https://doi.org/10.1604/978071468436Second Edition.

UN Security Council. "Statement by the President of the Security Council." S/PRST/2021/15, 09 August 2021. https://undocs.org/S/PRST/2021/15.

United Nations Office on Drugs and Crime, *World Drug Report 2020*. https://wdr.unodc.org/wdr2020/field/WDR20_BOOKLET_1.pdf.

United Nations Office on Drugs and Crime. *Global Maritime Crime Programme: Briefing Package*. https://www.unodc.org/documents/Maritime_crime/UNODC-GMCP_Briefing_Package.pdf.

United Nations Office on Drugs and Crime. *Promoting the Rule of Law and Countering Drugs and Crime in South Asia: Regional Programme for South Asia 2018-21*. 2018. https://www.unodc.org/documents/southasia//Promoting_the_ Rule_of_Law_Final_Rev.pdf.

United States Government. *Maritime Security Sector Reform Guide*.

Upadhyaya, Shishir. "Maritime Security Cooperation in the Indian Ocean Region: Assessment of India's Maritime Strategy to be the Regional "Net Security Provider"." PhD diss., University of Wollongong, 2018. https://ro.uow.edu.au/theses1/297.

US Defence Intelligence Agency. *Joint Military Attaché School*. https://www.dia.mil/Portals/27/Documents/About/JMAS/JMAS_Brochure_JUL_2020.pdf.

US Joint Forces. *Joint Publication 3-13 Information Operations*. https://www.jcs.mil/Portals/36/Documents/Doctrine/pubs/jp3_13.pdf. [Web page no longer available]

US Navy. "Navy, Marine Corps, Coast Guard Release Maritime Strategy." *America's Navy*, 17 December 2020. https://www.navy.mil/Press-Office/Press-Releases/display-pressreleases/Article/2449829/navy-marine-corps-coast-guard-release-maritime-strategy/.

Wilson, Brian. "The Turtle Bay Pivot: How the United Nations Security Council is Reshaping Naval Pursuit of Nuclear Proliferators, Rogue States, and Pirates." *Emory International Law Review* 33, no. 1 (2018): 1. http://dx.doi.org/10.2139/ssrn.3329212.

Index